the new girl

the new girl

Girls' Culture in England
1880~1915

sally mitchell

COLUMBIA UNIVERSITY PRESS

new york

Columbia University Press

New York   Chichester, West Sussex

Copyright © 1995 Columbia University Press

All rights reserved

Library of Congress Cataloging-in-Publication Data

Mitchell, Sally, 1937–

The new girl : girls' culture in England, 1880–1915 / Sally Mitchell.

p.   cm.

Includes bibliographical references and index.

ISBN 0–231–10246–1 (alk. paper). — ISBN 0–231–10247–X (pbk. : alk. paper)

1. English literature—19th century—History and criticism.
2. Girls in literature. 3. English literature—20th century—
History and criticism. 4. Young adult literature. English—History and criticism.
5. Children's literature, English—History and criticism. 6. Girls—England—
Books and reading—History. 7. Girls—England—Conduct of life—History.
8. Women and literature—England—History. 9. Young women in literature. 10.
Sex role in literature. I. Title.

PR468.G5M58 1995

820.9'352042—dc20

95–10929

CIP

∞

Casebound editions of Columbia University Press books are printed on permanent and durable acid-free paper.

Printed in the United States of America

c 10 9 8 7 6 5 4 3 2 1

p 10 9 8 7 6 5 4 3 2

contents

acknowledgments

DURING THE YEARS THAT THIS BOOK HAS SLOWLY GESTATED (WITH interruptions for union activism, service as director of undergraduate studies in Temple's English department, and various other scholarly projects) I have presented segments of work in progress at meetings of the Northeast Victorian Studies Association and the Research Society for Victorian Periodicals; at the annual CUNY Victorian Conference (by the invitation of Anne Humpherys); at a University of Pennsylvania Seminar in Language, Culture, Gender, and Power (organized by Joan Shapiro); in the Paley Library Distinguished Faculty Lecture Series at Temple University; and as an invited guest lecturer at the University of New Mexico in Albuquerque (through the agency of Carolyn Woodward). Responses to these presentations provided me with useful ideas and showed me what areas needed further development. I particularly remember comments made by Karla Walters, Rachel Blau DuPlessis, Margaret Beetham, Phyllis Rackin, and Louis James—and I apologize to other helpful discussants whose names have escaped me.

Temple University supported the project with a study leave, which allowed me to spend six months in England reading books and periodicals that can no longer be found except in British copyright libraries, and with a Faculty Summer Research Grant in 1994. Photographs taken from books and periodicals in my own collection were quickly and ably made by Temple's Department of Photographic Services. Other illustrations were supplied by the British Library, by its Newspaper Library in Colindale, and by the Bodleian Library at Oxford. The sources for all illustrations are identified in the captions.

I made heavy use of the Fawcett Collection in London as well as the British Library (in both Bloomsbury and Colindale) and the Bodleian, and I particularly admire the willing helpfulness of librarians who fetched great piles of books that had apparently been gathering dust ever since they were cataloged. (Extremely popular turn-of-the-century girls' books are not easy to find: many of them were no doubt read to pieces, and many more vanished in wartime paper drives. The volumes deposited in copyright libraries, however, are virtually untouched.) Dorothy Hearn made arrangements for me to use the archives of the Girls' Friendly Society (Queen's Gate, London). I had extensive help, as always, from the Interlibrary Loan Services of Temple University's Paley Library. In addition, London bookseller Elizabeth Crawford provided prompt and valuable service on transatlantic telephone orders for books important to women's history.

While in London in 1989 and on subsequent shorter summer trips, I stayed at the British Federation of University Women's residence at Crosby Hall (now, alas, defunct). In addition to discovering helpful sources on the history of women's colleges and their early students, which I found in the Federation's library, I enjoyed friendship and good scholarly conversation at the dinner table. From the "Crosby Hall crowd," I must make special mention of Rosemary Cowler, Nancy Fix Anderson, Phyllis Wachter, Carolyn Woodward, Carolyn Edie, Arlene Jackson, Marie Roberts, and Charlotte Templin. In Philadelphia I was energized by the dogs and people who take morning walks along the Wissahickon, and especially by Ruth Gayle and Garbo.

As always, Martha Vicinus dropped casual remarks that proved enormously helpful. Co-teaching Introduction to Women's Studies with Luci Paul, of Temple's psychology department, gave me a chance to pick her brains about the new research on girls' psychological development. Nina Auerbach has asked a few usefully awkward questions while we've gossiped over Mexican food. Several current and former graduate students—especially Andrea Broomfield, Kelley Graham, Lauren McKinney, and Esther Schwartz-McKinzie—have let me talk about my work as well as theirs. Andrea Broomfield did an enormous service in reading the entire manuscript and pointing out some holes I'd left and many errors I had overlooked. Finally, I am particularly thankful to Mary Prior, in Oxford, for more than thirty years of friendship—and for her expertise in women's history and in the use of archival and autobiographical sources.

An earlier version of chapter 2 appeared as "Girls' Culture: At Work" in *The Girl's Own: Cultural Histories of the Anglo-American Girl, 1830–1915*, edited by Claudia Nelson and Lynne Vallone (Athens: University of Georgia Press, 1994); the material is reprinted here by permission of the University of Georgia Press. I am also grateful for permission to reprint portions of the first chapter that were included in "Children's Reading and the Culture of Girlhood," *Browning Institute Studies* 17 (1989): 53–63.

the new girl

one

Girls and Their Culture: The Case of L. T. Meade

BY THE FIRST DECADE OF THE TWENTIETH CENTURY, "BOOKS FOR Girls" had become a standard category on the lists of British publishers. The genre included school stories and tales of heroic action in the Indian Mutiny or the Boer War, holiday adventures that showed girls on their own in dangerous places, career books featuring young artists and nurses and typists in detective firms, and tales about young teens who sold papers on the streets or ran away to join the circus. Girls' magazines were circulated in large numbers, ranging from glossy shilling monthlies intended for daughters of the rural gentry to halfpenny weekly tabloids for servants and factory girls. Much of this reading material was not "approved"—except by girls, who apparently controlled enough of their time and spending money to make their books and magazines a source of profit for publishers and authors.

Thirty years earlier the concept of girlhood as a separate stage of existence with its own values and interests was only beginning to take shape. When the impact of commercialization and competition led publishers to identify readers in a category different from both the adult audience and the general children's audience, they used expressions such as "the girl from 8 to 18" and "those who have left the schoolroom but not yet entered society." Early fiction for girls generally emphasized home life and home duties. By the end of the century, however, many books dwelled on the values, ethics, and interactions of girls themselves, with hardly any adults present.

IN THE PARK.

"In the park." By the mid-1890s bicycles supplied girls with transportation and the freedom to move about in public.

From *Girl's Own Paper* 18 (1896–1897): 9. Reproduced by permission of the Bodleian Library, University of Oxford, shelfmark Per. 2537.d.1/18.

My study proposes that over the years between 1880 and 1915 both working-class and middle-class girls increasingly occupied a separate culture. Compulsory schooling; changes in child-labor laws and economic circumstances; the new female occupations of nursing, school-teaching, and clerical work; the diminishing proportion of working-class girls employed in domestic service relative to other occupations; and the opportunity of extended academic or professional education for some among the middle classes meant that a great many more girls had some period of transition between "child at home" and the assumption of wholly adult responsibilities.

The new girl—no longer a child, not yet a (sexual) adult—occupied a provisional free space. Girls' culture suggested new ways of being, new modes of behavior, and new attitudes that were not yet acceptable for adult women (except in the case of the advanced few). It authorized a change in outlook and supported inner transformations that had promise for transmuting woman's "nature." Some women who were already adult when the alterations became visible responded with approval and even envy; Mary Anne Broome, for example, used the term *New Girl* and was convinced, in comparison to her own pre-1850 childhood, of "the superiority of the modern girl," who "is more sure of herself" and knows that marriage is not her "invariable destiny."[1]

I do not claim that most—or even many—girls of the period actually lived a dramatically altered life. Carol Dyhouse and others have demonstrated that most girls remained enclosed in family roles and governed by traditional expectations about marriage, maternity, and appropriate feminine skills and behavior. I am, however, asserting that girls were consciously aware of their own culture and recognized its discord with adult expectations. They perhaps suspected that they could be (new) girls for only a few brief years, before they grew up to be (traditional) women.

The girls' culture I will describe is evident in books, magazines, clothing styles, clubs, sports, schools, and memoirs. Although the dream/ideal of girlhood in its archetypal form perhaps never did exist, or existed for only a very few girls, it had (like the suburban nuclear families of U.S. television a generation ago) a cultural reality. The idea of the new girl exercised an imaginative and emotional power with fertile potential for nurturing girls' inner selves. The new girl's life was as fictive for the thirteen-year-old scullery maid as for the well-to-do daughter under the care of a private governess—yet both girls knew (and perhaps dreamed) about some of its freedoms. Whatever their actual circumstances, girls' culture told adolescents at the end of the nineteenth century that their lives would be different from their mothers' lives and that they could mark out a new way of being in the world. Because the commercial girls' culture of books and magazines and weekly papers described a new life of schools, sports, independence, and training for a profession, a girl's outlook was no longer limited to the ideas and models available in her own family and neighborhood. Girls welcomed the potential for change in their circumstances; their awareness of new possibilities shaped their inner lives.

How can I make this argument when most of the surviving artifacts of girls' culture were produced by adults and sold for profit? Precisely because that is the case: the books and magazines that portrayed the new girl were profitable only when girls made them so. I have drawn primarily on cheap and popular books and magazines, and especially on the series that have never been "approved literature" and have therefore slipped almost out of living memory. I concentrate on stories girl readers remembered. Some are vividly recollected in autobiographies and memoirs. Others were treasured long after they had been outgrown—and women of later generations who found them among a box of grandmother's things have also sometimes felt an almost guilty pleasure in their emotional indulgences.

Even though children's fiction became less obtrusively didactic over the middle years of the nineteenth century, those who wrote for the young almost invariably continued to convey values and instruction through their choice of character, structure, and plot. Toward the end of the century, however, a divide opened between the fiction endorsed by adults and the books most loved by girls. Adult readers frequently condemn the unreality and escapism in children's popular fiction (especially series fiction), while the stories for young people that literary critics praise are often located in a land of lost innocence—a feature of childhood that adults value. It is therefore possible that the ethics (and the evasions of reality) in the world of girls' popular fiction represent a serious critique of adult beliefs.

My analysis of popular fiction rests on two basic assumptions. The first is that successful mass fiction must speak to the readers who

Girls' Own Paper.

ART STUDENTS AT BREAKFAST IN PARIS.

London.

"Art students at breakfast in Paris." A spirited illustration from *Girl's Own Paper* in 1902 presents young women who are decidedly not shut up at home, under parental protection, and waiting for marriage.

From *Girl's Own Paper* 23 (1901–1902): facing page 210. Reproduced by permission of the British Library, shelfmark P.P.5993.w.

choose to consume it. We may once have been taught that great literature endures because it is universal; more certainly, however, fiction that becomes very popular and then fades into obscurity draws on the values, interests, and concerns of a specific group of readers at a particular time. My second assumption is that readers—and in particular, readers in their teens—choose books that meet their psychological needs and provide emotional satisfaction. They may quite possibly ignore overt "messages" if the right emotional cues are there. Hesba Stretton's *Jessica's First Prayer* [1867], for example, was approved by evangelical adults because the girl hero found God—but its enormous popularity among several generations of girls reflects not only their craving for the tears released by the story of Jessica's miserable life but also their triumph in her ultimate power over all the adults in the tale.

I believe that reading—and its emotional and imaginary constructs, removed though they may be from readers' material circumstances—has an effect on girls' inner lives, their personal horizons and standards, their image of self and potential. This, of course, is virtually impossible to demonstrate. However, there is certainly evidence that fiction influences readers' daydreams and (before the age of self-consciousness dawns) is used naively in "plays" shared with friends. One amusing example, among the many to be found in memoirs (and in our own recollections), is reported by Beryl Lee Booker, who recalled that she and a group of friends at Baker Street High School indulged in a fantasy-play based on *The Three Musketeers* that "involved the use of strong language, spitting, and smoking."[2]

Thus I'm not particularly interested in what authors were trying to do—except in cases where the author's own life experience suggests an interpretive edge—but in what girl readers were taking and using from their stories. History, autobiography, and memoirs demonstrate some of the conditions under which girls of various classes lived; the fiction girls loved suggests their dreams. In looking at the correspondences and differences between life and fiction, I am interested in suggesting how girls themselves may have seen their world. Insofar as they can be inferred, I will trace the fantasies, the dreams, the mental climate, and the desires of girls themselves, not the advice, exhortation, instruction, and belief about girlhood that adults provided.

One major class difference—and also a site of contestation during the period between 1880 and 1915—is the definition of *girlhood*. The word *girl* became dramatically visible about 1880. Advice books that in the 1860s had titles such as *Hints on Self Help: A Book for Young Women* (Jessie Boucherett, 1863) were—though directed to much the same group of readers—more likely two decades later to use the new term: *English Girls: Their Place and Power* (Isabel Reaney, 1879), *What Girls Can Do* (Phillis Browne, [1880]), or *What to Do with Our Girls* (Arthur Talbot Vanderbilt, 1884). The trend is even more evident in works of fiction: where an occasional earlier title had contained the word *girl*, it was used for literally hundreds of books in the last quarter of the century.

6

Yet the word signifies (at least partly) a state of mind rather than a chronological or legal concept: most working-class children were at work by twelve or fourteen, while a middle-class daughter might remain in her parents' home and entirely under their supervision until her middle twenties or even later. Even our own sense of the differences between *girl*, *adolescent*, and *woman* does not depend entirely on physical or psychological or legal definitions. The concept of life stages—and the boundaries between them—is culturally determined, just as gender is. Cultural factors are especially important in marking transitions. The age at which young people are seen as sexual beings is, quite evidently, not necessarily linked to puberty; both the gendering and the sexualizing of people in their second decade of life is subject to wide historical and cultural variation.

Elementary education became available to every child in England in 1870 and was made compulsory (although at first only between ages seven and ten) in 1880. The concept of an age for leaving school seems to provide one terminal boundary for childhood. Census figures almost immediately showed a sharp decline in the number of younger children at work. Further acts and local ordinances during the period until the First World War steadily limited the kinds of employment open to youngsters and increased the age and educational achievement required for leaving school.

Other matters covered by law set additional boundaries between child and woman. After 1885 the age of (hetero)sexual consent was sixteen, though there was a gray area between thirteen and sixteen: a man who had sexual relations with a girl under thirteen committed a felony, but if the girl was between thirteen and sixteen the offense was a misdemeanor and the man's belief that she was sixteen or older provided an adequate defense. To be married, however, a girl needed her father's permission until she was twenty-one: she could consent to nonmarital sex at sixteen but had to be five years older before she was "mature" enough to give herself (and her property or the economic value of her services) in marriage.

Lawbreakers under the age of fourteen were handled by the juvenile justice system and could not be put in adult prisons. The Poor Law made parents liable for maintenance of their children until the age of sixteen. By 1900 the official school leaving age was fourteen, although exceptions often were made for pupils who had reached a minimal standard of proficiency and whose earnings were needed. On the other hand, 22 percent of fourteen-year-olds remained at school in 1911, even though they were legally eligible to leave.

Meanwhile, the age of menarche was declining (probably because of improved nutrition) and the age at first marriage was rising; by the Edwardian years the average for English girls was twenty-five. Thus the space between sexual maturity and marriage was growing. The writer who used the name "Eugenius" for a *Westminster Review* essay on "The Decline of Marriage" in 1891 worried about the "advance of culture," which, he said, made educated women too fastidious and also too comfortable (in their professions and clubs) to marry, although he simultaneously praised clubs for working girls because they "[prevent] early marriages by creating sources of mental and social interest."[3]

Thus the categories delineated by age, occupation, class, education, sexuality, and various aspects of the legal system are overlapping and indeterminate. Indeed, Kirsten Drotner suggests that middle-class girls at home—though childishly dependent and protected—might have been more integrated into adult life than their brothers who were away in the distinctively young person's world of boarding school.[4] I would argue, however, that a comparable world for girls was found in girls' culture: whether they were at work, at home, or at school, girls could be defined through their shared stories, feelings, interests, self-image, language, and values.

In addition to the outpouring of publications for girls who could buy books or belong to libraries, new and distinctive girls' papers appeared for working-class teenagers. Unlike the penny romances and novelettes that had been consumed by working women and workingmen's wives since mid-century, the papers of this new type had stories about girl detectives in disguise as lady's maids and "boy" circus acrobats who turn out to be the Duchess's long-lost daughter. Thus the fourteen-year-old kitchen maid had a certain freedom of choice in her imaginative life and her self-identification: she could (for a halfpenny a week) be a woman who read romance and household hints or a girl who consumed tales of school and adventure and, therefore, shared in the developing girls' culture.

Middle-class Molly Hughes closed the autobiographical volume on her childhood and called herself a girl when she began attending North

London Collegiate School at sixteen. The oral histories of working-class women collected by Elizabeth Roberts suggest that for them "girl-hood" stretched from school to marriage.[5] Going to work, said the manager of a working-girls' club in 1890, "means a decided advance in the life of a girl. She ceases to be a child."[6] Yet she need not be in any hurry to become a woman. Girls who had friendship and recreation, club managers believed, would "not need the idle companionship of lads."[7] Girlhood was of value in itself, not merely a transitional stage to hurry through:

> Have we not seen a change in the views of marriage amongst girls of the educated and professional classes? When they had no other employment but fancy work, tea parties, or walks on the parade, or in the park, what could they think of but flirtations and possible marriages?[8]

But when and how can the woman at work be seen as a girl? This is part of the interest in girls' culture. At the end of childhood, the middle-class girl went from home (or homelike) education to secondary school, while the working-class girl was finished with her schooling. In either case, the new girl moved from family into a quasi-public space. Girlhood, in its archetypal form, is bounded on each side by home: by parental home on one side, by marital home on the other. In the space between the two family homes—for however many years that space might last—the new girl has a degree of independence (supervised though it might be by the mistress at work or at school). She is freed from the direct rule of her mother and father, and her independence, though not literally new among the working class, is newly idealized, becoming an icon for girls of all classes.

It may be for this reason that there was an outpouring of employment handbooks, advice manuals, guides to manners or health, and volumes about girls' activities, hobbies, clubs, and games. These are another part of my evidence for the development and features of girls' culture. The new girl moved into spheres where her mother had no advice to give; she did things her mother had not done and faced issues her mother did not face—if not in reality, at least in fancy. Advice manuals are perhaps more significant as markers of culture and imaginative life than as actual agents of instruction, and through them as well as

9

through fiction the daughter at home in a provincial town with a daily routine virtually indistinguishable from her mother's at the same age could be, in her mind, a new girl.

As a first step in discussing the creation of girlhood—and the values, attitudes, and understandings this creation encoded—it is instructive to consider the case of L. T. Meade. Born in an Irish rectory in 1854 as Elizabeth Thomasina Meade, she moved to London at twenty-one to live independently and pursue a career in literature. After marrying solicitor Alfred Toulmin Smith in 1879, and even after giving birth to three children, she continued an active professional life, dictating to shorthand writers for two hours in the morning, attending to household duties, spending the afternoon in town as an editor, returning home for dinner, and then, afterward, correcting the typescript of the work she had dictated in the morning.[9]

Thus, in the mid-1870s Meade had many of the characteristics that would make her a New Woman when the term became popular in the 1890s. Although some library catalogues still list her books under "Smith"—her husband's name—she used L. T. Meade not only as a pseudonym but also, in all aspects of her public life, as a professional name. Unlike the majority of women authors earlier in the century, Meade never claimed that she took up writing only because she was forced to support herself or because she wanted to do good. In an interview for a girls' magazine in 1900 she presented herself as someone who wanted to earn her own way in the world even over the opposition of her father, who had objected vehemently, saying that there "never yet has been a woman of our family who earned money."[10] Meade promoted higher education for women and healthy sports such as swimming and bicycling; when she was well past middle age her book jackets continued to describe her as "devoted to motoring and other outdoor sports." Furthermore, she served on the managing committee of the Pioneer Club, where independent professional women who took "an active personal interest in any of the various movements for women's social, educational and political advancement"[11] met for social events and debates on issues of the day. Pioneer Club members—who included Sarah Grand and Mona Caird—wore as insignia a silver brooch made in the shape of an axe.

An extremely prolific potboiling novelist, Meade published at least 250 books. (There were fourteen titles in 1900 alone.) She wrote "city arab"[12] tales for the Sunday-school trade, stories of aristocratic life, romances, sensation novels, "novels of today" about doctors and preachers who take drugs, an antivisection book, and novels about "emancipated women devoted to the cause of their sex."[13] There are enough titles about sorcery and the supernatural to earn her an entry in science fiction directories. Standard references on mystery say that Meade was the first to feature a female gang leader: Madame Koluchy, head of a sinister Italian criminal organization, was a kidnapper, bank robber, blackmailer, murderer, and (in the words of Jessica Mann) "the first criminal in fiction to hide behind the useful disguise of a beauty therapist."[14]

Meade apparently invented the subgenre of medical mystery. Her "Stories from the Diary of a Doctor" ran in the *Strand* from 1893. This is the period when a certain Doctor Watson was also narrating mysteries in the *Strand*—Meade's twist was to base the plot on new scientific discoveries or bizarre medical information.[15] She got the material from two collaborators. One was a divisional surgeon for the Metropolitan Police; the other used the pseudonym "Robert Eustace." The same "Robert Eustace" later fed scientific information to Dorothy Sayers, who pays tribute to Meade in her introduction to *The Omnibus of Crime* (1929).[16]

Meade was known best, however, as a writer for girls. In 1887 she founded *Atalanta* (1887–1898), a sixpenny monthly with an ambitious plan and a good deal of high-caliber work. In addition to printing her own stories and articles, Meade secured material from a list of contributors including E. Nesbit, Frances Hodgson Burnett, Sarah Tytler, Amy Levy, John Strange Winter, Rider Haggard, Grant Allen, and the American Mary E. Wilkins (later Freeman). *Atalanta*'s contents and advertising, as well as the rules for its contests and contributors' pages, suggest that the readers Meade hoped to reach were daughters of the gentry and upper middle class between about fourteen and twenty-five—intelligent, serious girls who needed only support and guidance in order to become women on the new pattern. In addition, *Atalanta* was carried by public libraries and was therefore available to working and lower-middle-class girls.[17]

Atalanta under Meade's editorship promoted the concept of a women's culture worth emulating. There were series on women novel-

The cover of *Atalanta* magazine. For middle-class girls, both athletics and classics were key signifiers of their brothers' masculine world.

ists, artists, and philanthropists. Frequent articles—some of them written by headmistresses such as Dorothea Beale—described the new academic girls' schools. The Oxford and Cambridge colleges for women were made interesting and attractive in essays written by former students and also by Meade herself; the "Brown Owl" column sometimes provided college news and alumnae notes. An offering in 1890 by Professor R. K. Douglas that claimed that higher education harmed young women by promoting rivalry, damaging health, preventing marriage, and destroying "grace" brought forth an outpouring of indignant letters, including one from a girl named Evelyn Sharp, who would subsequently become a journalist, novelist, lecturer, and militant suffragist.[18]

One of Meade's primary concerns was that girls should do something worthwhile—and worth money—after they left (as she put it) "school . . . or school-room."[19] Dorothea Beale proclaimed that the "once fashionable, but miserable doctrine . . . that a woman who had money or a place in society ought to live an idle life, on pain of losing caste, is almost obsolete, since the daughters of Cabinet-ministers and bishops and judges have thought it an honour to join the body of working women."[20] Meade commissioned articles on employments and careers from women who could give authoritative practical advice about training and earnings. Millicent Garrett Fawcett, for example, wrote about the civil service, Dr. Edith Huntley on medicine, and Ethyl Comyns—proprietor of a typewriting agency—on the requirements for successfully learning and practicing a new and promising women's career.

Atalanta also had a "Scholarship and Reading Union," which appears to be intended for girls educated at home and for young women interested in continuing study on their own. Meade secured articles on British authors from appropriate authorities: Anne Thackeray on Jane Austen, Mary Ward on Elizabeth Barrett Browning, Thomas Hughes on Charles Kingsley, Charlotte Yonge on John Keble, Andrew Lang on Walter Scott. Each was followed by two essay questions; readers who paid a fee of five shillings per year would have their essays returned with comments. At the end of the year, those whose had submitted regularly were eligible to write a final essay on the year's work, with a scholarship worth twenty pounds a year for two or three years as prize. Readers up to the age of twenty-five were invited to compete.

Atalanta, however, survived for only eleven years, and Meade had given it up by 1893. Her reputation as a girls' writer rests more centrally on her own very popular books. Readers of *Girl's Realm* in 1898 named L. T. Meade as their favorite author. Another survey in 1906—reported in *The Nineteenth Century* and questioning only girls between fifteen and eighteen who were enrolled in high schools—put Meade in fifth place; among these more educated girls, she came behind adult popular novelists Edna Lyall, Henry Seton Merriman, Anthony Hope (*The Prisoner of Zenda*), and Marie Corelli.[21] Violet Trefusius, a "sophisticated upper-class schoolgirl at the turn of the century," remembered that at fourteen she was reading important contemporary novelists—but still was "not too old to surreptitiously enjoy L. T. Meade."[22] The columns of girls' magazines that allowed readers to offer books for trade reveal a steady demand for Meade (and a notable willingness to give up sets of Walter Scott, Charles Dickens, and even Charlotte Yonge in order to secure her books).

L. T. Meade made popular (although she may not have invented) the chief varieties of formula fiction that came to dominate girls' voluntary reading for fifty years after her death. By 1929 she was on the Wilson Library Bulletin's "Not to Be Circulated" list of books that children's librarians should remove from the shelves because they had no literary value. Meade shared this honor with Tom Swift, Jack Harkaway, Horatio Alger, and the Stratemeyer syndicate books such as the Bobbsey Twins.[23] How did she get from the Sunday school prize lists to the despicable (at least in adult eyes) category of "formula trash"? *A World of Girls,* which Meade published in 1886, is generally described as the first school story for girls.[24] Now certainly there had been novels such as *Jane Eyre* and a number of girls' books with "School" in the title; I will come back to the nature of the school story as a genre.

Meade wrote about the intense friendships and rivalries of adolescents. "I have fallen in love," says one girl about another in *A Sweet Girl Graduate* (1891). The whole action of *The School Favourite* (1908) turns on the relationship between two girls who kiss, fondle, and climb into bed together. Gillian Avery remarks that Meade's "school books are interesting in the way they show the emotional turmoil of adolescent girls as one of these might herself have written of it."[25] She wrote career stories about nurses, teachers, settlement workers, art students, journalists. (One is about a typist in a detective firm.) Rosa Nouchette Carey also wrote—somewhat earlier—about young women who took up some work other than governessing, but in Carey's books the difficulty of making that decision and then overcoming the family's objections generally forms a major portion of the story. The difference in Meade is the simple assumption that girls will support themselves; the matter-of-fact appearance of bicycles and high schools and sharing a flat; and the practical details about training and opportunities.

In *Four on an Island* [1892], some children are cast away and survive largely through the efforts of the fourteen-year-old tomboy who is their leader. Meade followed this with other books about children left on their own through some unlikely circumstance that let them be self-sufficient and have a good time. It became commonplace by the turn of the century to suggest that girls liked their brothers' books better than their own. Meade, however, interpreted this as girls' desire for "plot, plenty of it, peril, a keen sense of danger"—and believed this yearning could best be satisfied by truly exciting books with a strong girl as hero.[26] A 1911 story entitled *"Ruffles"* was about a fifteen-year-old girl who solved mysteries and drove her family's "new Napier car" when she had an urgent mission to undertake. The tone leads me to suspect there might have been sequels had Meade not died shortly thereafter. In fact, of the girls' formulas popular during the next fifty years, the only one I have not yet found in Meade is the pony book—but her tomboy heroes are often splendid horsewomen.

John Cawelti suggests that formula fiction allows changing values to be assimilated into traditional imaginary constructs. The formula creates its own world, which becomes familiar by repetition, and then the new material can be integrated in a nonthreatening way.[27] In the case of Meade, the situation is somewhat complicated, because she's creating the formula at the same time. But she is also using a great deal of material that is already available to her.

She deliberately echoed literature her readers knew. In 1889, for example, she gave a book the title *Polly: A New-Fashioned Girl*. Now the heroine of Louisa May Alcott's *An Old-Fashioned Girl* (1870) is named Polly, and Alcott's title is ironic: Polly is old-fashioned because she works hard and supports herself, unlike the parasitic social butterflies of the American Gilded Age. Meade's *Polly* also recycles a beloved plot:

Dr. Maybright's wife dies, leaving him with nine children (and their number is soon increased to eleven by adding two orphans from Australia). In Charlotte Yonge's *The Daisy Chain* (1856) Dr. May's wife dies, leaving eleven motherless children to bring themselves up. Another Meade title with echoes is *Merry Girls of England* (1896). Unlike Sarah Ellis's *Women, Wives, Daughters*, and so forth of mid-century,[28] the merry girls don't have any father or brothers to love and serve: they put their modest inheritance into stock for a farm, where they make themselves a pleasant home and do a thriving trade in butter and eggs.

Meade used gypsies and other standard conventions of popular melodrama. She drew on tracts for the sequence of reform-crisis-illness, but Meade's stories close with the sufferer surrounded by loving schoolmates instead of by angels. She picked up the ingredients that had already become stereotyped in boys' school stories: the stolen exam or tampered essay; the prize giving; the innocent girl wrongly accused of theft or cheating; the boating accident; the runaway lost in the storm, rescued by the person she has wronged, and "brought back to school half dead."[29]

Meade herself evidently added several incidents that became essential in girls' books: the drama society presentation (borrowed perhaps from Charlotte Brontë's *Villette*)[30]; the midnight feast; the clique or secret society. Her schoolgirls play relatively decorous games, most often tennis. But a young woman "highly commended" for her Reading Union essays in *Atalanta* magazine was one Angela Brazil, age eighteen.[31] Brazil was originator of the "hearty, hockey, honor of the house" fiction that dominated schoolgirl magazines between the wars.

Finally, another set of clichés central to Meade and the girls' formula is, I think, more significant: the brief moment of anger that is revealed as major cruelty when a girl realizes how badly she has hurt someone's feelings; the spoiled rich girl used to having her own way; the "Wild Irish Girl" (or American, or Spanish, or Tasmanian) who has to be broken in to an English school and manages to teach the English girls something about emotions and frankness while she's at it; the child who is overburdened by working for a scholarship because she will have to support herself; and the casual criticism of a friend's dowdy clothes, followed by a scene in which the girl faints from hunger because her widowed mother is ill.

Girls' schools tended to be more democratic (or at least more broadly middle-class) than boys' public schools, and Meade set her stories not only in boarding schools but also in day schools, where girls came from a greater range of backgrounds. When she has a character talk about reasons for sending girls to school the first argument is always that it teaches them to get along with each other.

Most of the plots in her schoolgirl world hinge on friendship and feelings. The only really bad girls are those who sow dissension and deliberately make others unhappy. I would suggest that this is a way of assimilating the female world of family and relationships to the male world of school. The boys' public school was seen as both model of and preparation for the adult male world of politics, the army, and the empire. For girls the only parallel model was the old-fashioned family-style boarding school in which a very few girls of mixed ages lived in the proprietor's house. Meade wrote about those schools in some of her earlier stories. By the 1890s, however, books such as *Wild Kitty* (1897) described schools with six or seven hundred pupils. Meade took the organizational structure of the "men's world" and grafted onto it the emotional content of the "woman's world" of friendships, feelings, and the care and development of relationships.

The psychological subtext of these books is also interesting. Typically, a story begins at some point after mother has died. Father goes off to inspect mines in Australia or climb in the Himalayas, throwing the girl abruptly out of family privacy and into the public world of a school. High jinks and stolen exams and crushes and so forth occupy most of the book. At the end, the girl has been lost on the moors or is near death after being caught by incoming tides, and, as people cluster around realizing how much they value her, her father reappears. He is there when she opens her eyes and finally tells her that he cares.

The fantasy can be astoundingly transparent. In *A World of Girls* Annie disguises herself as a gypsy to rescue a stolen child. She goes into a burial mound, through a deep round tunnel, and emerges with the toddler; she falls ill, can't rest, brain fever threatens. Someone places the child on her chest so she'll know it's safe, and that is when her father shows up. After the dark passage that is both death and birth, she is resurrected as mother with child, and her father is at the bedside.

Yet I don't think we should be too patronizing about the obsessive retelling of this story. Anna Freud suggests that when the oedipal fantasy appears at adolescence it serves to overcome the real and actual fear of the father. Other analysts see the father as a stand-in for lovers that are still too dangerous to imagine: fantasies of winning father's admiration signal the onset of mature heterosexuality. Furthermore, there is an additional subtext. These girls earn their father's love and attention. "Earn" is important. The father does not come to the rescue—the girl rescues herself or is helped by other women. With Daddy's reappearance the girl is recognized by the masculine world.

This reading is supported by the flaws of mothers—when there are any. (The absence of mother is a striking feature in girls' popular fiction down to our own day.) Those mothers who do appear are apt to be "bad" in interesting ways. They disapprove of study; they let young girls wear adult clothes and go to adult entertainments; they get into debt or do other stupid things with money while they giggle and say "I don't understand anything about business—poor me—don't trouble me about details." Furthermore, as the precocious infant in *Daddy's Girl* (1901) says, "Mother likes me when I'm pretty, father likes me anyhow." These mothers represent a dysfunctional feminine ideal. Carroll Smith-Rosenberg has suggested that the generation gap between mothers and daughters—the expectation that adolescence would be marked by friction and rebellion—arose when the old "female culture" began to disintegrate: when daughters were no longer trained by apprenticeship to become women in their mothers' image.[32]

What the formula school story does, then, is to create a community where the important rules are the children's own ethics and mores. The new girl's popular fiction emphasizes peer standards, not adult standards—that is surely one reason adults came to ignore or despise it. Meade, for example, ranks courage higher than obedience. And more than anything else, her school stories value cohesion, formation of a group, loyalty, and care of girls for one another. Does this contradict the message of the "father/rescue" fantasy? Meade is often inconsistent. In some years, after all, she wrote more than a dozen books. Yet perhaps it is not so much inconsistency as a layering of competing moods, emotions, and messages, an addition of new ideas and new

A Sister of the Red Cross

Thomas · Nelson · & · Sons ·

A Sister of the Red Cross. One of L. T. Meade's most popular books glorified the nurse as a wartime hero.

From the author's collection.

models of girlhood on top of—instead of as replacement for—older and more conventional emotional satisfactions.

It often seems that Meade shifts her focus and evades her central story. Books open with one heroine who then almost disappears while someone else takes over. Often the pseudoprotagonist is an average girl—a wholesome, naughty, daring, responsible, honorable girl—and the replacement is initially dislikeable, a girl who is utterly selfish, or so needy she's incapable of caring for others. Ultimately the root of her disobedience is understood and she is taken into the group. Or there may be a pair of other girls, whose character traits bracket the "heroine" in the way that *Nancy Drew* uses boyish George and silly-femme Bess to mark the edges of Nancy's androgyny. Sometimes the interesting character is a girl who does not live in an adequate family and who behaves in astonishingly unconventional and forward ways, which are made admirable by her "unnatural" circumstances. This girl, however, is not the putative focus of the story—all of the interesting plot involves her, but the "heroine" is someone the reader can safely identify with. Some sequences of action begin and then vanish without resolution.

In other cases, Meade fails to write the book that seems to be promised. *A Sister of the Red Cross* (1900), for example, has a dedicated, career-minded nurse and another woman who goes to South Africa as a newspaper correspondent. However, more than half of the pages are about a third girl, a spoiled twit whose only goal is marriage: pages of ballrooms and dressmakers' shops and endless descriptions of her feelings during the siege of Ladysmith, where she spends her time weeping in a hotel room. The moral intent is obvious—but why must so much time be spent on this character when there are two splendid New Women in the book? It almost seems that Meade is afraid of what she starts to do.

Sometimes she subverts her message. Horrible gypsies and wild-women tell girls to trust themselves and do great things: the message is important to the girl, but the messenger is discredited. A misunderstood child runs away and is sold to the circus. This of course is terrible: she's virtually a slave, and her family is prostrate with grief. But she's also a star, an astonishing success, the most courageous young girl ever seen in a bareback act (*A Little Mother to the Others*, 1896).

It may indeed be Meade's very failure to pursue the implications of her plots and to look head-on at what she writes that allows her to introduce daring material. For example, there is not usually any romance in her girls' books. Two that do end with a wedding (somewhere beyond the last page) involve extremely independent women—the Red Cross nurse acquires a young officer with a VC; Maggie, in *A Sweet Girl Graduate*, makes a conquest of the senior wrangler (an extremely Christian gentleman who is about to become a don).

Is that a disappointment? Or does it make emulation safe? *A Sister of the Red Cross* provides some fairly realistic details about nursing wounded soldiers. When a family emergency arises in *A Sweet Girl Graduate*, Priscilla does not go home to look after her young sisters; the book explicitly shows that it would be wrong—not right—for her to choose self-sacrifice and waste her talent. She meets her friend Maggie's beau when a jealous classmate has fooled her into arriving at a fancy tea party dressed for walking in the rain in stout boots and an old brown dress—but she entrances him with her free and intelligent discussion of an unresolved problem in Homer. Narratives such as these may be important for showing that a career or an education does not destroy "femininity."

New images and models are implicit in Meade's plots and dropped without comment, as a matter of course: athletic triumphs, girls whose money is put in their own hands (without trustees), bicycles, unchaperoned friendships, girls willing to pawn their clothes rather than write home for money, adults (both men and women) who are wrong and must be disobeyed. By focusing on other things, Meade lets these be part of the automatic, unexamined, natural world.

Building on Alcott and Yonge, L. T. Meade made the new girl into a conventional protagonist. Her typical fifteen-year-old climbs trees and vaults over dikes—she is very often seen in motion in the first sentence of the book. Athletic energy is not something she will have to tame in order to mature, and it is not even terribly important: it is simply assumed. She's never a grind, but she takes real pleasure in intellectual pursuits. Disobedience is no longer something to grow out of. It has become a positive trait. Meade said, in a 1903 article on her craft:

> The girls for whom I write love a naughty heroine, but she must be naughty in a certain way. She must never be sly or vindictive. . . . She must be as daring as she likes, and even a little imperative to her elders; but her heart must be warm, and she must be true to her friends.[33]

Meade is really very good at adolescents—a word just then coming into use. She once told an interviewer that her children had "fully paid their own expenses for education" in the opportunity they gave her to observe juvenile nature.[34] She created characters who are willful, selfish, forgetful, snobbish, priggish, stubborn, rude, changeable, who act out their anger and distress—basically decent girls who do some really dreadful things.

In 1900, when Meade was turning out these books by the dozen, there were only 20,000 English girls at recognized grammar schools; by 1920 the number was 185,000. L. T. Meade wrote for the first generation in a new world. She did for girls what others had done earlier for boys: wrote about a separate culture with its own values, customs, and social standards. Sometimes the adults are weak, or stupid, or simply wrong. She produced books about girls who go to school and college and work and live together in flats—and solve mysteries—and run away from home and ought to because conditions there will not let them develop.

She made the new world safe by using familiar incidents and fantasies, by distracting the eye and diffusing the interest, in stories so centered on things that could only matter to people under sixteen that the books are almost unreadable for the rest of us. Like much popular fiction, Meade's books are far too culture-bound to revive. But the title of her first big success is almost irresistibly appropriate. L. T. Meade did indeed take a leading role in creating *A World of Girls*. Furthermore, in the illustrated series on girls' schools which she produced for the popular *Strand* magazine in 1895, she asserted that "girls, so trained, must surely be the New Women for whom we long."[35]

Meade's feminist intent was compromised, however, by the emotional pull of traditional conventions, by her unthinking echo of gender, class, and imperial stereotypes, by the very shock of change—and, certainly, by her need to earn money through writing what readers and publishers wanted. Such, indeed, is the story of the girls' culture: occupied by change, moving erratically toward the modern world, self-consciously "new" but still driven by powerful (and unexamined) old feelings. These are the themes that will be examined in more detail as we look at the new girl expressed in girls' culture during the years that bridge the nineteenth and twentieth centuries.

two

At Work

THROUGH MOST OF THE VICTORIAN PERIOD, GENTRY AND MIDDLE-class girls were expected to stay home until they married. Inside her father's house, the girl was exhorted to "create feelings of greater . . . love"[1] and

> pay her way by filling in the little spaces in home life as only a dear daughter can, by lifting the weight of care from her mother, and by slipping in a soft word or a smile where it is like oil on the troubled waters of a father's spirit.[2]

By the early years of the twentieth century, however, advice manuals and mainstream periodicals were using the language of moral imperative in precisely the opposite direction: when a girl leaves school, she "must find work," either paid or unpaid, which will provide regular duties and teach her essential skills and habits that she cannot learn in the shelter of her family.[3] No matter how wealthy she may be, insists another conduct book, "every girl by the time she reaches eighteen must know how and where she may place her talents in order to earn money, position and content."[4] Popular girls' books came to construct paid work—even for a suddenly impoverished heroine—as not merely a necessary evil but also a great adventure. One girl who finds a job waiting tables in a fashionable tea shop tells her friend, "It's going to be simply screaming fun! I'm going to have the time of my life."[5]

Over the space of a single generation, public ideology about a girl's place, role, and occupation had shifted. It is important to understand that there was no change in the real numbers. Three-quarters of all unmarried English females over the age of fourteen had been in the labor market ever since the census began asking. During those very mid-Victorian years when the "ideal woman" lived in decorative leisure, that life was possible because one-third of all girls between fifteen and twenty were working as domestic servants. The change is one of perception, attitude, and expectation: in 1905 it was seen as usual for girls—those girls visible to the man or woman doing the writing—to work outside the home; in 1880 it had been seen as unusual.

This chapter explores the nature of that change in expectation. How does the idea of paid work affect the culture of girlhood? Looking at advice manuals, popular fiction, and especially at girls' magazines in the period between 1880 and 1915, I have identified a number of contested and conflicting messages. The feminine ideal of service and self-sacrifice is reconstituted to encompass women's employment. The independence required in a public role encounters the "sweet dependence" of femininity. There is an imaginative reshaping of courtship and heterosexual companionship. Personal relationships at home are ambiguously distinguished from business relationships in the workplace. Feminization alters certain occupations and affects wages. The very concept of "the girl" interacts with all of these changes.

In middle-class advice manuals, the alteration was just becoming visible during the 1880s. According to the author of *What Girls Can Do*, many people still look down on the "young person" at work as opposed to the "young lady" at home, but girls themselves feel "respect and even . . . envy" for "their companions who are busy, independent, and self-supporting."[6] The vocabulary is fairly easy to unpick: *young lady* is the stereotype of leisured femininity, particularly the newly idle dependents that had become a status symbol for middle-class men. *Young person* is drawn from the factory acts. In those laws, children, whose work was increasingly regulated, were under fourteen; men and women were nineteen and upward; and the "young person," aged fourteen to eighteen, was in an intermediate and partially protected category.[7] In fiction of the period the term is an insult, a class marker much resented by pupil teachers or apprentice dressmakers.

The class label of *young person* also erases gender; one of the magic ways that nineteenth-century stereotypes manage to ignore women's labor is by overlooking the sex of female workers. The medical books that recommend avoiding physical activity during the six months that mark the "transition from girl to woman" and instruct adolescents to "give up all violent exercise"—as well as "excessive intellectual work"—during "those few days each month when . . . special care is called for"[8] are not intended for the thirteen-year-old down in the kitchen who works a sixteen-hour day.

But if young person and young lady are fairly transparent concepts, girl is not. The word became enormously popular in the last quarter of the nineteenth century. Young lady and young person—like lady and woman—had class referents; *girl* is inclusive. It takes in workgirl, servant girl, factory girl, college girl or girl graduate, shop-girl, bachelor girl, girl journalist, and office girl. It includes schoolgirl as well, but she is not a child; a "schoolgirl," in Victorian usage, is probably over eleven.

The "girl," then, is neither a child nor a (sexual) adult. As "young person" unsexed the worker, so, in a somewhat different sense, did terms such as *college girl, girl graduate, working girl,* or *bachelor girl.* The "young lady" at home is on the marriage market, but a "girl" is not husband-hunting. The ascription of immaturity and transition gives her permission to behave in ways that might not be appropriate for a woman.

At the same time, the understanding that girls could—indeed, should—earn their own livelihood released them from an obligation to remain childish. In the 1860s even a feminist such as Jessie Boucherett of the Society for Promoting the Employment of Women could write that if a father wanted his daughter at home "to amuse . . . and cheer him," it was her duty to obey.[9] By the end of the 1890s, however, the *Monthly Packet*—a high church and conservative magazine for young women—reported that fathers who had formerly "scraped together" an annuity so their "unmarried daughters might pinch out an uneventful existence" were now investing that money in training so the daughters could support themselves.[10] A sixteen-year-old middle-class girl startled her parents by finding paid employment for the paper *Woman*; she recalled in her autobiography that "the money was very useful and even nice girls were . . . beginning to go about by themselves and to be independent."[11]

Was it, however, acceptable for a girl to work if she did not need the money? "Conscientious girls," wrote Evelyn March-Phillips in 1897, "are deterred . . . by the accusation that . . . they are 'taking the bread from out their starving sisters' mouths.'" Why is it, she wonders ingenuously, that "we do not hear it said of a young man that because he has £500 a year, or £5000 for that matter, he is guilty of unfair competition, if he goes into the Army or is called to the Bar"?[12]

This debate surfaces frequently from the 1890s on. In almost every case, the answer is the same: it's perfectly all right to take the job, provided girls understand their "real moral obligation . . . not to sell their labour below the market-price."[13] A wealthy girl in a schoolgirl novel is coached by her friends on the importance of asking for full salary: "If you don't need the money, give it away to the Governess' Institutions—Convalescent Homes—whatever you like; but, for pity's sake, don't take less than your due."[14] Margaret Bateson, writing in *Girl's Own Paper* in 1896, set one pound a week at the lowest beginning salary a middle-class girl should accept.[15] Clementina Black enlisted religious rhetoric in teaching girls to demand fair pay:

> To do work at a price by which we could not live, because we happen to be otherwise supported, is to make it impossible for some other unsupported woman to live by work of that sort. If actions are to be measured by the sufferings they cause, few actions are more wicked than those which tend to lower the payment of labour; and such an action is committed by every woman who lets herself be ill-paid for her work.[16]

The language of suffering and virtue, however, is only one part of the story. Money in the pocket also leads to feelings that had been suppressed or denied when "sweet dependence" was the ideal. These subversive emotions are found more often in fiction than in essays. One example, plucked out of many: in a story from an upper-middle-class girls' magazine, a widow—that is, someone who has been not only a daughter but also a married woman—says to a newly orphaned girl, "If you will believe me (and I speak from experience), the bread we earn for ourselves is sweeter than other people's money buys for us."[17] An anonymous girl contributor, writing in *Girl's Own Paper*, revealed a pride touched with rebellious arrogance:

wherever we see a girl petted and thought too pretty or too delicate or too anything else to work, she is invariably discontented and unhappy—and why? Because she is not fulfilling her mission in the world.

If, as people say, we are robbing our brothers of their work, it must be because we take more pains with the work and do it better than they. Therefore let them look to it.[18]

As the idea of earning one's own bread grew increasingly attractive to girls of all social classes, a new genre of "career novels" became popular. A selection of titles indicates the work that appealed: *Miss Secretary Ethel* (Ellinor Adams, 1898), *A Woman of Business* (Mary Bramston, [1885]), *A Ministering Angel* (Ellen Clayton, [1895]), *The Probationer* (Amy Irvine, [1910]), *Dr. Janet of Harley Street* (Arabella Kenealy, [1893]), *Pickles: A Red Cross Heroine* (Edith C. Kenyon, [1916]), *Catalina: Art Student* (L. T. Meade, 1896), *Mary Gifford, M.B.* (Meade, 1898), *Nurse Charlotte* (Meade, 1904), *A Sister of the Red Cross* (Meade, 1900), *Elizabeth Glen, M.B.* (Annie S. Swan, 1895), *Mrs. Keith Hamilton, M.B.* (Swan, 1897), *Mona Maclean, Medical Student* (Graham Travers, i.e., Dr. Margaret Todd, 1892), *The Newspaper Girl* (Alice Williamson, 1899).

There are far more books about doctors than about schoolteachers, though by 1889 a grand total of seventy-two women physicians were on the medical register.[19] Aside from the drama of women's recent struggle for entry, medicine could be described (in the language of sentiment and service) as "one of the best openings for women" because "it is a useful occupation" and "provides full employment for all a woman's faculties both of heart and head." Note the order—heart first. And one could almost miss the next sentence, tagging along with less emphasis: "There are very few, if any positions open to women where they can so soon make themselves independent as in the practice of medicine."[20]

The crosscurrents generated by the older ideal of service and the newer ethic of self-sufficiency are also evident in the *Girl's Own Paper*, which was the first broadly successful magazine for girls. Priced at one penny a week, it was intended for a lower-middle-class audience. The letters column, however, shows that servant girls read it, and autobiographies reveal subscribers also among professors' daughters and others from the professional class. *Girl's Own Paper* (like *Boy's Own Paper*) was published by the Religious Tract Society in order to provide

"Helen pays a visit to the publishers." Career novels generally featured the more glamorous ways of earning a livelihood.

From *The Four Miss Whittingtons* by Geraldine Mockler [1899].
From the author's collection.

the increasingly literate young people who benefited from the 1870 Education Act with healthful alternatives to the romantic novelettes and blood-and-crime "penny dreadfuls" that were the most readily available cheap reading matter. In a daring and rather controversial move, however, the RTS deliberately kept the new publications free of almost all overt religious instruction, concentrating instead on interesting and entertaining articles about topics that appealed to young people, and on fiction that demonstrated approved social values within an exciting narrative. The formula evidently worked: in an 1888 poll of one thousand girls between eleven and nineteen, almost a third listed *Girl's Own Paper* as their favorite reading.[21]

In the 1885–1886 volume of *Girl's Own Paper*, five stories center on girls who earn money and seven on girls "at home." None of the working girls, however, is really in the world of commerce—there are three varieties of governess, a dressmaker who does pin-money work for friends, and an aspiring novelist who becomes a children's writer after conquering her inappropriate desire for fame. "The Stay-at-Home Girls," in a serial of that title, look after their invalid mother and do charity work; the story is designed to provide instruction about how to set up a penny bank, start a Band of Hope, and do other approved social work. In this volume from the mid-80s, many essays supply information for working girls, but the weight of emotional energy in the fiction lies with home and unpaid community service.

A decade later, the volume for 1894–1895 has, numerically, quite similar proportions. The working girls, however, are far more evidently out in the world—they include a hospital nurse, an elementary teacher, a telegraph clerk, and a shop worker. Furthermore, almost all of the home girls would have been called employed by the census of 1871, which still had a category for unpaid household work. One manages her brother's estate, one has been running the farm since her father's eyesight failed, another is raising an orphaned stepfamily, and yet another is an overworked secretary for her brother the scholar. Indeed, these "nonworking" heroines would be better off with the regularized duties and free time of a paid job. Their physical and emotional labor at home, performed with little recognition or reward, may be valorized by its appearance in fiction—but it no longer glows with peace and happiness.

In the earlier decade paid work had been meliorated through a homelike setting that emphasized emotional service, imitated family relationships, and provided a shield against public visibility in the role of worker. In the 1890s, by contrast, the fiction explicitly teaches girls to put a businesslike detachment between their personal lives and their work lives. A character who had first worked as a companion and later in a shop explained that though her social status was "lowered" she

> would much rather there was nothing but a "money" bond between me and my employers. At "Aylmer Court," when Lettice and her mother were unkind to me, it always hurt me because once I had been their friend and equal. Now at the Gallery I am just paid so much to do certain things, and so long as I do them to the very best of my ability, Mr. Jobling has nothing to complain of. From ten till six I am at his orders, but all the rest of the time I am independent, and I needn't feel grateful to him, because my salary is fairly earned and just a matter of business.[22]

I have so far been looking primarily at middle-class readers and middle-class work—this is the arena in which the change of outlook was most evident. What about girls who had always expected to support themselves, as had their mothers before them? A new phenomenon from the 1890s was the halfpenny weekly paper for working-class girls. These are eight-page tabloids, often on pink or green paper, with titles like *Girls' Best Friend*, *Girls' Friend*, *Girls' Reader* and *Forget-Me-Not*. Purely commercial enterprises, the halfpenny weeklies featured serials, horoscopes, and contests to generate circulation; they had none of the underlying educational and religious purpose that sustained *Girl's Own Paper* and the middle-class monthly magazines such as *Atalanta* and *Girl's Realm*. Many of the halfpenny papers were published by Alfred Harmsworth, later Lord Northcliffe, inventor of the mass media conglomerate—and the fortune and peerage to be made from it. Harmsworth was a marketing genius who used the contests, clubs, and advice columns to find out what readers wanted and even what language to cast it in.

In middle-class fiction, serving in a shop is respectable only if the shop sells toys or old lace or art goods or very expensive hats (presumably because the customers are largely female and upper class). Office work is a little suspect; the "secretaries" are generally private secretaries (working for a scholar or statesman at his home—with his wife's

OUR ARTIST.

TOO INTENT TO BE DISTURBED.

"Our artist: Too intent to be disturbed." The girl professional at work does
not need protection or a chaperone.

From *Girl's Own Paper* 17 (1895–1896): 561. Reproduced by permission of the British
Library, shelfmark P.P.5993.w.

31

presence in evidence), and the girl in a business office is apt to find the conditions fairly sleazy.

In the workgirls' papers however, "business" has entirely favorable meanings. The columns with advice about training and opportunities use "business" where middle-class magazines would describe the same work as a "career" or "profession." The jobs in a *Girls' Best Friend* series on "Businesses for Girls" include telegraph learner, Post Office sorter, and "typewriting girl in Parliament"—a post established two years ago, according to this 1898 article, for which one must have short-hand at 120 wpm and type 80 wpm on a Remington typewriter.[23]

The titles of the novels cited earlier showed us that middle-class girls, who would probably become typists and teachers, were fantasizing about medicine, art, and journalism. Girls who read the halfpenny papers—which sold sewing patterns to make "overalls for shop and factory" and nursery maids' dresses sized for ages twelve, fourteen, and sixteen—had a comparable fantasy in the idea of office work. But popular fiction also finds ways to cast a haze of glamour around the work we actually do. Just as the middle-class typist has an exciting persona in a novel about a statesman's private secretary, the workgirls' papers offer glamorized versions of domestic service in serials about the shipboard stewardess, the "Complexion Specialist," the waitress in an elegant tea shop, or the detective under cover as a lady's maid.

The halfpenny papers contain an extraordinary number of stories about circus performers. I'm a little puzzled about what to make of them. Is it the tomboy appeal? The performance and public attention—without having the right accent to be an actress? The courage? The "Queen of the Ring" in the first volume of *Girls' Best Friend* turns out to be the long-lost daughter of the Countess of Chippenham. At the conclusion she is "happy in the love of her mother . . . so happy that she has already refused to listen to the importunities of her many suitors."[24]

That makes us stop to consider the fourteen-year-old sent away to live-in domestic service. Many of the workgirl serials are "family romances," in the Freudian sense, that discover good parents elsewhere, but more simply they're also about being restored to a family. They make us see how young these working girls are. Indeed, it is not so much restoration to a nuclear family that provides the emotional fuel of these tales (and of the otherwise puzzling stories set in "convent schools" where girls have been sent for punishment) as it is a longing for mother. In contrast to the paternal recognition that caps the middle-class fantasies of L. T. Meade, fathers in working-class periodicals may remain unmentioned, but a good mother's embrace often supplies the happy ending.

The fiction in workgirls' papers often has a delightful physical energy. Girl detectives grapple with muscular (although female) suspects. In "Emma Brown of London; or, The Girl Who Defied the Kaiser," which began in *Girls' Reader* in January 1915, a servant runs away, gathers a band of nondescript Frenchmen and her trusty bulldog, and leads them to victory against the Germans.

It may be more raucous in workgirls' fiction, but with the independence and self-confidence that come from paid employment, a barely covert rebelliousness enters all kinds of writing for girls. Take a didactic book such as M. H. Cornwall Legh's *An Incorrigible Girl* [1899], in which a drunkard's daughter is sent to a county council rescue home where "wild girls could be . . . tamed, and the daughters of 'undesirable homes' rescued from them just in time, and all be turned into, what everybody said were so much wanted, well-trained domestic servants."[25] Narrative doubt wells up in the rhetoric—"undesirable homes" is in quotation marks; irony tinges the interruptions of "just in time," "what everybody said were so much wanted."

That tone becomes even more marked after the turn of the century. Although the lines of influence are impossible to trace, it is evident that the sassy smart-mouth manner of the working-class girl is on its way toward becoming a degree of acceptable "smartness" in *any* girl, a mark of her self-assurance—and a mark of the distance between the new girl and the old feminine ideal. We recall that L. T. Meade, one of the writers most popular among girls whose families could afford to keep them at school during their teens, had remarked that her readers love a heroine who is "a little imperative to her elders."[26]

When girls entered the workforce, the perceived social ranking of the various jobs open to them was only tenuously related to pay. Once the value of board and lodging is taken into account, real earnings were probably highest in domestic service and in factories—particularly unionized textile mills. Yet these two kinds of work had the least desirable image. Girls found domestic service demeaning because of the supervision, the dependence, and the irksome rules about "no followers"; yet many of the same girls saw the factory as "not genteel" because of the independence it promoted.

Ladies who did social service thought factory work was dangerous because girls and men worked in the same shops (and could be seen larking around when they poured out of the gates). These women tended to overlook the risks of privacy in domestic service. When religious tracts show a servant girl endangered by "rude" behavior it's usually the footman who is to blame, not the man of the house.[27] Mainstream publications for working girls were less reticent. *The Girl's Encyclopedia* [1909] provides a section on employment law that tells the young worker that "cruelty, violence, impropriety or familiarity (such as a kiss) done to a girl by one of the other sex against her will" is punishable, and gives the address of an agency for the protection of women and children.[28]

Among working-class girls, both dressmaking and shop work seemed more attractive than domestic service or the factory, yet both had poorer wages and working conditions. One young dressmaker wrote:

> The girls are kept working till half-past ten or eleven, day after day, through the best part of the season. That may not sound much, but it is bad enough when you have to do it. Where I am there are twenty girls, sitting round three oblong tables, in a room not bigger than an ordinary drawing room. You can think what the air is in July, when we have all been working in it for twelve hours . . . and then when eight o'clock comes, and you are dying for a breath of fresh air, you are told you will have to stop an hour longer, or perhaps two, or even three hours.[29]

Shop work also meant long hours, close supervision, fines that ate the wages, and (in the most desirable stores) the expense of dressing well. "Why," a writer in the *Monthly Packet* asked, "do so many women crowd into it? . . . First, there is the fact of social status. . . . The shop assistant all her life belongs to a higher caste, so to speak, than the domestic servant." She wears better clothes, has a better chance of marriage, and "looks forward to having her free Sunday. . . . The idea of a number of young people, all working and living together, is lively and amusing."[30] Once they had experienced the conditions of shop work, however, sales clerks tended to grow disillusioned. Factory girls, Evelyn March-Phillips reported, often continued to work after they married, but shop assistants saw marriage "as their one hope of release."[31]

Status interacts with questions of gender, sexuality, and the ideology of difference. Emily Pfeiffer in 1888 pointed out that men use an arsenal of sentimental arguments to protect girls against "unwomanly" callings—that is, in her words, "precisely such as offer the highest rewards in money."[32] The *Girl's Own Paper* reported a "widespread feeling, especially amongst the lower middle-class, that a woman becomes unwomanly when she enters into the same field of labour as a man, in direct competition with him."[33]

This is certainly one reason why the new occupations created in the 1880s by the typewriter and the telephone were particularly welcome. They were almost immediately labeled as women's work. Typing solved "the problem of finding suitable employment for ladies" because—like piano playing—it was "suited for their nimble fingers."[34] The telephone receptionist needed a clear speaking voice; employment guides said it was especially appropriate for "the daughters of professional men who have received few educational advantages."[35] Other occupations that required some training and offered the opportunity for earning one's independence failed to seize the popular imagination. *Girl's Own Paper* in 1880, for example, recommended horticulture, wood-engraving, bookbinding, and pharmaceutical dispensing[36]—but the "girl gardener" and her like did not become recognizable figures in fiction or other cultural artifacts.

Did a girl's social position come from her own work or from her father's occupation? The case of elementary teaching is interesting. The elementary schoolteacher was likely to be the daughter of a tradesman or even a laborer. Usually herself from a state-supported school, she began at fourteen as a "pupil teacher"—but after passing an exam at eighteen, she went to a training college and, later in the period, sometimes to a university.

The social class of young teachers created a dilemma for the Girls' Friendly Society, an Anglican organization designed to provide "friendship" between young ladies at home and girls from the working class.

WOMEN WHO WORK.

THE time was when no woman worked unless dire necessity made her. In that case, if she were one of the class designated "ladies," she cross-stitched impossible flowers in wool for private sale

The Typewriter

amongst her friends, or she essayed to teach the "young idea how to shoot." In either case, days of unsatisfactory drudgery with small pay were the result, because adequate training was absent even in the case of the governess, who administered "rule of thumb" as freely as did the cook. Happily, things are now changed, and there are a variety of occupations open to women who have the laudable desire to work.

Typewriting appears to have "caught on" with young girls more quickly than any other form of modern occupation. Probably that is because their fingers are nimble for the work, it is sedentary in character, does not take very long to learn, and serves as an equipment for a variety of posts. The fair typist, her fingers dancing

quickly over the tiny ivory keys, is to be seen in the merchant's office, in the editor's sanctum, in the classic seclusion of the author's study, and amongst the Blue Books in Government offices. The click, click of her machine is not unmusical, either, when one gets used to it ; at least, it will bear comparison with the monotonous playing of scales and five-finger exercises, or with the unmusical rendering of musical pieces, and besides, it has the advantage of being useful.

In London, the headquarters of women who type-write are in and around Chancery Lane. There, throngs of girls are to be seen each morning hurry-ing along to the offices of the typewriting firms where they are employed, or to the school where they go for instruction. And although the pay is never high, the competition to obtain a typewriter's post is always keen. In spite of the labour of deciphering and copying manuscript much corrected and often well-nigh illegible, the fair typista show no falling off in numbers, and continue, in fact, to hold the field against the male competitor whose fingers nature did not intend, it would appear, for work requiring a touch so delicate as that needed by an expert typist.

In addition to all this, the fair typewriter has actually figured in the region of romance. I read quite a charming love-story the other day, in which the heroine was a fair, brown-eyed girl of gentle birth acting as secretary and typist to a middle-aged man,

The Hospital Nurse

"Women Who Work." Career guides by the 1890s generally featured type-writing as a splendid opportunity for respectable independence.

From *Young Woman* 3 (1894–1895): 230. From the author's collection.

The people on its rolls were listed as either "associates" (the ladies) or "members" (working girls). Elementary teachers were insulted if they were put in the member category and often ceased attending. But according to one of the clergy wives who organized the GFS: "It is only necessary to go once to any 'Centre,' where large numbers of pupil-teachers of both sexes gather for lessons, . . . to realize how very much the tone of these girls needs raising."[37]

Now, compare that with the recollection of a pupil teacher: "All of us were desperately anxious about qualifying, getting to College, getting jobs in a wider world. . . . This idea . . . of success and independence made us capable of living laborious days and nights and shunning most of the delights of youth."[38]

What we see here is one example of the problems in recovering the history of girlhood: virtually all of our information comes from adults, who may well be unreliable or at least selective in what they observe or recall. The class bias in the language of the GFS report is evident. In objective terms, pupil-teacher centers were essentially coeducational Saturday secondary schools; the pupils were boys and girls between fourteen and eighteen who worked all week as classroom aides. They probably did talk to each other without much restraint—they were teenagers, after all, who had many experiences in common. Yet memoirs by those who were once pupil teachers emphasize seriousness, ambition, and the real bliss of having adequate teaching and of learning with other students who cared about the same things.

On the third hand, almost all of the autobiographies and memoirs about life as a pupil teacher were produced by women who remained single and had long careers in education, and who did their writing in the 1950s after they'd retired as superintendent of curriculum for Liverpool or headmistress in Camden Town—a self-selected group of bookish and ambitious girls who perhaps didn't join in whatever rowdiness and flirting there may have been.

One final suggestion about the "tone" that shocked the clergy wives: virtually every recollection of pupil-teacher life in the last decades of the nineteenth century that I have discovered mentions—with bated breath and great excitement, as a thrilling, liberating, and highly secret experience—reading Olive Schreiner's *The Story of an African Farm*.

Heterosexual relationships clearly stood on a piece of the contested ground that was reshaped by the impact of work on girls' culture. Both fiction and essays exposed the fear that self-support made girls less willing to marry, and that independence rendered them less attractive to men. A particularly poignant example appears in "The Girls of To-Day, by One of Them," in the *Girl's Own Paper* for December 2, 1899: "If we do not work . . . we are told that we cannot make good wives; and if we do work, that we shall be unable to make our husbands happy because they want companions more or less frivolous when they have been at work all day."[39]

On the other hand, as the middle-class work ethic came more and more to mean paid work, a certain distaste attached to the young lady whose exclusively social life could be seen as open commerce on the marriage market. The novels about students and bachelor girls celebrate comradeship between women and men. Because they are less artificial than "courting," such friendships will ultimately promote healthy marriage.

These characters have a "detached Amazon look,"[40] the look of someone who is not thinking about men and sex. Girlhood's innocence is invoked to permit their unprotected independence. An extraordinary number of the heroines are described as boyish—but there seems to be no disparaging overtone. "Girl" suggests prolonged latency rather than inappropriate masculinity. The lack of erotic tension enables wholesome working relationships with men; by calling her a girl, fiction evades the "danger" that a woman with economic and social freedom might prefer not to marry.

Paid work also enabled physical separation from home. The earlier advice manuals were sometimes blindingly naïve in their insistence that girls stay in the parental dwelling. The author of *Girlhood*, in 1869:

> Many working girls, as soon as they earn a few shillings, . . . leave their homes, and go into lodgings. We know that there is some excuse for this—that too often their homes are not happy places, and that they can really be more comfortable, as well as more independent, in strange houses. And yet, would it not be better—if not for themselves, yet for their brothers and sisters . . .—if they remained with them, and tried to make the home better and more comfortable?[41]

Three Girls in a Flat. The dust jacket of Ethel F. Heddle's 1896 novel, one of the many popular books about working girls on their own.

Reproduced by permission of the Bodleian Library, University of Oxford, shelfmark 2537.e.558.

Charitable ladies who actually worked with the poor recognized what both girls and their mothers knew: a one-room or two-room cottage was not a suitable place for teenagers of both sexes (plus, indeed, father himself). This was one of the primary reasons that mothers wanted their daughters to go into domestic service instead of other work—it got them out of the house. When industrial wages rose sharply toward the end of the century, working-class girls began to prefer jobs in man-ufacturing or transport, which could pay enough to live away from their parents.[42] The proportion entering domestic service declined—and women in search of servants to hire learned to de-emphasize the value of domestic work as training for marriage and suggest instead that it offered an adolescent experience like that of girls from other classes. The girl in service, one guide pronounced, "learns self-dependence and the habit of discipline, just as the home-taught daughter of richer par-ents generally gains by going to a boarding school."[43]

In fiction, working girls discovered the pleasures and responsibili-ties of the latchkey or the shared flat. Series in *Young Woman* and *Girl's Own Paper* gave instructions about cooking meals on a hot plate and dividing the chores. Novels coached through example: how to make cupboards from cheese boxes, where to get stamps for the lease, ways to conceal the bed when using the room for other purposes.

In the process, social and moral standards undergo another vast but almost unremarked change. In fiction of the 1890s, working middle-class girls can and do invite men friends into their rooms as long as it's clear that there is no romantic involvement. The seventeen-year-old of *A Home Ruler*—one of the many novels about gently raised young women who take to self-support after becoming penniless orphans—responds to the family doctor's criticism of her unchaperoned friend-ships by telling him that she is "a working woman and an artist. It is only rich idle people who have time for . . . all those sort of things."[44]

Many girls' novels voice at least a rhetorical heroism in the girl-woman's independence. A character in one L. T. Meade novel says that she and her like "struggle to succeed, because we want to join the brave band of those women who have learned to help themselves, and can fearlessly stand alone."[45] On the other hand, I have found no mention of the political reason for leaving home: after the local government reforms of the 1890s, unmarried women occupiers—even if they had only one room as a separate dwelling—were eligible to vote in school board and county council elections.[46]

Listen, however, to the resonance in a serial called "Handsome Harry, the Girl-Man," which ran in *Girls' Home* from November 19, 1910. Harriet Nash is fired for resisting the manager's sexual harass-ment and is unable find another job. Discouraged, hungry, looking for

VOL. I.—No. 39.]   ONE HALFPENNY—EVERY THURSDAY.   [NOVEMBER 26TH, 1910.

Handsome Harry wears her brother's clothes and enjoys a man's job.

From *Girls' Home* 1 (1910): 317. Reproduced by permission of the British Library, Newspaper Library, Colindale, shelfmark 661.

something to pawn, she pulls out the box that her brother left behind when he went to sea. Nothing but clothes . . . Oh! With her brother's wardrobe and her hair chopped off, she discovers that life is much more pleasant. She enjoys freedom of movement, the absence of insults from men, a very good job as a trolley driver, and some healthy competition with her workmates in an athletic club.

Working-class papers were frank about the marriage question, often printing short paragraphs such as this one from *Forget-Me-Not* headed "What Girl Marries Soonest?" The answer: not the idle girl but the "business girl," who "is continually thrown right with men all the time" because "propinquity is the greatest of all match-makers . . . any sort of girl who is not actually hopelessly plain may marry any man she pleases with whom she works."[47] *Forget-Me-Not* was also, however, blunt about the dangers of romance: "Don't marry a man for a livelihood," it warned in 1901; "there are better, safer, and more honourable ways by which women can earn a living nowadays."[48]

The fear that a massive realignment of gender roles lurked in the offing was muted, in middle-class fiction and even in "Handsome Harry," by insisting on the youthfulness of girls. Real career work that pays a decent income must be justified by invoking other powerful traditions to provide reassurance that the worker has some good reason to remain single. The doctor in L. T. Meade's *Mary Gifford, M.B.* (1898) takes up an East End practice begun by the man she loved, who has died; the social worker in *A Daughter of the Democracy* (Ethel Forbes, 1911) also remains single because of her lover's death. Family tragedies or eugenic imperatives require other admirable professional women to live solitary lives.

While the stereotype of femininity as equivalent to service and self-sacrifice was partly reshaped by the culture of work, attitudes about certain kinds of work were simultaneously revised by women's entry. We might call this something like "frontlash"—as women move into a new profession, the conception of that profession is altered to show how it serves the womanly ideal.

The woman physician, for example "will have the delightful consciousness of being useful to her fellow-women . . . and the satisfaction of making herself independent, so as to be able to stretch out a helping hand to those that need it."[49] Notice the instant melioration of financial independence with yet more service. Employment guides recommended new careers by pointing out their links to the traditional emotional labors girls and women performed at home. "Mental Nursing," for example, "calls for considerable self-sacrifice" and requires the nurse "to adapt herself to the varying mood of her charges."[50]

The character of schoolteachers changed markedly when the profession was feminized. The number of elementary pupils almost tripled between 1875 and 1914.[51] To create a national system of schooling, make it compulsory, and extend its length at both ends required vast numbers of new teachers—at wages that could not attract adequately educated men. Teaching became a job requiring cheerfulness and love of children,[52] though as a man's profession it had needed intellect, system, order, and force of character.

Much the same thing happened with clerical work. The number of female clerks exploded from 6,000 in 1881 to 125,000 in 1911.[53] Early in the Victorian period boys who began as clerks might expect to rise into management, but as businesses and civil service expanded, clerical work was subdivided and made routine; upward mobility became rare; and the pay eroded to working-class levels. While this was happening, the description of clerical work became more and more aligned to the feminine ideal. The "lady clerk," according to an article in *Young Woman*, "must learn to do exactly what she is told" and "to work in silence."[54] Advice to boys taking up clerical work had emphasized brains and energy, alertness, confidence, and seeking opportunities to take the initiative.[55] The value of obedience (or lack of initiative) comes in with women.

As has become evident, although the number of unmarried females in the work-force did not change significantly, the proportion working in white-collar jobs—as teachers, nurses, shop assistants, clerks, civil servants—underwent dramatic gains between 1881 and 1911.[56] Compulsory and longer schooling gave bright working-class girls the literacy to enter these occupations. It would seem also that they brought some of their values about independence, sexual responsibility, and economic self-interest with them into the culture of white-collar working girls.

Furthermore, as we now realize, the mid-Victorian "ideal" of womanhood (fragile, dependent, protected) had excluded three-quarters of the unmarried female population, who labored in factories, on farms, in workshops and private houses. As work became part of girls' culture, girlhood was increasingly conceptualized as an age class without reference to economic status.

When the middle class began to approve of paid work for its own girls, "going to work" was seen as a temporary stage, a learning experience. The fact that work provided "training"—for one thing or another—made it acceptable. The concept of the worker as a girl, not a mature woman, removed her from the sexual marketplace, and bought her a new freedom in social and living arrangements. The culture of work promoted a girl's self-dependence, provided a new estimate of her capabilities, and reshaped her romantic expectations.

These gains, however, had their corresponding cost. To think of the worker as a girl is to emphasize lack of maturity, lack of skill, need of supervision, emotional (rather than intellectual) labor. It encourages separate job categories, impassable barriers to advancement, deskilling, separate pay scales. Margaret Bateson, writing in *Girl's Own Paper* in 1896, discussed the problem of reduced wages in any field that became identified as women's work and gently suggested the value of "combination."[57] Clementina Black—who had daringly (if unsuccessfully) presented a motion on equal pay for equal work at the 1888 Trades Union Congress—perceived that both opportunities and wages suffered from the assumption that "girls" were working. She protested that many female employments "offer no opening for the future. For instance, shop girls, nurses, and teachers of all sorts are preferred moderately young; after a certain time of life they have a difficulty in finding fresh employment and their earnings tend rather to diminish than to increase."[58]

The social and economic forces that encouraged occupational segregation and the habit of paying females less than a living wage were not created by the working girl, and they continued to hold sway long after she learned to call herself a woman. Yet although it was economically damaging to see "going out to work" as merely a transitory phase, the world of work was indeed one of the key components that created a culture of girlhood as a distinctive—and extended—passage between puberty and marriage.

three

College, and a Hero

ON SATURDAY, JUNE 7, 1890, CAMBRIDGE STUDENTS ASSEMBLED TO
learn the results of their exams. The hall, according to the *Cambridge
Review*, was "absolutely crammed with men, so tightly packed as to be
incapable of individual motion." Women, not admitted to the floor of the
senate house, took places in the gallery. Although for them no degrees or
fellowships rested on the outcome (women were not full members of the
University until 1948), Newnham students were "there to a woman,"[1]
waiting for a drama they expected yet hardly dared anticipate.

The examiner in charge, W. W. Rouse Ball,[2] began reading out male
names, in order of rank. In the mathematical tripos—generally con-
sidered the world's most intellectually demanding examination—the
senior wrangler (the man at the head of the list, virtually assured of an
academic appointment at Cambridge or perhaps an invitation to head
the math department of a young North American university) was, as
expected, Geoffrey Bennett of St. John's, one of five students who
began to study math together at University College, London, when
they were as yet too young for Cambridge matriculation.[3]

Mr. Ball reached the end of the list. It took some time for the senate
house to grow quiet enough that he could continue. Although women
were not officially ranked, it had become the custom to read out their
names and report the place each would have taken: "between twentieth
and twenty-first" or "bracketed with eighth." At last Mr. Ball was able
to begin. "Women," he announced. The men shouted, took off their

hats, demanded that he say "ladies" instead, and made other rowdy end-of-year undergraduate noises. Marion Cowell, who was in the gallery, wrote to her mother:

> The examiner, of course, could not attempt to read the names until there was a lull. Again and again he raised his cap, but would not say "ladies" instead of "women" . . . He signalled with his hand for the men to keep quiet, but he had to wait some time.[4]

Finally his next words could be heard: "Above the Senior Wrangler . . ."

A "great and prolonged cheering"[5] overwhelmed the examiner's voice and drowned out the name; it continued, swelling over the rest of the names, pouring into the street, sending telegrams and newspaper reports around the English-speaking world. Women and girls "cried for joy."[6] Even more than an outstanding individual achievement and a moment of great symbolic importance for women's education, this was an instance in which the narrative's emblematic power was extraordinarily sweet and satisfying.

The twenty-two-year-old who achieved the unique honor was Philippa Garrett Fawcett (1868–1948). Her mother, Millicent Garrett Fawcett (1847–1929), lectured and wrote on women's causes, and would soon be leader of the National Union of Women's Suffrage Societies. Her father, Henry Fawcett (1833–1884), was elected to Parliament in time to vote with they "ayes" when John Stuart Mill proposed amending the 1867 Reform Bill to grant women the vote and, in the cabinet as postmaster general, had significantly expanded women's opportunities in the civil service. Philippa's maternal aunt, Dr. Elizabeth Garrett Anderson (1836–1917), was largely responsible for women achieving the right to become registered medical practitioners. Philippa herself, as an infant, was present at the meeting held in her parents' drawing room in 1869 when a group of reform-minded Cambridge men joined with Henry Fawcett (who despite becoming blind in young manhood was Professor of Political Economy as well as a member of Parliament) to discuss a plan of lectures for ladies—the seed from which (ultimately) Newnham College flowered.[7]

The extraordinary aptness of this particular girl's success probably created the "delirium of joy."[8] In addition, her triumph seemed finally to demolish all of the tired arguments about women's intellectual limits. Although scores were not public, academic committees have always been prone to leak; before long people with contacts in Cambridge understood that Fawcett's victory was neither narrow nor a gift. Her marks were said to be "13 per cent. better" than those of Bennett[9] (with whom she had shared those early math classes in London). One examiner reported that her work was "similar to that of her father"—who had also, in his undergraduate days, been regarded as possible senior wrangler—but "with greater mathematical knowledge."[10] Even more significant, given the widespread assumption that women were emotionally unsuited for competition, Henry Fawcett—unlike his daughter—was believed to have missed the highest honors because of "excitement and mental disturbance."[11]

Philippa Fawcett was not the first Cambridge woman to achieve a notable triumph. In 1887 Agnata Ramsay of Girton had written the only examination paper put into the first division of the first class in classics, an achievement celebrated with unusually good grace by *Punch* in a George Du Maurier cartoon showing her being ushered, in solitary splendor, into a first-class railway carriage marked "For Ladies Only." Furthermore, many other Newnham and Girton students turned in stunning achievements in June 1890. The *Englishwoman's Review* for July 15, 1890, called it a "record absolutely without precedent." Sixteen women in addition to Fawcett were among the top hundred in mathematics; Margaret Alford of Girton was bracketed with the senior classic; women won honors at every class in both natural science and history. In the words of the *Englishwoman's Review*: "Miss Fawcett alone, or Miss Alford alone, might have been regarded as exceptions, special instances of the hereditary genius, . . . but when so many others range in positions comparatively close behind them, both in Cambridge and in London University, there can be no refuge in the proverbial exception."[12]

The uniquely satisfying wording of Fawcett's triumph was, of course, made possible only by women's official exclusion: no man could ever be placed—in the phrase that also appeared in the *Times* list of examination results—"above the Senior Wrangler." The journal *Education* reported that "the moral importance of her victory is far and away greater than that of a dozen Senior Wranglers of the opposite sex."[13] An early historian of the women's movement wrote:

HONOUR TO AGNETA FRANCES RAMSAY !
(CAMBRIDGE, JUNE, 1887.)

"First Class, Ladies Only." In an unusually celebratory cartoon from *Punch*, George Du Maurier recognizes Agnata Frances Ramsay's achievement as the only candidate to place in the first class in Cambridge's Classical tripos in June 1887, although he misspells her name.

From *Punch* 92 (1887): 326. Reproduced by permission of the Bodleian Library, University of Oxford, shelfmark Per. 2539.d.1/29.

Gone now were the arguments that women were incapable of advanced abstract thought; gone was the notion that arithmetic was too severe for females. Nothing more appropriate or satisfactory could possibly have happened, and the rejoicing which found expression in bonfires in the Newnham garden was echoed all over the country.[14]

For the next decade or so that scene—the reading of names in the senate house, the expectation, the undergraduates' roar, the triumphant bonfire and fireworks and dancing that lasted into the night—was multiply renarrated in memoirs and fiction and essays about college life. The events at Cambridge in June 1890 gained, for a short generation, the stature of heroic myth, encapsulated in the instantly recognized reference: "above the senior wrangler."

Even by 1915, no more than a few thousand women had been students at Oxford or Cambridge, taken examinations for a London degree, or attended classes at one of the mixed-sex provincial universities. Nevertheless, the knowledge that women had surpassed men in institutions central not only to the intellectual but also to the political and cultural life of the nation gave the idea of "college" an enormous impact on a thoughtful girl's sense of potential. As a pioneer student wrote in 1914, even though only "one girl in a hundred has any sort of University career, the other ninety-nine are unconsciously affected by it, and their standard of life and its work altered."[15]

The first students gathered at Hitchin (Girton's initial location) in 1869, but although intellectual magazines discussed women's higher education during the 1860s and 1870s, the surge in interest did not reach a wide public until the next decade.[16] In the 1880s girls' magazines and fiction began assiduously to spread information about women's share in a previously male right (and rite). Articles on women's colleges were published in the earliest issues of *Girl's Own Paper*. On July 22, 1882, a full-page woodcut of "Sweet Girl Graduates"[17] in cap and gown appeared. A dissenting essay on "The Disadvantages of Higher Education," which argued that "it has yet to be proved that Cambridge examinations assist women in their household duties,"[18] was effectively demolished on the contributors' page by fourteen-year-old Bertha Mary Jenkinson, who quoted Scripture, gave examples of women's achievements, and pointed out that moral as well as economic dangers arose when women were unable to support themselves.[19]

The college mythos failed to make its way into workgirls' papers (except, rarely, in a joke or cartoon), but its frequent appearance in the (more expensive) monthlies *Atalanta*, *Young Woman*, and *Girl's Realm* suggests its appeal for girls educated at home in vicarages and country houses, town-bred middle-class daughters, and even board-school girls with intellectual ambitions and a prospect of teacher training. "College" supplied an imaginative frame that let a girl reconceptualize her sense of life's potential. The "girl graduate" or "college girl" was something new (and, for a time, fluid). She was not bounded by home and family duties, yet her class and moral status were secure. At college girls had companionship and community. Individual achievement was admired; girls who disciplined incursions into their space and time were heroic rather than selfish.

Although college was (economically and practically) out of reach for the vast majority of girl readers, it provided a screen to project desires, a script with images, places, and situations where victories could be envisioned. College, thus imagined, was a vastly improved home with minimal supervision, congenial companions, private space, and individual self-development—without any corresponding adult burdens. Just as the fin de siècle New Woman typically had the social status to claim as privilege the self-support, independence, and unchaperoned passage through city streets that were a necessity for working women, the new girl in her college version was safely supervised at a discreet and unobtrusive distance.

Within the imaginative space of girls' culture, "college" meant escape from home, economic potential, freely chosen friendships, a whiff of heterosexual romance, and a certain amount of quiet subversion. A female head topped by mortarboard—we must remember how startling the image once was—appeared in cartoons and advertisements, on book covers, decorating the title of the monthly magazine *Sisters*, and even at the head of an "Our Girls' Parliament" letters column in the penny weekly tabloid *Our Girls*. And the "Parliament" motif suggests recognized subtexts to be read—almost always—in and through the college student. Girls' culture made it known that students at Newnham and Girton emulated national politics in serious debate.

"Sweet girl graduates." A triumphant illustration in *Girl's Own Paper* marks women's admission as full members of convocation at the University of London, which made them eligible for all degrees and privileges of the university.

From *Girl's Own Paper* 3 (1881–1882): facing page 682. Reproduced by permission of the Bodleian Library, University of Oxford, shelfmark Per. 2537.d.1/3.

(Philippa Fawcett served as home secretary in Newnham's 1888 Liberal Unionist "government."[20]) Light-hearted stories made the subversion overt; in May Baldwin's *Golden Square High School* (1908), for example, a girl explains that the mock Parliament exists " 'so that we may be at home in the real Parliament when we get there.'"[21]

As the first university-based college for women, Girton occupied a particularly strong emblematic space. The earliest novel to make capital of the name was Annie Edwardes's *A Girton Girl*, serialized in *Temple Bar* in 1881 and published in three volumes in 1885. An avatar of contemporary stereotypes (and their cash value), Edwardes's book is about a girl turned into a man-hater by disappointment in love. Her intellectual ambitions disappear as soon as a better suitor appears; on her only visit to Cambridge, midway through the third volume, she doesn't even set foot inside Girton.

Soon thereafter, however, several American novels republished in England assembled the motifs that became commonplace in British girls' fiction: a mix of students from varied backgrounds, the joy of learning and the pleasures of community life, caricatured objections from absurdly conventional men, the reform of a girl whose "short hair" and "masculine stride" prejudice people against the college, and the delicious sense of leading the way toward a new future.[22] Before long the physical layout and customs of Girton, Newnham, Somerville, and Lady Margaret were reflected in scenes so broadly known as to become clichés: the fire brigade, the debates, cocoa parties (which had become coffee parties by 1911), long walks along the river, rooms decorated with Morris papers, Burne-Jones prints, and a terra-cotta rag rug, the tensions and glories of examination week. Even such specific incidents as a ferry accident during May week in which the chaperone Alice Gardner was rescued by two male undergraduates found their way very quickly into fiction.[23]

Although the charm of college life glamorized certain "unfeminine" qualities, the subversive savors—of feminism, exam success, equality—were quickly submerged beneath comforting reassurances. It was often difficult for girls to attend college, even in families where brothers were habitually sent. Gertrude Bell wrote to her father at age seventeen (in 1885): "Above all don't laugh at me, I really think I seriously want to go."[24] Evelyn Sharp, who won an honorable mention in

Atalanta's 1890–1891 scholarship competition,[25] "never managed quite
to live down [her] resentment"[26] that her parents would not send her.
"Everyone," wrote Constance Maynard of her time at Girton in the
mid-1870s, "had come to College by her own strong desire, everyone
had come in the face of a little laughter, . . . and the atmosphere was
charged with electricity."[27]

Despite the narrow accommodations and penny-pinching meals so
memorably described in Virginia Woolf's dinner at "Fernham"—
Margaret Haig Thomas, later viscountess Rhondda, left Somerville in
her first year because of its ugliness and bad food[28]—the single most
striking motif in early college stories and memoirs is the bliss of pos-
sessing one's own room. Emily Davies called it the most distinctive
feature of college as compared to family life.[29] Helen Swanwick
remembered her first day at Girton in 1882:

> To have a study of my own and to be told that, if I chose to put
> "Engaged" on my door, no one would so much as knock was in itself so
> great a privilege as to hinder me from sleep. I did not know till then how
> much I had suffered from the incessant interruptions of my home life. I
> could have worked quite easily in a mere noise. I never found it at all
> difficult to do prep. in a crowded schoolroom. What disturbed my mind
> were the claims my mother made on my attention, her appeals to my
> emotions and her resentment at my interest in matters outside the fam-
> ily circle.[30]

In my first reading of college fiction, I was bothered by the attention authors lavished on furniture and wall-hangings. I remember won-
dering whether one *Girl's Own Paper* piece was really a college story, or
if it was an article on interior decorating in disguise. Rereading the article, however, I realize that the wealth of detail creates an emotional
glow that affirms the intense pleasure of controlling one's own space.
It is perhaps difficult for us to appreciate the urgency of girls' joy in
privacy. A passage from a delicately bound little 1903 volume probably
intended as a confirmation present might help. Although occasionally,
the writer says, it may be "good discipline" to be "left alone for an hour
or two," one should never allow oneself to expect it; if the experience
is "continually repeated, it becomes a hardship to be interrupted," and
a girl "will grow irritable, selfish, and self-centered."[31]

"Phil had made her room look as much like a Girton study as possible."
Amy Clarke's 1896 novel *A Clever Daughter* suggests the influence of college as an idea and the extent to which other girls knew about college life.

From the author's collection.

The college room encoded college liberation. Eleanor Lodge—the ninth child in her family—went to Lady Margaret Hall in October 1890 and found it "simply a revelation . . . of what life might be."

> The very fact of having a room of one's own, a place where one not only could work, but was expected to work, the possibility of independence, of arranging one's time for oneself, of getting up and going to bed according to one's own ideas and not those of others, made each day an adventure and a joy.[32]

Constance Maynard remembered that her sense of delicious independence began when girls assembled at a center in London to take the entrance exam: "Even the trifling fact of turning out alone into the streets of London, choosing a shop and ordering coffee for luncheon (sometimes, O vanity, even an ice!) was to me a sort of presage of the liberty that now would be mine."[33] Another woman recalled her first night at Newnham in the 1890s: "I drew the curtains and lit my lamp and sat and looked at my fire. I didn't do anything else the whole evening, it was so blissful to look at one's *own* fire."[34]

The regulations of college life were made familiar through essays and fiction. At Girton in the mid-1870s, according to an American journalist:

> Students are required to enter their names on the marking-roll three times daily, and to be present at lectures, unless especially excused by the Mistress. They must not accept evening invitations more than on an average once a week; they must not receive visits from gentlemen in their rooms; and they must always be within the college gates by six o'clock in winter, or before dark in summer, except when they are out visiting, in which case notice is given to the Mistress of their destination, and they may be out till eleven.[35]

The reporter called these rules "as slight as possible." We need to notice that they do *not* forbid walking in Cambridge alone in the daytime, or visiting with men in the college's public areas, or going out in the evening so long as notice is given. In girls' novels, the regulations felt like "absolute liberty."[36] Even the intellectual freedom to read on their own was thrilling; Jane Harrison remembered that Cheltenham students were forbidden to buy books because of "Miss Beale's horror of what she called 'undigested knowledge.'"[37]

An 1876 essay provided a typical schedule, which fiction repeated, with some variations, for the next forty years. Students rose at seven, had prayers in the lecture room at eight, and ate breakfast from 8:15 until 9:00. They worked independently in their own rooms until lunch, which was available from noon to three. After lunch most students had an hour's walk or other exercise and then attended a lecture. The instructor reviewed students' work, answered questions, and then lectured on "portions of the subject, or methods of treatment which are not found in the class books in use." Dinner was at six, followed by evening study. At nine or thereabouts, students would often make tea or cocoa over their own fires and invite friends. "These gatherings," said the essayist, "take the place of the men's 'wines.'"[38]

In later years women could attend lectures with men, and the women's colleges also developed their own qualified instructors. (Philippa Fawcett, for example, was on the staff at Newnham from 1890 to 1901.) This shifted the hour for lectures, since instruction no longer depended on the generosity of dons who volunteered to repeat in late afternoon at a women's college the work they had done with a class of men in the morning. Even in the mid-1870s many professors admitted women to lectures, though they usually required that a chaperone also be present. (University wives and other sympathetic older women generally performed this service, though in the 1880s, Janet Courtney, studying philosophy at Lady Margaret, had to hire a chaperone, since she couldn't find a volunteer for subjects such as logic.[39]) Others professors, however, remained adamant. At Oxford, John Ruskin said he could not

> let the bonnets in, on any conditions this term. The three public lectures will be chiefly on angles, degrees of colour-prisms (without any prunes) and other such things of no use to the female mind, and they would occupy the seats in mere disappointed puzzlement.[40]

Of the first four women's colleges, Girton was most like the men's. By 1890 each student had a "set" made up of bedroom and study; the other three colleges had bed-sitting rooms. In addition, Girton required that all of its students work for regular university examinations under the same rules as men. Newnham, Somerville, and Lady Margaret offered residents the opportunity to do shorter courses and special "women's examinations."[41]

Thus there were shades of connotation in the college stereotypes. Girton was strictly intellectual (and perhaps dangerously "masculine"). In Amy Clarke's *A Clever Daughter* [1896] the self-centered, selfish, ambitious girl aims for Girton, while the home-loving foil who wants education to be "better able to do women's work in the world" plans on Newnham (which was, perhaps not incidentally, the author's college in 1875–1876 when she was Amy Key). Oxford had stricter regulations for walking in town and going out in the evening. The Oxford colleges remained more "homelike." In the 1890s Somerville and Lady Margaret each had about 40 students in residence; Girton had 100; and Newnham had 150.

Cambridge kept a higher intellectual reputation even after Oxford also began admitting women to exams. Since university regulations required that examinations be taken within ten terms (customarily a preliminary May term plus three full academic years in residence), women who came up without knowing the Latin and Greek required of all male students were at a great disadvantage. Some of them spent two years learning the classics needed for the Previous ("Little-Go") exam, which men often took in their first May term. These women would then have only one year to prepare for their major, or tripos, subject. From 1875 to 1903 Cambridge university allowed women to take a modern languages and literature examination in place of Latin and Greek. Newnham used the privilege, Girton did not. At Newnham, in addition, some students spent only a year or two in residence and took the Higher Local instead of other examinations. A university-administered exam on the order of A-levels in Britain or College Board subject tests in the United States, the Higher Local had a specific practical value: by the middle 1880s it was becoming the essential qualification for teachers in the reformed girls' secondary schools.

Women who arrived at college with inadequate preparation were, understandably, under a great deal of pressure. One anecdote about Philippa Fawcett's tripos success was that Newnham principal Anne Clough had said in her speech to the rapturously celebrating students: "I am sure . . . it is a great lesson to you all—to go to bed early!"[42] The story was widely circulated, as were pictures of the slim and upright Miss Fawcett, who was also a hockey star. Given the nineteenth-century belief in gentlewomen's fragility, colleges needed to combat the myth that strenuous study would ruin women's health, especially their reproductive health.

Very early in the debate, Harriet Martineau suggested that women's illness was caused by idleness and depression, rather than overwork, and slyly suggested that the "Ladies' Colleges in Harley Street and Bedford Square" were worth the expense simply to avoid doctors' fees, since the companionship and the stimulus of working for examinations would give girls an aim and keep them occupied.[43] An American reporter pointed out that English colleges, unlike those in the United States, had no "system of marking at recitations"; thus a woman "temporarily out of sorts" could miss lectures if necessary.[44] As late as 1912, however, the "risks" of menarche remained in people's minds.[45] Even some proponents of women's education thought examinations were too stressful (and that competition was unfeminine). Frances Marshall, whose fiction was published under a male pseudonym, clearly approves of Cambridge life for the girls in her novels yet can write that examinations

> were literally sapping the blood out of the girls' faces. Their hearts were stout enough, and they wouldn't have given in for the world; but day by day they grew whiter, and their eyes grew heavy, with dark lines beneath them, and the sweetest natures grew nervous and irritable beneath the strain.[46]

The popular college-girl novels and stories, by and large, had very little to say about books, study, lectures, examinations, and intellectual life. Nor, for that matter, did the typical male "university novel." A conventionalized genre from mid-century, university novels dealt in athletics and pranks, drinking, gambling, risky connections with town girls, and (sometimes) attacks of Christian seriousness to bring about a satisfactory resolution. College-girl stories had a similar focus on the social side of university life—though there was, needless to say, a different set of excitements, dangers, and pleasures.

Fiction about girls' education did, however, usually point out the economic benefits. The career goals of a boy's university career were generally unstated: the real aim of three years at Oxford or Cambridge was to practice supervised independence away from home, get older, and come to know the men who would be the political and cultural leaders of one's generation.

So, in a much more compelling fashion, was college society enormously appealing to girls. It may be hard to appreciate just how isolated many of them were. Emily Davies said that college would most benefit the "two thousand sisters of the two thousand undergraduates who, at any given time, are under instruction at Cambridge." Most of them, she continued, could not even use the lectures and libraries available in cities because they were "scattered about in country houses and parsonages, and in the families of professional men and retired merchants and manufacturers in the villages and smaller towns."[47] A girl raised virtually without peers and educated by a governess was simultaneously "individualized" and unaware of her individuality, enmeshed in adult control and without private choice, and subject to a sense of isolation and uniqueness in thought. Women's college life was more communal than men's. Men largely ate and entertained in their own rooms; they could choose a "set" and be exclusive in their friendships. Women, by contrast, had all their meals in the common dining room.

Most women students came from the professional and upper-middle class.[48] An American was surprised to find so few students from "families of high position"; girls of "the wealthier class," she said, were in the majority at Vassar and Bryn Mawr.[49] She seems, however, to have overlooked the difference in class structure; English "families of high position" were seldom the social equivalent of "wealthier" Americans. The expense, however, was prohibitive for many middle-class families. Somerville in 1879 would have cost, at a minimum, £75 a year,[50] while an 1887 advice manual suggests that one year's "board, lodging, and instruction"—exclusive of "personal expenses, such as washing and books"—at any of the Oxford or Cambridge women's colleges would come to £105.[51] Although Newnham—and perhaps the other colleges as well—had a lower fee for students who were preparing to teach,[52] even one year at college would cost more than the beginning annual salary a college-trained woman could expect.

On the other hand, relatives or trustees might provide college fees for a girl who would need to support herself. The practical advantages were indisputable: the new girls' secondary schools demanded qualified teachers. With suitable certificates it was (for the first time) possible for a young woman from the middle class to prepare for a career that would provide an adequate income and some independence. "A good Cambridge certificate," reported the *Englishwoman's Review* in 1881, "is equivalent to an increase of from £50 to £100 in the salary which a future teacher can obtain."[53]

Even given the relatively narrow social range from which students were drawn, the freedom to choose her own friends was another significant liberation. Many secondary schools did not allow girls to walk home together without their parents' written permission.[54] Pupils at Kensington High School, indeed, were "forbidden to hold any communication with each other during school hours."[55] But on the first night of term, readers learned, "college corridors rang with light-hearted laughter and merry greetings as old chums met again, and 'freshers' made the pleasant discovery that Newnham is a world where formal introductions are dispensed with."[56]

Women's colleges were proud of their diversity, limited though it may have been. An article in an 1896 issue of *Sisters* reported that one of "the ladies who took the B.Sc. degree at Durham University last week was Kate Colborne, of Sunderland, the first girl in England who has gone from a *Higher Grade Board School* straight to the University and taken her degree."[57] College novels typically have multiple heroines, who validate plural roles for women: the scholarship girl who will teach, the rich girl devoted to social work, the beauty who will marry.[58] Anne Jemima Clough, sister of the poet and longtime principal of Newnham, named social breadth first when describing what women gained by college life:

> Our colleges have gathered together women from very varied homes, from different classes in society, with their special tastes and opinions, and, lastly, from different countries. These women have lived together and studied together as friends and comrades; they have learnt to plan and work together and to carry out schemes among themselves. Their studies have taught them energy and self-control; their examinations have taught them the power of collecting their thoughts rapidly, of putting them into words, and of exercising their memories.[59]

Opponents of women's comradeship worried about what girls might learn. Charlotte Yonge initially believed girls in groups "always hurt one another in manner and tone."[60] By the time of her final novel, however, a term at Oxford leaves her heroine "much improved . . . even in appearance and manner."[61] Mary Agnes Hamilton, a Newnham student in the earliest years of the twentieth century, recollects that she was "blankly ignorant about sex" and that Newnham conversation in her period also avoided religion: "If we left religion alone and sex to wait for the revelations of possible matrimony, we made up for this by an intense concern with politics."[62]

Joan Burstyn has outlined the Victorian arguments against college for women. Marriages, it was said, would become unstable, because educated women would argue with their husbands. Qualified women would also take men's jobs and depress their salaries. Educating women would divert scarce resources from men who—because of their superior intellectual and creative potential—would better profit from the training. Furthermore, Darwinism (as interpreted by conservative voices such as the *Saturday Review*'s) demonstrated that evolutionary advance grew from an increasing divergence of male and female; allowing the sexes to become more alike would risk degeneration. Finally, sexual and reproductive "dangers," which had generally been veiled at mid-century, were openly discussed once the threat of women's competition became more real. Physicians asserted that girls between fifteen and twenty must establish healthy reproductive systems; if they used their energy on intellectual achievement they risked breakdown, masculinization, sterility, or becoming the mothers of sickly children.[63]

Frances Power Cobbe (among others) snickered at some of these objections. Did people who believed that educating women would "obliterate the natural differences," she asked, have eyes, scientific knowledge, or even common sense?[64] Some fair-minded men also doubted that male intellects were inevitably superior. In 1880, when Charlotte Scott was the first Girton student to rank among the first class in mathematics, the *Times* pointed out that "for a young woman under twenty-two to have been eighth Wrangler implies very much more than for a young man of the same age to have been Senior Wrangler" because "mathematical talent in a boy is fostered and nursed and forced by anxious masters and parents. In a girl the fire of mathematical genius might burn and blaze for a long time without being so much as suspected."[65]

Charlotte Scott's bracket, incidentally—the official eighth wrangler of 1880—was George W. Johnson, who worked actively in Josephine Butler's campaign to repeal the Contagious Diseases Acts, edited her memoirs, and published, in 1926, a book entitled *The Evolution of Woman: From Subjection to Comradeship*. Scott herself earned a D.Sc. from London University in 1885 and became professor of mathematics at Bryn Mawr. The *Englishwoman's Review* commented: "It is to be feared that the States will tempt from us some of our most learned women, as more valuable University posts are open to them across the water."[66]

Fiction regularly supplied concrete images of women's achievement for the enlightenment of girls who did not read the *Times* or the *Englishwoman's Review*. One novel describes photographs in the reception room at Newnham:

> Some of the women here had been wranglers, senior classics, had taken First Classes in science, history, moral philosophy.... No college in the University during the same period, covering the same number of years, could show such a roll of distinguished names.[67]

Even the readers of *Girl's Own Paper* knew that the reason women were allowed to take exams but were not awarded degrees was that degrees "would admit them to the governing bodies of the Universities."[68] An 1893 novel by Frances Marshall gently mocks the gentlemanly protection of turf. The "Master of St. Benedict's" regards "every concession made to the weaker sex as a step towards that dreadful time when a female Vice-Chancellor will confer degrees in the Senate House, and a lady D.D. will occupy the University pulpit."[69] In another novel Marshall explains ironically that women don't need the "stimulus" or "reward" of a degree; unlike men, women "are strong enough, persevering enough, diligent, self-sacrificing, and quite ambitious enough to be able to do without such spurs to learning."[70]

Women took pleasure in circulating sly stories. Vera Brittain begins her 1960 history of Oxford women with the once-familiar narrative of A. M. A. H. Rogers, who placed first in the Oxford Senior Local examination in 1871. Worcester College asked Rogers's father "to convey to the successful candidate" the offer of a scholarship—hastily with-drawn when told that the initials belonged to Annie Mary Anne Henley Rogers.[71] Many early students saw themselves—as Lilian Faithfull, who entered Somerville in 1883, put it—as "members, however young and obscure, in a great forward movement for the women's cause."[72]

Though college-girl fiction is seldom aggressively feminist, it might be called "safely" feminist; it almost inevitably carries whiffs of quiet subversion. Women at Oxford and Cambridge realize that they do not, actually, want to be college men; they begin to take a condescending tone about male students' childishness. In one novel the visitors to a women's college walk "up a stairs cleaner than it would have been in the men's colleges."[73] In another, in lectures "while the girls were intent taking notes, the men were whispering together and laughing."[74]

The capitulation of a girl scholar who had vowed never to marry quickly became a romantic cliché—but it did not inevitably encode female subordination. In a lighthearted version produced by E. Nesbit for *Atalanta*, the climax comes when Laura Wentworth swims "swiftly and steadily" out to sea to rescue her despairing suitor, finally towing him back to shore (and marrying him).[75] Surprisingly, a very similar scene ends Charlotte Yonge's last novel, *Modern Broods* (1900). The university student Agatha, on her way to New Zealand with her friend Dolores to give a course of lectures on electricity, saves a young man after a shipwreck—a man who had failed the civil service exam and was (as girls had once done) living at home doing nothing. She, however, doesn't marry him—she becomes a scientist instead.

Other turns of story put new twists on the convention of female moral superiority. Girls make good use of college while their brothers or cousins fall into disgrace. Furthermore, women gain confidence when mental training and college debate have taught them to trust their own authority. The central conflict in Frances Marshall's *A Proctor's Wooing* (1897) is a gender-based divergence in moral reasoning. The proctor maintains that although Walter Severne had honorable motives for breaking a Cambridge rule, he must nevertheless be sent down, while Geraldine Annesley argues that observing the letter of the law will ruin several lives and nullify Walter's chivalry. Charlotte Yonge's early heroines need moral advice from fathers, husbands, and clergy-men. Her last book proposes that education prepares women "to take their place among men, and temper their harshness and indifference to suffering with the laws of mercy and humanity."[76]

Thus even while using traditional plots and values, college stories suggest new ways of being for girls. College life cast its glamour around certain "unfeminine" characteristics and cultivated new behaviors. Emily Davies in 1863 had reported the stereotypical fears: "Much learning would make her mad. . . . She would lose the gentleness, the grace, and the sweet vivacity, which are now her chief adornment, and would become cold, calculating, masculine, fast, strong-minded, and in a word, generally unpleasing."[77]

Novelists took care to give their leading characters a certain amount of gentleness, grace, vivacity—but also to promote some alternative excellences. College students learn equality, fairness, wider sympathy, sincerity. They are admired for intellectual humility and for frankness about what they can and can't afford to spend. An overindulged daughter in *Girl's Own Paper* learns that money won't buy her a better room, does poorly in her first examination, and loses her sense of self-importance. In consequence she learns to make do with the space she has, dress modestly, and pay more attention to ideas than objects. The moral, of course, is intended for girls at home and even girls in domestic service—but the college heroine has become a desirable model to emulate.[78]

Many college-girl novels preach humility: girls must not trust the reputation they had acquired as the cleverest girl at school or the star of a country neighborhood. Ultimately taking a place won fairly through effort, independent thought, and self-discipline restores their confidence. Girls at college, said Constance Maynard (an early Girton student and later mistress of Westfield), learn public spirit, persistence, self-restraint, toleration, and courage.[79] This is an interesting combination of virtues: middle class and military, Protestant and manly, very British public school, and yet exemplified in college fictions as quite appropriately female.

The caricature of educated women as physically unappealing was a code for their lack of interest in men, a screen for men's fear that they could not win women who had other alternatives, and a club to discipline the average girl. Even pro-college novelists could be infected. Frances Marshall's first version of Dorothy Piggott, the Newnham wrangler whose story borrows Philippa Fawcett's, is "a plain-looking girl, with absent, preoccupied eyes. . . . Her clothes were ill-fitting, and put on with a slovenly disregard for effect; there was a button or two short on her jacket, and holes in her gloves."[80] Dorothy Piggott, however, ceases to be so willfully unattractive in later novels.

One writer in a girl's magazine in the 1890s suggested that the caricature once held some truth:

> In the early days of University education for women . . . some students seem to have thought that they could best show their superiority over their more frivolous sisters, by disregarding their appearance, and by being uncouth and ungracious in their manners. This was undoubtedly a great error, but it is a kind of error almost inseparable from the initiation of a new "movement." For there is under those circumstances a reaction against the old order of things, and a tendency to rush to extremes in the opposite direction.[81]

By the turn of the century, girls' fiction no longer made intellectual characters plain. "The Girton Girl" of E. Nesbit's 1895 *Atalanta* story is

> no mere book-worm, but a healthy young girl. . . . She rode, she sang, she swam, she danced, she played tennis, she could pull an oar or a trigger with strength and accuracy—she could construe one of the hardest bits of Aeschylus, and could prune a fruit-tree with equal grace and readiness. But one thing she never did—she never flirted.[82]

Fiction's emphasis on womanliness, beauty, and romance was implicitly designed as a counterweight to spinster-phobia. The impression that intellectual women were both uninterested in marriage and unappealing to men was probably the most powerful prejudice against women's education. Eliza Lynn Linton argued that a college-trained woman should "justify the cost of her education" by remaining celibate so as "to devote herself to its use."[83] Girls were evidently infected by the belief that it was an either/or choice. *Atalanta* reported that members of a girls' debating society in the late 1880s rejected the idea of college because women's "domestic qualities" would suffer.[84]

The *Girl's Own Paper* evocatively turned the stereotype on its head in a sequence of drawings under the title "The Child: How Will She

Develop?" The mannish and discontented woman who is shown giving a harangue in front of a poster that proclaims "WOMEN! ARISE!!! TO SUPPRESS THE ENEMY—MAN!!!"—had spent her young womanhood in "Waste of Time" (reading, alone, in a chair with cushions); the fine woman, who marries and has a happy old age surrounded by children and grandchildren, is the one wearing cap and gown in the drawing "At College. Congratulated."[85]

Hardly anyone dared suggest that it did not matter if educated women remained celibate, although *Westminster Review*, in discussing higher education for women, pointed out that male bachelors had included Michelangelo, Raphael, Handel, Beethoven, and Turner.[86] Frances Power Cobbe (herself single) argued that "there *are* purposes in the order of Providence for the lives of single women and childless wives, and they too are meant to have their share of human happiness."[87]

That ideology was not popularized in girls' culture. "The Girton Girl" of E. Nesbit's 1895 *Atalanta* story proclaims women's "right not to marry, . . . to live our own lives, and do our own work." She's incensed that "a girl who doesn't succeed in getting a situation as domestic slave is spoken of as a failure."[88] As is typical in fiction, however, the language of resistance is subverted in the story's ending. Or is the swiftness the last-sentence marriage itself a wink at its irrationality, leaving the feminist speech untouched to be pasted up over mirrors and inside diaries? Either interpretation could be given contemporary weight.

Eugenicists by the 1890s worried about the stagnant marriage rate and blamed the universities: educated men could not find a "like" wife and Girton or Newnham women, when they have "acquired a permanent interest in classical or scientific literature, cannot be expected to sink these tastes and their fascination in the cause of matrimony."[89] It may be especially worth noting that in the year after Fawcett's success in the Cambridge tripos, girls were once more being advised to avoid mathematics because it would make them "masculine" and "unwomanly"—and that the warning was cast as coming from the mouths of young men.[90]

Yet a contradictory fear also arose: college girls were away from their families' supervision and protection while at an age to marry. Rita

McWilliams-Tulberg suggests that this was probably the major objection to Girton in its earliest phase.[91] College novels certainly did nothing to allay this fear. The piquancy of throwing together young women and young men of courting age and giving them like interests and plenty of opportunities for unsupervised daylight meetings in chapels, at lectures, or walking along the river provided a pleasant new set of conventions for romantic fiction.

Cambridge was not as straitlaced as we perhaps imagine. It was the professors—afraid of disturbance among male undergraduates—who demanded chaperones at lectures, not the women's colleges. Mixed social events were held; girls visited with their brothers and their brothers' friends. Cambridge dons began to find brides among women students. The Master of Trinity married Agnata Ramsay of the "First Class—Ladies Only" *Punch* cartoon.[92] Florence Brown delayed announcing her engagement to moral science lecturer Neville Keynes because Anne Clough did not want Newnham to be "regarded as a marriage market,"[93] but when Mary Paley passed her tripos and joined the Newnham staff as a lecturer in economics, Clough set aside a college sitting room where Paley and her husband-to-be, lecturer Alfred Marshall, outlined *The Economics of Industry*.[94]

Reproductive fears continued to be used to frighten ambitious girls and their parents: if a girl

> goes in for competitive examinations, with their exhausting strain and feverish excitement—if she takes up a profession where she will have to compete with men and suffer all the pain and anxiety of the unequal struggle—let her then dedicate herself from the beginning as the Vestal of Knowledge, and forego the exercise of that function the perfection of which her own self-improvement has destroyed.[95]

In 1887 Eleanor Sidgwick (a scientist who, in 1892, would succeed Anne Jemima Clough as Principal of Newnham) devised a questionnaire to study the health issue. She sent two copies to each student and alumna, asking for the second copy to be filled out by a sister or cousin who had not been to college. Thus Sidgwick secured a control group and discovered that the students were in significantly better health. Furthermore, those who were married had more children and fewer childless marriages than their peers.[96] Eugenicist Francis Galton was so impressed with Sidgwick's report that he proposed "a dower fund as an equivalent to fellowships" to encourage female students to marry and breed.[97]

College fiction promptly dramatized this information for readers who would not see statistical reports—and perhaps made it available for girls to use in persuading their parents. "The women's colleges," says the narrator of *A Proctor's Wooing*, showed that students' offspring

> were not only none the worse for the mental strain their parents had suffered during the early years of womanhood, but they were stronger, and more precocious, and healthier, than other babies!
>
> There was a collection of photographs of the babies of old Newnham students on the walls of the Principal's room. No argument could be more convincing than those baby photographs.[98]

A subsequent statistical analysis by Eleanor Sidgwick, however, showed that while two out of five Girton students who took ordinary degrees had married, among those who won honors the proportion was only one in ten. Contemporaries found it difficult to avoid concluding that education made women "more fastidious in their choice" because they did not need "to rely on matrimony as a means of support."[99] Lecturing at University College Liverpool in 1896, Sidgwick—who was not only Principal of Newnham but also wife of political economist Henry Sidgwick, a leader among the Cambridge men who were trying to open degrees to women—emphasized that only half of all girls in the classes from which Cambridge drew students married.[100] One can only guess that some girls chose college because they had already formed an intention not to marry. As Martha Vicinus demonstrates, colleges, schools, and other communities of women provided not only paid work but also many of the emotional benefits of family life, whether or not erotic satisfaction was also involved.[101]

These suggestions, however, remained unstated; proponents of college education emphasized the "normalcy" of college girls and their "normal" girlish interest in woman's "normal" destiny. Conservative educators such as Elizabeth Wordsworth began to argue that college was valuable "not only as finding occupation for unmarried women, but as affording—may one dare to say it?—excellent training for future wives and mothers."[102]

Fiction about college girls reflected the contradictions abroad in girls' culture: unexamined beliefs about women's role; voiceless physical desires that, with no other identifiable outlet, took shape in fantasies of marriage and motherhood; the excitement of new possibilities; the emerging acceptance of female individuality and even ambition. When people are moved by progressive ideas yet anxious over changes for which there are no visible precedents, it is not surprising if popular fictions supply fuel for new fantasies while at the same time providing the comfort of familiar feelings. Sometimes even the most glowing pictures of college life, such as Alice Stronach's autobiographical *A Newnham Friendship*, conclude on a note of sadness: "Our work, our latch-keys, our independence, our comradeship even, are all very well for a time, but not for always. And they cannot complete us; they cannot do for us what marriage . . . and motherhood . . . ."[103]

By the century's end it could be argued that women's visible success—including the publicity earned by Philippa Fawcett—had already aroused a backlash. College women were no longer rare. *Englishwoman's Year Book* for 1899 contains nine pages in small print of examination pass lists and university scholarships; by 1900 over 30 percent of University of London graduates were women.[104] The very real danger of female competition led to noisy public unpleasantness in 1896–1897 when proposals to grant degrees to women were defeated at both Oxford and Cambridge. At Cambridge, over two thousand undergraduates signed a petition demanding that women be kept out, and their victory was celebrated in a special pictorial supplement to the *Daily Mail*.[105]

Reactionaries discovered powerful "evidence" in the American experience that degrees for women led to "extreme laxity in divorce, . . . the institution of female clergy," and other "aberrations." Higher education was "a phase of the tendency which leads women to wear men's clothes, to play men's games, to smoke, and to advocate relaxations of the ties of marriage and maternity."[106] In an "advanced" novel of 1907, an Oxford woman studying for her exams is possessed by a second personality who takes a First and later reemerges to betray the man she has married.[107] On the one hand, this is a rather interesting novel about split personality that belongs with other psychological studies written in the first decade of the twentieth century, while on the other, it is a clearly reactionary reprise of the clichés about examinations leading to mental breakdown and about the educated woman's unfitness for marriage.

In young women's novels (rather than adult fiction) schoolgirls in the years leading up to World War I go unexceptionally on to college. Women, says a tutor in one of these books, "are coming to carry their learning easily—not as though it were not natural to them."[108] It can be argued that college stories and girls' magazines had helped create that acceptance. Yet the fiction—which emphasized fun, romance, and social life—also made education seem less important. In a 1913 book published by the Religious Tract Society, the aunt who will eventually pay her niece's college expenses asks

> "Would you kindly explain for what reason you are anxious to go to Cambridge? I had imagined that it was for education, now it appears that balls and picnics are the attraction. Which of the two is it of which you are really thinking?"
>
> "Oh, Aunt Maria, I'm a human girl! Of *both*!" cried Darsie, laughing. "Education first, of course, because of the result, and all it will mean afterwards, but if you want the truth, I shouldn't be so keen if it wasn't for the fun!"[109]

Some college tales that used transparent versions of Philippa Fawcett's triumph made revealing alterations. In *A Junior Dean* Dorothy Piggott waits alone in a cheerless room while the undergraduates demand that "Ladies" be substituted for "Women" and finally hears that she is "Bracketed—Second Wrangler," a considerably less impressive success than Fawcett's. (Curiously, once the author has chosen to diminish the woman's mathematical success the narrator reveals an acid suspicion of Cambridge authority: "Rumour, which has always something of the truth in it, had been busy as usual, and had counted up all Miss Piggott's marks, and all the Senior Wrangler's marks, and it had found out—never mind what it found out. He took all the glory and the distinction."[110]) And in *A Newnham Friendship* the celebrated wrangler named Pippa is described as daughter of a man "who had done splendid public work for his country"[111]—leaving us to wonder why Millicent Garrett Fawcett was erased from her daughter's triumph.

At the end-of-the-year banquet in *A Newnham Friendship*, one speaker says that the world still awaits "the regeneration which . . .

would come only from 'three consecutive generations of single women'"[112]—that is, women without family ties to lead social service reforms, control school boards, and so forth. Fiction does little to encourage their production. The hard-working girl who achieves professional success appreciates the honor of her advance and values her stature as a model for future generations but is aware of its cost in loneliness.

Yet it is also transparently evident that the fantasy of romance and marriage is the only narrative available to girls that responds to their adolescent physical and emotional drives. The stories women writers did not know or could not tell account for curious displacements and bittersweet resolutions. The climax of *A Sweet Girl Graduate* (1891), for example, is triply distanced: Priscilla Peel, acting the Prince to Maggie Oliphant's Princess in a college production, sees the man who (also?) hopelessly loves Maggie at the back of the auditorium and woos her for him by "communicating the sensations which animated her own breast" through Tennyson's words[113]—a scene silly in the telling but strangely moving when read in context. In L. T. Meade's *A Princess of the Gutter* (1895), the Girton graduate does settlement work with the help of a slum girl and the girl's "adopted" child: a happy family is thus formed by doubly displacing the relationship between Joan and Martha and the source of the baby they raise. Ellinor Davenport Adams's *A Queen Among Girls* (1900)—a novel with even more than the usual quota of tears and self-sacrifice—ends with a family visit to Rome in which the novel's surviving characters seem to be disposed in three couples: two educated women, two younger boys (one a gentle artist and one lame), and two middle-aged bachelor uncles.

The emotional ambivalence—and the paucity of available endings—probably accounts for the contradictions in Frances Marshall's books. A Cambridge-educated woman who wrote as "Alan St. Aubyn" and was treated as a man by reviewers,[114] Marshall had a man in the title role of her typical university novel, a Newnham girl as viewpoint character, and a story involving the girl's brother or cousin in all the old sensational material of gambling, actresses, boat races, debts, duels, and suicide attempts. Women are shown to be better than men at governance, organization, intellectual effort, and steadiness—yet the books arrive at a romantic resolution that seems to demand the appearance of male superiority. Woman's sphere (as Virginia Woolf would shortly say) is evidently to reflect men at twice their natural size.[115] Marshall's quasi awareness of the problem gives her novels a distinctively edgy tone.

At the end of *A Proctor's Wooing*, Geraldine Annesley has convinced Walter Severne that he is the "chosen leader of the New Women's movement"; she becomes don at a women's college and he a fellow of St. Crispin's:

> For his chivalrous championship Walter has won the hearts of a thousand Cambridge women whose cause he has espoused, but he is willing to barter them all for the love of one. He has still a goal to reach; he will reach it some day, with the world applauding. When an overwhelming majority of the senate throw open wide the doors of the University for the admission of women to full membership, he will get his reward— not till then. Perhaps it will not do him any harm to wait.[116]

I cannot decide if Frances Marshall would have written the last sentence had she realized that Walter and Geraldine would need to wait more than half a century to marry—she might, in fact, have enjoyed the irony. The English novels did not find a way to reach a triumphant climax such as the one from an American college-girl story in which fragments of conversation are overheard at a Vassar alumnae meeting at Delmonico's:

> "discovered an asteroid . . . school for Apache and Comanche children . . . Margaret Sterling's lecture on the Abolition of the Death Penalty . . . the surgeon of the Women's Hospital . . . studying theology and has already had a pastorate offered her . . . fashion editor of . . . a work on abstruse mathematics . . . which Joseffy played at his farewell concert . . . succeeds wonderfully as an architect . . ."[117]

As is so often the case in nineteenth-century fiction, even the texts that can be read as subversive or advanced do not accurately reflect women's significant achievements. Without any "role model" in fiction, the girl hero we saw at the beginning of this chapter remained single and carved out a new professional space. After leaving the staff of Newnham in 1901, Philippa Fawcett went to South Africa with her mother, who had been appointed to a government commission of inquiry to investigate conditions in the concentration camps where the wives and children of Boer soldiers were held. She remained behind to supervise the establishment of public elementary education in the Transvaal and then, in 1905, became the first woman to hold a senior administrative post with the London County Council. Before retiring as principal education officer for higher education in 1934, she oversaw the development of London County Council's secondary schools (including the emphasis on an academic curriculum for girls' schools), established two teacher-training colleges, and worked out schemes of articulation that made it possible for pupils to pass, on merit, from local elementary schools into (ultimately) London University.[118]

Popular culture, in contrast, mediates, meliorates, makes small steps thinkable, and perhaps moves the mean. To create a socially comfortable role for new girls who would become new women—independent, educated, intelligent, self-fulfilled, economically self-sufficient—it was probably necessary to reassure both girls and their parents that the role was appropriately feminine, with all the complex social and emotional burdens that "feminine" encoded. There was simply no other script available for a happy life. The "forward" and "advanced" novels about new women and modern women were problem novels—and their endings usually made the prospect of carving an unconventional road very frightening indeed.

Seen from our perspective, the college girl portrayed in girls' culture had a long and comfortable adolescence. Unlike the working-class girl (who had to bring in wages from age twelve or fourteen) and unlike the stereotypical daughter at home (whose energy might be entirely consumed by boredom alternating with undefined emotional duties), fiction's college girl had an obligation to develop herself and prove her mettle within a sheltered setting that provided independence, friendship, and the safe excitement of pioneering an admirable new role. Even if the vast majority of middle-class girls experienced college life only in imagination, its embodiment gave them mental space to think of themselves in new ways.

four

Schoolgirls, School Stories, and Schoolgirl Culture

CAN IT BE ARGUED THAT SCHOOLS WERE RESPONSIBLE FOR CREAT-ing girlhood? Girls' education changed dramatically in the second half of the nineteenth century. Schools categorized girls by age and assembled them in groups where they shared experiences, exchanged ideas, and created fashions in language, feeling, and attitude that coalesced into a distinctive culture. Even by the end of the period, however, less than a quarter of all girls between twelve and eighteen attended any sort of school. School stories, on the other hand, were avidly consumed by daughters at home and by working girls. Although these stories had little relation to most girls' reality, they spread school mores, the image of girls in groups, and the culture of schooling as an institutional separation of adolescents both from their families and from the world of paid labor. It was thus primarily in fiction that school became a privileged space for girls' interactions and ethics.

Girls' school stories, Mary Jackson suggests, originated with Sarah Fielding's *The Governess* (1749), which is "made lively by some amusingly naughty if unladylike conduct in her characters."[1] But although occasional books about girls at school had been published for more than a century, the "school story" as popular light reading for girls had its real genesis in the 1880s. This is a full generation after the development of comparable books for boys. Furthermore, Isabel Quigley's study of the genre claims that while some boys' school stories have attained "literary" quality (as in Kipling and Wodehouse) the ones girls loved have no interest for adults.[2]

Any generalization about girls' education during the nineteenth century will have copious exceptions; there was no "system" and no firm expectation. For every upper-class memorist with bitter complaints about the governess who used a question-and-answer manual to teach unconnected snippets of information there will be another who was well educated by a mother or father with a good library. The small private boarding schools where middle-class girls often spent a year or two in their teens also varied widely. Widowed or orphaned gentlewomen often advertised for "a few select girls to educate in a home-like setting." Such a school depended almost entirely on the quality of the proprietor's own education. Meanwhile, working-class girls seldom went to school once they were old enough to earn something or to mind younger children while their mother worked.[3]

Nevertheless, as background for the late-Victorian reforms, the "typical" education of English girls might be summarized as follows. Until (and even beyond) the First World War wealthy families generally educated daughters at home. An English governess might be employed to teach ordinary subjects and provide companionship. Often there would also be a French or German governess for a time, as well as visiting masters for music, dancing, or special subjects. School of any sort was seen as risky by families at the upper reaches of society. Loelia Ponsonby, whose father was equerry to Queen Victoria, "recalled that her parents had felt self-consciously 'modern' in sending her away to school" in the years just before the war.[4]

In the prosperous and professional middle classes, girls also received much of their education at home, perhaps sharing lessons from a governess with their brothers until the boys went away to public school. They might then attend a private day school near their home and, finally, be sent to a small boarding school for a few terms in their teens. Girls in the lower middle class might be taught by mother, sister, or nursemaid until about ten, and then sent to a local day school for four or five years.[5]

By mid-century, it was generally agreed that middle-class girls' education needed reform. The first new-model day school providing a truly secondary academic curriculum was North London Collegiate

School, established in 1850 by Frances Mary Buss. The Schools Inquiry Commission of the mid-1860s recommended that a fee-paying girls' school on the model of North London Collegiate be established in every town of more than four thousand inhabitants.[6] The Girls' Public Day School Company, founded by Emily Shirreff and her sister Maria Grey in 1872, provided a mechanism for day schools that were "public" rather than "private." Public schools, in Britain, are owned by trusts or companies and controlled by a board of governors; private schools are run for profit by their proprietor. In most small schools the proprietor was also the head—and sometimes the only—teacher.

By the end of the century there were three types of reputable secondary school for girls. Day schools—often called "high schools"—were modeled on North London Collegiate. These schools were essentially middle class but did not usually exercise social exclusion in selecting pupils. The fees were relatively low because most girls lived at home.[7] Day schools were seen as especially appropriate for adolescent girls because they preserved home ties, permitted family control of friendships, encouraged pupils to spend time on domestic duties, and allowed maternal supervision of a girl's health and temperament. The aim of high schools, in the language of the *Englishwoman's Year Book*, was "to give girls an education comparable to that received by boys in public schools and grammar schools, which shall fit them in the future to take up professions, each of which again requires special study."[8]

The second variety of reformed secondary school was on the model of Cheltenham Ladies' College, where Dorothea Beale became principal in 1858. Cheltenham and its imitators retained some features of a finishing school: they were socially selective in admissions, and the life of boarders was constructed to nurture ladylike deportment. However, the ladies' colleges also furnished an academically demanding education. Cheltenham even prepared girls to take University of London degree examinations, though the great majority of students were doing secondary rather than university work.[9]

Finally there was a new type of boarding school, which came eventually to predominate in girls' fiction and provides our own usual mental image of "boarding school." Established later in the century—the earliest include St. Leonard's (1877), Roedean (1885), and Wycombe Abbey (1896)—these schools were deliberately modeled on the boys' public schools, with all the paraphernalia of uniforms, games, houses, prefects, and so forth. They ultimately came to stress the separation of home and school and the suppression of some "feminine" and "domestic" traits. Their expense reinstituted a kind of selectiveness that was also comparable to Eton, Winchester, or Rugby.

All varieties of reformed secondary school loomed much larger in public consciousness than in actual numbers. Most middle-class girls still attended small private schools, many with only six or eight pupils.[10] Advertisements in a magazine such as *Sisters* as late as 1896 use two key words to distinguish educational style: "home school" and "collegiate school." The new (collegiate) schools were efficient only if they were big enough to form classes grouped by ability and subject. The curriculum was largely shaped by the Oxford and Cambridge Local Examinations, which provided outside certification of secondary schooling. Success in the Locals allowed admission to university or some kinds of professional training, supplied qualification to teach in many schools, and provided entry to some branches of the civil service. A typical plan of Local Examinations from the last quarter of the century required candidates to "pass acceptably in at least four subjects taken from not less than three different categories" of the four outlined here:

I.   (1) Latin; (2) Greek; (3) French and German
II. (1) Scripture knowledge; (2) English; (3) History
III. (1) Mathematics (elementary); (2) Mathematics (additional)
IV. (1) Natural Philosophy; (2) Heat and Chemistry; (3)
     Botany; (4) Physical Geography and Elementary Geology[11]

Following the example of North London Collegiate, a typical school had four subject-lessons a day, from 9:00 A.M. to 1:00 P.M., with a short break at 11:00. Calisthenics or drill might be added in the morning. Students were generally expected to go home at 1:00 P.M. for their midday meal and to spend the afternoon on household duties and preparing lessons. Most day schools, however, also offered an afternoon session with optional subjects (such as art and music) and individual tutoring for remediation or special subjects.[12] There might also be a time set aside for charitable work (e.g., an afternoon sewing session during which girls worked at petticoats and layettes for the poor while being read to from an improving book).

By 1899 the afternoon session was generally no longer optional, and the curriculum, according to the *Englishwoman's Year Book*, would include "the ordinary English subjects;[13] mathematics, including conics and trigonometry; French and German; Latin and Greek; biology, chemistry, physics; political economy; harmony and class singing; drawing, painting, gymnastics." Some schools also offered "technical" courses such as "cookery and dressmaking, book-keeping and shorthand."[14] Reformed boarding schools generally had much the same plan for lessons, with additional physical activities and organized games in the afternoon and supervised prep time in the evening.

The new schools developed an entirely new type of teacher, wholly unlike the "distressed gentlewoman" of earlier years. She was well educated, well paid, and professional in her conduct and status.[15] In 1891 the average salary of Girls' Public Day School teachers was £113 a year[16]—about twice the average earnings for a working-class man, though inadequate as a middle-class family wage.

Only 15 or 20 percent of English girls, however, had any education at all during their adolescent years. Secondary schooling requires children to postpone earning until their late teens, and the fees were a further burden for lower-middle-class or working-class families. In 1899 Girls' Public Day Schools charged nine to fifteen guineas per year and high schools run by the Church Schools Company from four to eighteen guineas.[17] Children of the poor, the working class, and some of the lower middle class attended state-supported elementary schools. Elementary education was made compulsory between ages seven and ten in 1880. Only in 1891 did it become free. The leaving age was raised to twelve in 1899; to fourteen (with many exceptions for pupils who had reached a certain level or whose earnings were needed) in 1900; and to fourteen for everyone in 1918.

Although the government provided funds only for elementary schools, a few local authorities established "Higher Grade Board Schools" because of what the *Englishwoman's Year Book* called the "steadily increasing demand for a cheap education beyond Standard VII."[18] Some working-class girls had, furthermore, been receiving the rough equivalent of a secondary education through the pupil-teacher system initiated in 1846. Elementary-school children with academic promise were kept at school from thirteen to eighteen, earning a modest stipend for teaching younger children in the daytime and taking additional lessons from the head teacher in the evening or at a regional pupil-teacher center on Saturdays. The scheme altered in details over the years, eventually leading to daytime teacher-training colleges, some of them attached to universities.

There was, however, no articulation between the (state) elementary and the (fee-paying) secondary schools. In some subjects, elementary girls at twelve were more advanced than high-school girls of the same age, but the elementary child would be completely unacquainted with other subjects that had been studied in the preparatory departments of a high school.[19]

The 1902 Education Act finally instructed local authorities to make sure secondary schools were available and to coordinate all forms of education. As a consequence, additional girls' schools with low fees were established all over the country, and many existing high schools chose to receive government aid in return for providing free places to elementary-school girls who passed an entrance examination. Another act in 1907 required that prospective elementary-school teachers be given scholarships to high schools or grammar schools instead of serving an apprenticeship as pupil-teachers. By 1911, London County Council operated fourteen girls' secondary schools; Philippa Fawcett supervised their establishment. In other places, the former higher-grade board schools were converted into county high schools that charged a very modest fee (perhaps three or four pounds per year) and provided ample free places with government funds.[20]

During the first decade of the twentieth century, then, girls of all classes whose parents could afford to postpone their earnings were able to have virtually the same secondary education. (This may well be one reason that parents of the upper middle class began to patronize the more exclusive "public school" variety of boarding school.) Home education became less common. The *Englishwoman's Year Book* for 1899 reported on the rapidly diminishing number of governesses.[21] The periodical *Monthly Packet*, which found its primary audience among gentry and vicarage daughters at home, ceased publication in 1898; the middle-class *Girl's Realm* in 1901 discontinued its "Reading Union" because, according to the editor, schoolwork no longer left girls time to write the required essays.

The list of public (i.e., not proprietary) schools in the *Girls' School Year Book* jumped from 119 in the 1906 edition to 147 a mere five years later. The established high schools put up new buildings and were "crowded with pupils."[22] Between 1897 and 1920 the number of girls receiving secondary education surged from around 20,000 to 185,000.[23]

Long before school attendance really became commonplace, however, schoolgirl stories were spreading the culture of girlhood—and, as they became in the literary sense "less realistic," they might also be seen as more and more closely related to girls' desires and dreams, rather than to adult programs. In the 1880s, when L. T. Meade turned school into a place of fun and adventure, most fictional schools had fewer than thirty pupils and a headmistress who exercised strong personal influence. The early stories found it acceptable for girls to be at boarding school only if unusual circumstances required them to live away from home or to be prepared for self-support. The very plots that authors contrived to make fantasies of school life possible, however, may encode otherwise unexpressed feelings about the family situation.

As the years passed, fiction's teachers and headmistresses grew less visible and far less important. By the 1890s, stories often used a high school setting and made the conflict between home and school explicit. These high school stories are more overtly feminist than a lot of girls' fiction, though the feminism may be diluted in overlapping layers of tale and interpretation.[24] After 1900 schoolgirl stories began to feature boarding schools modeled on boys' public schools. These tales have attained "classic" status, and although somewhat less interesting in terms of social history, they encode strongly suggestive psychological themes.

A typically negative pre-1880s school story is Sarah Doudney's *Monksbury College* (1878). The "College," a school with thirty students, is too "large" for the mistress to exercise adequate influence.[25] The pupils bicker and learn bad things from one another; because they lack maternal supervision they can't mature in appropriately feminine ways. Another example, Mary Gellie's *The New Girl* (1878), is a sour tale of rivalry without a single likable character. Interestingly, it has almost all of the ingredients from which the school story genre evolved—competition, prizes, heavy adolescent emotionalism, even the scene in which a pupil is trapped by the incoming tide while gathering specimens for an aquarium and falls ill as a result—but they are cast in an unpleasant light. Bertha, who is working for a prize so she will be able to support her feeble-minded young brother, is eventually taught that she would do better to stay home and make him happy.

The high schools established in the 1870s sought to avoid the moral and emotional risks of boarding (as expressed in antischool stories) as well as counteracting the reputation for snobbery and useless accomplishments that had long clung to schools for young ladies. In an advanced (even "dangerous") decision, the Girls' Public Day School Company made its schools free of class and denominational restrictions. An air of daring is evident in early fiction and memoirs about the high school experience. Maria Grey wrote that Chelsea High School (the company's first school) had girls of "every class . . . from an earl's daughter to a very small tradesman's in the neighborhood."[26] The first Jewish girl came to Chelsea in 1873. Scholarships were established for pupils from the local elementary school.[27] Helen Swanwick describes her experience at Notting Hill High School: "I sat between the daughter of a publican and the daughter of a laundress, and I never succeeded in beating the former. The daughter of a viscount was at the bottom of the class."[28]

Early pupils were proud of their schools' democracy. Dame Meriel Talbot, who had a long career in public service, believed that it was an enormous advantage to have met girls from "every kind of home" at Kensington High School.[29] Molly Hughes at North London Collegiate in 1881 was overjoyed to discover that "no one asked where you lived, how much pocket-money you had, or what your father was—he might be a bishop or a rat-catcher."[30] The schools deliberately fostered egalitarian attitudes. The second number (April 1876) of North London's school magazine features a moral tale about a girl who is rude to a servant, learns of the servant's family troubles, feels greatly humiliated, and resolves never again to let her feelings get the better of her.[31]

Democracy and independence energize the high school fiction of the 1890s. Freedom to choose friends was a heady experience for girls previously taught at home or at private schools selected for their social tone. Another exciting lesson was the training in self-sufficiency. In Alice Stronach's autobiographical novel about Newnham College, the high-school girl is easily distinguished from other "freshers" because she's quicker to be independent.[32] Helen Swanwick, sent to Notting Hill High School at fourteen after two miserable years at home, delighted in the "defined rights and duties instead of the irregular, vague and mostly sentimental exactions of home" and in being "an equal member of a corporate body."[33] (She was also, incidentally, a school friend of William Morris's daughters.)

In *The Four Miss Whittingtons* (Geraldine Mockler, [1899]), four orphaned sisters with an inheritance of £400 make a tough but sensible decision to spend their capital on training. Sixteen-year-old Barbara learns at North London Collegiate that she must not stay up late doing Greek on her own but rather mind her health by going out for games. Having discovered how to take care of herself, she earns a scholarship to Newnham. Similarly, in a 1906 novel poverty forces Dora Cockburn and her mother to move to Chelsea lodgings after her father's death. Dora finds work at the high school a "revelation and an increasing delight" after the "dull routine" of lessons with a governess.[34] She learns to be self-reliant and to go about London on her own, and after winning a £50 essay prize is allowed to travel "Bohemian style" to the Continent with a slightly older girl artist friend who has sold a picture.

The story's ending, however, papers over the compromise between old and new ideals: Dora inherits riches from a lonely old man she's befriended. Although Dora proves herself by learning independence, doing well in a democratic high school, and earning her own money, wealth arrives not from her "new woman" efforts but from her "old woman" ways: she has been kind, daughterly, and attentive as an emotional caretaker. Yet we must also see that although the fantasy-reward is earned with traditional womanly skills, Dora befriends the old man only because she had learned to make independent (and snobbery-free) choices.

Ellinor D. Adams's *A Queen Among Girls* (1900) has a similar reward (heart's desire achieved by feminine service) in a story that emblemizes the high school's balance of new intellect with home values. Orphaned "Gussy" Pembroke is brilliant, popular, and kind but fails in sisterliness toward her affection-starved younger brother. When he suffers an injury, she leaves school and works as a governess so that he can have art training rather than the conventional education their guardian would prefer. After Gussy is thus feminized through sacrifice and maternalism, an uncle offers her the money to attend Girton.

This conflict between family and ambition is the most typical plot in high school novels, and its resolution—at least in the fantasy supplied by fiction—is "yes, both": the new girl and the traditional woman can be united in the same body. Novelist Amy Clarke used the double signifier of her husband's name and her own University of London degree on title pages, where she was always "Mrs. Henry Clarke, M.A."[35] In her 1896 novel *A Clever Daughter*, "Phil" is a high-school girl whose ambition for a Girton scholarship makes her blind to her mother's need for help at home. But, in a significant central ambiguity, Phil's mother supports her: "Why should Phil not have her chance as well as her brothers? No one thought of keeping Percy away from school when the wheels of domestic life dragged heavily."[36] The message seems to be that Phil should perceive and imitate her mother's silent self-sacrifice. An exemplar is provided by the teacher at Phil's high school who (although she was senior classic at Cambridge) lives at home and takes "a little crippled sister" for "her special care."[37] Her mother's collapse finally opens Phil's eyes; she gives up her scholarship exam, helps her brothers with their lessons—and then, as in *Dora* and so many other stories, once the girl has learned home duties a benevolent friend makes possible her resumption of triumph at school.

These plots exemplify the high schools' raison d'être: day schools encourage a girl to accept family responsibility and learn domestic skills while she gains the education to become a self-supporting and responsible woman. At the psychological level—as light reading—they supply the fantasy that one *can* have it all: parental love and true womanliness without giving up ambition, success, and new-woman independence. Yet although the high school tales contain the most revealing social history and also have the most interestingly conflicted messages, the day school phenomenon is less familiar to us than the other varieties of English girls' education. Our attention has been occupied by governesses, unreformed boarding/finishing schools, and the elite imitations of boys' public schools. The high schools' flowering as democratic proto-feminist institutions was brief, although since girls who attended high schools between 1890 and 1910 became head teachers in the new state-supported secondary schools, their influence on the twentieth-century shape of British education probably deserves reconsideration.

Traditionalists never liked girls' high schools. Elizabeth Sewell—herself an educational reformer—criticized the secular teaching and the subjects "beyond a woman's need." She was also suspicious about the moral character of teachers who preferred day schools and had their evenings free.[38] The class mixing and class mobility became problematic for middle-class parents once working-class pupils began to exceed token numbers. A 1903 article in the *Woman's Library* suggests—as if it were an interesting relic of a bygone era—that the "democratic character of the high schools had its attraction, when the reaction against false notions of gentility was at its strongest."[39] Janet Courtney argues that when board-school children began advancing to high school level, "clergymen and doctors and lawyers, whose daughters in the 'eighties went to the High Schools, began to strain their resources to send them to schools of the type of Roedean and Wycombe Abbey."[40]

As it had in marking the establishment of high schools, girls' fiction lagged by a decade or so. Around 1910, however, the boyish sports-mad boarding school came to occupy in girls' popular reading the central role that it retained for the next half century, even though only a tiny fraction of girls who read the books ever attended such a place. Going away to school, in this fantasy, meant entering an almost pure realm of girls' culture; the typical story has little reference to home and is sometimes almost without adults who have any significant role (even in the shape of teachers) in guiding the story's action or creating the characters' mores.

The classic development of the "hearty, hockey, honour of the house" girls' public school story took place in the 1920s, although Angela Brazil, one of the principal writers of the genre, published her first book in 1906.[41] After writing a few stories about old-style schools, Brazil began constructing tales set in upper-middle-class boarding schools with prefects and organized games. One appeal of public schools, at least in fiction, was their rules and impersonal governance, as opposed to the traditional "feminine" style of authority through emotion. Brazil wrote in 1925 that she envied the schoolgirls in her books: "If we had had prefects, and had ever been taught the elements

"The cricket-match." The frontispiece of Dorothea Moore's 1908 novel *A Plucky School-Girl* exalts athletics and comradeship.

Reproduced by permission of the Bodleian Library, University of Oxford, shelfmark 2537.e.1207.

of citizenship and social service, and that our school was a world in miniature where we might help one another, it would, I think, have brought in a totally different element."[42]

This style of governance (also typical in high schools) was seen as *public* rather than *familial*, and (in nineteenth-century terms) therefore more masculine than feminine. The crucial innovation lay in the transfer of responsibility from adults to girls. Sara Burstall, headmistress of Manchester High School, insisted on limiting the teacher's personal influence. "It is never right to say to a girl: 'Do this to please me' in any question of school work or morals," she wrote. "A mother may say this, but not a teacher."[43] In girls' public boarding schools the putative transfer of power was complete: in old-style private schools, girls were emotionally dependent on teachers;[44] in day high schools they remained dependent on their mothers though they exercised governance at school; but in large organized boarding schools the pupils (theoretically) administered discipline and took responsibility for all activities except for what went on in the classroom.

An 1864 essay by Inspector of Schools J. G. Fitch pointed out that intellectually boys learned system, which might not have immediate use, while girls were taught skills or facts that had temporary practical value. Thus, he said, boys study Greek to learn grammar and gain power over words, though Greek in itself has little use in adult life. Girls, on the other hand, learn conversational French or German without studying grammar. Their ability to speak a modern language is valuable if put to use, but otherwise it quickly disappears without leaving any transferable mental skills.[45]

By the turn of the century, many parents from the business and professional classes understood the intellectual advantage in giving their daughters a "boys' education." Fiction taught girls the difference between the two styles. The school in Angela Brazil's early book *The Fortunes of Philippa* (1907) is an entertaining mix of old and new: students do mathematics and curtsy to teachers; have chemistry laboratories and practice fine darning; play cricket and hockey but also use backboards; have excellent professors for languages and literature and are taught to pour tea, arrange flowers, and write invitations. In Jessie Mansergh's *Tom and Some Other Girls: A Public School Story* (1901) a girl begs not to go to "Miss Moorby's, at Bournemouth" but rather to "a nice, big, sporty school, where they treat you like boys, and not young ladies, and put you on your honour, and don't bind you down by a hundred sickening little rules."[46]

Those words encapsulate the imagined pleasures that made boy-style schools the model of girls' culture even for the great majority of girls who did not attend them. *Tom and Some Other Girls*—written by an extremely popular author who often published in *Girl's Own Paper*—is virtually a manual to the revised code of values. Girls are still taught to ignore their interests and suppress their feelings, but the impetus is manliness rather than martyrdom. They are taught "the feebleness of 'making a fuss.' If you are hurt—bear it! If you are teased—look pleasant! If you are blamed—do better next time! If you feel blue—perk up, and don't be a baby!"[47]

Sara Burstall wrote from an educator's viewpoint on the value of discipline. School training teaches

> that work must be done, whether we were ill or well, that our individual needs and fancies must be subordinated to the whole community, that we must do what we were told whether we agreed with it or not, that we must be accurate, tidy and business-like or suffer for the failure . . . that any one of us was of very little importance compared with the success and the well-being of the great organisation to which we had the honour to belong.[48]

Honor quickly became the key word in girls' school stories. Honor means fair play, defense of the weak, honesty, openness. It does not, however, necessarily mean obeying adult rules or subordinating oneself to teachers or mothers. *Honor* represents a corporate individuality. In Graham Moore's *The Human Girl* [1909], the witty tomboy narrator explains the vast distinction between "breaking rules" (which is all right, particularly when the rules are silly) and "cheating," which is very definitely not.[49] The feminist periodical *Englishwoman's Review* thought the book had

> rather too much encouragement of the idea that the girl and the mistresses are natural enemies; but with all their mischievousness the former never lose their sense of honour. Perhaps not the least merit of the tale is that it has no moral.[50]

The reverse of honor is *sneaking*, which means to whine, complain, tattle, or "say things behind people's backs that you can't or daren't or won't say before their faces."[51] Margaret Parker's *For the Sake of a Friend* (1896) delineates the suffering of a girl who heroically refuses to "sneak," even on a schoolmate who abuses her. As in many similar books, the denouement is reached through illness; the girls are overcome by guilt when their victim is injured. The typically "feminine" message—that girls must learn to care for others' feelings—is cast in the "masculine" public language of honor and chivalry.

Martha Vicinus describes the new-style girls' education as cultivating "a modern individuality; a girl was encouraged to take responsibility for her actions, to recognize their consequences for others."[52] In the archetypal high school story, the lesson applies to home; mothers or younger brothers suffer from the schoolgirl's selfishness (which is often simply a typical self-centered adolescent oblivion to others). In boarding school stories—whether those of L. T. Meade in the 1880s or those set after the turn of the century in the girls' public schools—the harm is done to other girls; and the care of others' emotions is understood and undertaken in an all-girl context.

The public school (in fiction and perhaps in actuality) was a female world that contained a variety of "masculine" and "feminine" roles. Pseudofamilies were established: older girls were assigned a new girl as "child." The new girl's hunger for mothering was satisfied while she learned to emulate her "school mother's" corporate values instead of her real mother's home ways. One of the first things twelve-year-olds learn in *A Plucky School-Girl* (Dorothea Moore, 1908), for example, is to give up crying and kissing. Yet romantic admiration was not wholly discouraged. A 1908 advice book explains:

> the romantic, sentimental feeling that one girl has for another . . . is not altogether a bad thing . . . for, if kept within bounds, it is very often an incentive to work and to higher efforts after good. . . . It is only when such a feeling becomes intensified and all-absorbing, so that a girl can think and dream of nothing save the adored one, that it is altogether wrong![53]

Fiction's imagined world was almost certainly more "boyish" than boarding-school reality. Girls in the stories go by such names as Phil,

Gussy, Terry, Tom, Harry, Cecil, Sidney, Ted, or Tony. The "feminine" charitable work (such as sewing for the poor) commonly undertaken by real schools rarely appears in fiction. Schoolgirl tales also support the period's high imperialism. One book, for example, uses narratives about girls to sweeten lessons in geography and history. "Lory—The Little Negress" is captured by Arab slave traders and becomes educated only when she is rescued by two English naturalists; "Sita—The Hindoo Girl" tells readers that "our religion, Brahminism, condemned women to total ignorance" and "offers a most serious obstacle to the progress of civilisation."[54]

The two most distinctively "masculine" elements of post-1890 schools were uniforms and team sports. Adolescent girls were first released from tightly fitted bodices and heavy skirts by the games costumes some schools adopted in the mid-1880s. "What freedom," wrote Winifred Peck, "what glory, to scamper about after one ball or another in sun or rain or wind."[55] Around 1900 games costumes started to be used for general school wear. Illustrations of the dark serge gym tunic or "gym slip," which falls in pleats from a straight yoke, show that it was virtually identical to the school uniform commonly worn by British girls through the 1960s and still required in the 1990s by many parochial schools in the United States. I wonder, however, whether late-twentieth-century schoolgirls' joy in getting rid of school uniforms when they leave adolescence comes anywhere close to the turn-of-the-century girl's dramatic liberation when she first dressed in a costume distinctively her own, which marked her as neither child nor woman, had pockets, made it possible to run and climb, and let her add a boy-style shirt and tie.

Even though historians tell us that most schools did not "go in for the hearty games-playing so beloved of the fiction writers,"[56] the point is that writers—and the readers who supported the market—did have that love. Games signaled the essential difference between old-style and new-style girlhood. On the sports field, girls performed feats their mothers and teachers could not share. They competed—aggressively—and were encouraged to strive for excellence. Their own leadership and their cooperation with one another made the difference between team success and failure. Popular magazines that wrote articles about girls' schools invariably included photographs of their teams. Games, wrote a late-nineteenth-century educator, not only develop health but also promote "most of the qualities, if not all, that conduce to the supremacy of our country."[57] For girls in particular, she continued, games encourage

> development of powers of organisation, of good temper under trying circumstances, courage and determination, . . . rapidity of thought and action, judgment and self-reliance, and, above all things, unselfishness, and a knowledge of . . . working with others for the common good.[58]

And so in fiction the hard knocks of hockey teach girls "not to be babyish and mind trifles, and to be better-tempered like boys, and bear the troubles of life."[59] One girl keeps another from running away by reminding her of "Newbolt's splendid lines about playing the game . . . it is more often struggling on bravely and cheerily in the midst of defeat than carrying out your bat with everybody cheering to the echo. If it were all winning, it wouldn't be hard at all to play the game."[60]

Twentieth-century boarding school stories emphasize fun; they have lost the ambiguous mixture of feminism with messages about true femininity that marked the high school stories. The exceptional circumstances needed to justify sending a girl away from home vanish. In Jessie Mansergh's *Sisters Three* (1900), for example, well-to-do girls living in the country make the following plea for school:

> "We are dull, father! We are tired of ourselves. You are all day long in your study, the boys spend their time out of doors, and we have no friends . . . and every day is like the last. . . .
> "Father, when girls are at boarding-schools they have parties and theatricals, and go to concerts, and have all sorts of fun."[61]

The girls in these stories are generally good-natured; the plots hinge on accident and misunderstanding rather than flaws of character—and the books' lack of interest for adult readers and their limited portrayal of "reality" means that we must find other ways to interpret them if we are not simply to dismiss them out of hand. We may find it easy to understand that middle-class girls who went to local day or grammar schools—and were, perhaps, torn between home and school mores— might adore the fantasy of boarding-school life. The popularity of

"The doings of a night." Another key delight in boarding-school stories is shown in the illustration facing page 170 of Dorothea Moore's *A Plucky School-Girl*.

these tales among working-class readers is somewhat more startling. Yet serials laid in boarding schools ran constantly in one or another of the halfpenny-weekly papers such as *Girls' Best Friend*, *Girls' Friend*, and *Girls' Reader*.

Halfpenny papers were profitable because of the growing pool of young readers made literate by compulsory education. Letters and advice columns suggest that they were read by servants, factory workers, and shop-girls; by girls who (in another common working-class pattern) "stopped at home" to look after younger children for a year or two after leaving school at twelve and before entering the full-time workforce when tall enough to convince child-labor inspectors that they were fourteen; and by older pupils in elementary schools. But audience size was not the only determining factor in the creation of new papers. Ever since the 1840s, when penny-weekly "family papers" and "novelettes" made possible by cheaper paper and printing began to tap the mass audience, women had been reading stories of love, sensation, adventure, and happy marriage, as serialized in *Family Herald*, *Bow Bells*, etc.

Soon after mid-century boys' papers also appeared (often called by the name "penny dreadful"); working boys were seen as a separate class with their own reading interests, but working girls presumably moved directly from childhood to womanhood, and read the same romantic tales as older working-class women. In marking out a separate style of fiction for "workgirls" rather than "working women" Alfred Harmsworth identified and perhaps even consolidated a new segment of the population. After the mid-1890s, a fourteen-year-old nursery maid who had time to spend with a paper while waiting to walk a child back from dancing class could choose whether to be a woman— who read about romance—or a girl who consumed stories of school.

The school stories printed in the workgirls' papers had no "realistic" link to readers' lives. Characters do not go to senior elementary schools or serve as pupil teachers. The school fantasy is a speeded-up and exaggerated version of the stories L. T. Meade invented in the 1880s. And they definitely appealed to readers—in a rare memoir of working-class childhood, Dorothy Scannell, one of ten children in an East End family, reports that her mother bought her a girls' paper weekly until one day when a teasing brother snatched it: "I should have waited for it back, but I was in the middle of a story about a boarding-school, and, snatching it back, it tore just as Mother came into the room. 'I will buy no more girls' papers if that is what is going to happen,' she said."[62]

Why were there no day schools in the workgirls' papers? The only reasonable answer is that boarding school stories filled some need; they satisfied girls' emotions and made them crave more and more of the same. (If they had not, a marketer as savvy as Harmsworth would have printed something else.)

Harmsworth's most popular schoolgirl hero was Pollie Green, who first appeared in *Girls' Friend* in 1908. Pollie is called "the prettiest, the wittiest and the sauciest girl we know," and "spends her time fending off a series of impudent school-mistresses, romantic suitors, rascally devious money lenders, and other opponents."[63] Her best buddy is a comic black girl named Coosha who shares Pollie's irreverence and her ability to turn the tables so as to one-up her "betters." The pair were so popular that their serialized adventures continued in *Pollie Green and Coosha*, *Pollie Green at Cambridge*, *Pollie Green in Society*, *Pollie Green Engaged*, and *Pollie Green at Twenty-One*. Harmsworth recycled the serials in *Girls' Reader* and *Girls' Home* and printed them once more in single volumes in the *Girls' Friend Library*.[64] As a character and a device for high jinks, Pollie has a good deal in common with Jessie Mansergh's *Pixie O'Shaughnessy*, who had been in *Girl's Own Paper* in 1900.

The author of the Pollie Green stories was "Mabel St. John," a pseudonym for Henry St. John Cooper, half-brother of actor Gladys Cooper, who claims in her 1931 autobiography that he "often wrote 10,000 words at a 'sitting,' and on one occasion when he was asked if he would do a 'rush' story for a Christmas Annual of 32,000 words in 24 hours, he did it in a little more than half that time."[65] The numbers don't add up; very few people can (physically) write or type ten pages an hour even when working from copy text, much less when composing. Tales of such feats (often told by those who wrote for the cheap press) were a means of disavowing literary pretensions and discouraging the writer's educated friends from reading the work. But flat characters and fast action do not, by themselves, guarantee popularity with the mass public. Why were working girls especially fond of Mabel St. John's school stories? It may be worth noting that Cooper also wrote, as Henry St. John, for the Harmsworth boys' papers—*Boys' Friend*,

Vol. I.—No. 6.] ONE HALFPENNY—EVERY THURSDAY. [April 9th, 1910.

"Were your clothes defaced—spoiled, as Miss Simms asserts?" asked Miss Patterson. Nellie's lips quivered. "No," she said quietly.

The Outcast of Crowthorpe College.

"The Outcast of Crowthorpe College." School stories in the work-girls' papers tended to emphasize the pupils' unkindness and their dislike for teachers.

From *Girls' Home* 1 (1910): 41. Reproduced by permission of the British Library, Newspaper Library, Colindale, shelfmark 661.

Boys' Realm, Pluck, Marvel, Union Jack. He was skilled at snappy dialogue, comic pratfalls, adolescent irreverence, exaggerated physical stunts, and poking holes in authority figures.

Mary Cadogan and Patricia Craig point out that schoolgirls in the halfpenny papers "hold in contempt all well-educated women, especially their teachers."[66] Although middle-class stories may also treat girls and teachers as "natural enemies," even Pixie O'Shaughnessy reveals an affectionate respect, at least for teachers of British nationality, beneath the fun. Some adolescents in middle-class schools seem to suspect that they may want to emulate the life of independence and authority that education has made possible for their active young teachers. Not so, apparently, the working girls; in their fiction teachers—representing authority—remain virtually another species.

I have already suggested that a college or school setting appeals to girls because it provides a separate world where their own interests and interactions can be carried on with little adult interference. The boarding-school fantasy lets girls imagine being free of parental control while not yet burdened by the hard work of supporting themselves. For girls already at work, the teacher-as-authority-figure may well have been a safe substitute for a feared or disliked forewoman or employer. To imagine revenge, evasion, talking back, seizing control from the "teacher"—all of these fantasy confrontations serve both as comic relief and as psychological escape valve. The boarding-school teacher is a particularly satisfactory figure on which to project these fantasies because she is not the dangerously real person who controls the reader's actual circumstances.

The same narrative can of course serve as fantasy expression for several (and even conflicting) needs at the same time. Another curious fact about the boarding schools in workgirls' papers is that many are convent schools, and the central characters stereotypically Irish. They may to some limited extent be intended to appeal to Irish girls working in England, but their cultural resonance is much broader. In middle-class fiction, Irish girls are typically adventurous and hard to discipline, even when they are upper class and Anglo-Irish; L. T. Meade's *Wild Kitty* (1897), for example, is used to dogs, horses, hunting and outdoor adventures on her father's estates and never does submit to the discipline of a staid English high school. As an outsider, she can be admirable even when passionate and undisciplined; the same characteristics would fatally mar a respectable English girl. Seen in this light, we perceive that the "Irish" girl of workgirls' papers has the rough, boisterous, self-sufficient, uninhibited ways often criticized in working-class girls, yet she remains a fine, wholesome person.

Another striking feature of the convent stories is the role played by the mother superior. In a typical convent school tale (as in the 1870s books about small boarding schools) the girls are jealous, spiteful, mean, underhanded troublemakers, and most of the teachers are rigid, vindictive, or dishonest. At the head of the school, however, is an extraordinary "good mother"—the mother superior—warm, loving, understanding, pure. These stories remind us that working-class girls were often sent out to service at thirteen or fourteen. Their situation reversed the usual middle-class pattern of boys at boarding school and girls at home. Especially among rural laborers, boys lived at home doing farm work while girls entered domestic service. The situation of the typical convent school story—however Harmsworth's writers happened to discover it—provides a screen on which to project feelings that a young servant might find too painful to face directly. A "bad mother" or terrible family situation requires a girl to leave home for a strange unpleasant place where she is mistreated, suspected of dishonesty, spied upon, badly fed and housed, and bereft of sympathetic friends. The "teachers" are cold, critical, and strict; her duties are hard to learn and sometimes almost unintelligible. In the fantasy life of her story-paper, however, she can return in her private time to the "good mother" who will make all well.

The overlap between the readers of workgirls' papers and of the stories I've been calling "middle class" seems principally to have occurred when girls from the lower classes read "up." Memoirs by middle-class and upper-class men recall illicit schoolboy reading of penny dreadfuls, but I have found no references to halfpenny workgirls' papers except in writing by women whose family of origin was working class. The reward labels often pasted into old books, however, show that elementary-school pupils were given boarding school stories as prizes.[67]

Certain of the fantasies that can be read into the workgirls' fiction also turn up in middle-class books and may be multiply accessible by girls of different classes. In May Baldwin's *The Sunset Rock* (1903), Edith Everard (whose father is a leading barrister) sticks up for Leslie Stuart, a board-school girl on scholarship. Eventually Leslie's father is discovered to be an earl—a very common event in cheap fiction, and one that may (for some readers, at least) be a coded recognition of the bastardy that does indeed cause gentlemen to have "long-lost relatives" among the impoverished classes. Thus the book provides a persona for working-class girls in Leslie (with a fantasy of class mobility and wealth) and a persona-with-a-moral for middle-class readers in Edith. Defending one's friends against criticism by parents and teachers as well as other pupils may be seen as class solidarity and also as a value that middle-class girls learn when they move from family to public circumstances.

Some books explicitly published as "rewards" provide stories suitable for pupil teachers and other upwardly mobile girls. Emma Leslie's *Elsie's Scholarship and Why She Surrendered It* [1898]—the copy I own was an attendance prize from a Wesleyan Methodist Sunday school—opens with Elsie's selection to take a scholarship exam; the first twenty pages provide good practical advice on preparation, test-taking strategies, etc. Since Elsie Winn is the eldest of five, she can remain at school past thirteen only if she wins. The story line works out a fairly realistic version of the family versus school conflict found in so many high school stories. Elsie gives up her chance at grammar school when her father dies; she has to look after the younger children while her mother supports them by dressmaking. The "love your brother" lesson—which seemed merely instruction in a gendered morality when it appeared in books for the middle class—is revealed as a real and hard necessity for Elsie.

Indeed, the high school stories discussed earlier might also serve simultaneously as moral instruction and as fantasy vehicles to valorize the working girl's strength and responsibility, thus giving her a means to read herself into the middle-class story. Elsie minds the baby, helps her brother, encourages an invalid girl in the neighborhood, and falls ill from semistarvation because she scrimps on her meals so her mother and brother will have enough—suggesting a possible realistic correlative for the omnipresent illnesses that close so many girls' stories. Ultimately Elsie is discovered by long-lost relatives—one more story of a mother who "married beneath her" that could, conceivably, conceal the lack of any marriage—and given the money to go to high school.

Elsie's Scholarship, I must emphasize, was published in hardcover and was therefore too expensive for a working-class child to own unless it was given to her as a prize. It is an 1890s book with a typical 1890s plot—a plot usually seen in a high school story with middle-class actors. The working-class setting of *Elsie's Scholarship* reveals that the high school narrative can be reread to reveal causes, outcomes, and signifiers that have psychological value as fantasy for working girls.

Stories about senior elementary schools, county grammar schools, and pupil teachers are extremely rare in any kind of girls' fiction. Charlotte Yonge recommends *The Girls of Flaxby* (1882), which was written by her disciple Cristabel Coleridge.[68] The central character, a doctor's orphan, at first feels superior to other pupil teachers but finds that they have a great deal in common—largely "thanks to the library,"[69] which has permitted all of them to read the same books.[70]

Middle-class girls' schools did have greater contact with the state system than traditional boys' schools had. The Association of Head-mistresses founded in 1881, for example, was open to the head of any girls' school, private, public, or state-supported.[71] In addition, the public-school ethos strongly influenced state-supported girls' secondary schools since the headmistresses and the initial cadre of teachers came primarily from high schools. Factors such as these may have some bearing on the apparent class fluidity of girls in fiction. Yet paradoxically, the great majority of girls who attended other schools—or none—chose and devoured the stories devoted to upper-class boarding schools.

By early in the twentieth century, school stories were the most popular light reading of girls from late childhood through the middle teens—whether or not they went to school, or what kind of school they attended, or even whether they liked or disliked education. Evidence can be found in such places as the "books to exchange" column of *Girl's Realm*, where girls beg to trade their copies of Scott or Dickens or Charlotte Yonge for school stories. The editor of the tabloid *Girls' Reader* writes on February 20, 1909, that girls "prefer above all others" the stories "dealing with school life."[72] As the stories became more and more formulized, adults increasingly criticized or ignored them; girls with educational ambitions hid their reading of school stories or pretended to look at them only because friends did.[73] Undeniably, the school story in its formula incarnation—whether the sporty boarding school volumes middle-class girls bought, traded, and had as treasured gifts or the sensational illustrated installments on cheap newsprint purchased with working girls' halfpennies—had very little to do with the lives of its eager consumers.

It also had very little, by this time, in the way of overt moral education—that was part of its appeal. The school setting moved the story's action away from the family and its conflicts. Its patent unreality—and the invisibility of home and family—helped diminish class specificity, which in turn supplied girls in vastly different social and economic circumstances with a vocabulary of common concepts, understandings, and peer-based ethical beliefs.

Most critics of children's literature value characteristics such as realism in setting and action or psychological accuracy in character development. They find a few boys' school stories of literary quality but none among those written for girls. The genre's importance, however, is not as realistic literature but in supplying materials for fantasy. School stories use a patently unreal world to expose desires and dreams about a real world. Like some recent science-fiction utopias, they create a women's society where girls have power over their lives, choices, and experiences. Readers could enjoy the fantasy without guilt because the stories explicitly did not present the real world's family tensions, or the working-class reality of beginning paid labor at twelve or fourteen, or any of the issues about sex and sexuality that remain undiscussed.

Gill Frith in the 1980s found that working-class girls in the comprehensive school where she taught still avidly consumed school stories. They were, she reports, "aware from the start that they are *fictions*. . . . They did not believe real boarding schools would be like the schools in the stories. . . . They were drawn to the stories because they were *fun*, because the girls in them were having the time of their lives."[74]

Some writers of escapist literature have consciously articulated that function. In the late 1960s, Harriet S. Adams of the Stratemeyer syndicate criticized the vogue for realistic children's fiction, which confronts young characters with serious social problems. "Why," asked Adams, "make children all weeping and worried? Children's reading should be pleasant and lighthearted."[75] Similarly, Margaret Cole, who spent her childhood immersed in what she called the "dream-literature of boys' boarding schools," suggests that the classical British detective novel (she and her husband, G. D. H. Cole, wrote twenty-nine of them between 1923 and 1942) is "a slightly more sophisticated version of the public-school story."[76]

One element that makes the school story satisfactory as fantasy is that rebellion, breaking bounds, evading rules, and defying authority have no ill consequences. Pixie O'Shaughnessy in the extremely popular tale originally written for the *Girl's Own Paper* is another "wild Irish tornado"[77] used to enact the unpermitted. (A typical Pixie prank is to lasso a mistress.) *Pixie O'Shaughnessy* is structured like situation com-

"BUT HORROR OF HORRORS! SHE SQUEALED IN FRENCH."

Pixie O'Shaughnessy lassoes the French mistress.

From *Girl's Own Paper* 23 (1901–1902): 88. Reproduced by permission of the British Library, shelfmark P.P.5993.w.

edy; since there's no dramatic question ruling its plot, the story can run virtually forever as a sequence of high jinks reinvigorated from time to time by adding new characters. In the sequels, however, Pixie eventually grows up and marries, as does the derivative *Pollie Green* of Harmsworth's papers. When the boarding school novels reached their classic form, between the wars, writers discovered the trick of never letting characters become adults. Similarly, in the United States, Elsie Dinsmore and the Little Colonel and Pollyanna—whose series had stretched into marriage and their children's adventures—were replaced in the 1930s by Nancy Drew and her like, forever just older than the readers, with access to some of adulthood's possibilities but none of its constraints or responsibilities. In *The Girl Sleuth: A Feminist Guide* (1975) Bobbie Ann Mason contends that perpetual girlhood leaves readers "free to entertain the possibility of an alternative identity to conventional womanhood."[78]

In the British school fiction, furthermore, as Rosemary Auchmuty points out, the characters

> inhabited a female world. All authority figures as well as colleagues and comrades were women. The action was carried on by women, and all decisions were made by women. Women rose to the challenges presented by ideals such as honour, loyalty and team spirit. All emotional and social energies were directed towards women, and women's friendships were presented as positive, not destructive or competitive, and sufficient in themselves.[79]

Indeed, not only are the characters all female, but the figures who have any importance are, with very few exceptions, very young. In a story such as Jessie Mansergh's *Tom and Some Other Girls* the only teachers who actually appear in scenes are of the "big girl" type; no longer do motherly women supply nurture and give advice. "The pervasive taboo against 'sneaking,' " as Gill Frith says, "is useful because it keeps the teachers *in the dark*, leaving action, responsibility, procedure and control in the hands of the girls."[80]

The war years and their aftermath witnessed a further modernization of schooling. By 1918 secondary education was nearly universal for middle-class girls, and those of the working class were required to attend school full-time until age fourteen. In consequence, a new variety of schoolgirl paper emerged (the so-called comics, British variety, that flourished until the 1960s). Schoolgirls were seen as definitely young: they fall into the category of childhood. In the 1880–1915 period, however, "girls" were not identical to children. The creation of new girls—most clearly seen and situated in schoolgirl fiction—both depended on and reinforced changing ideals and new roles for adult women.

five

To Be a Boy

MANY WOMEN WHO WERE GIRLS AT THE TURN OF THE CENTURY HAD longed intensely not to be. Gwen Raverat (daughter of a Cambridge don and granddaughter of Charles Darwin), for example, wrote in her memoir: "I wanted so much to be a boy that I did not dare to think about it at all, for it made me feel quite desperate to know that it was impossible to be one."[1]

Among daughters of privilege the memory may be tinged with the sentimental glow of golden late-Victorian and Edwardian years. In long, lesson-free summers girls and their brothers or cousins were left to their own devices in safe gardens and woods.[2] Emily Lutyens recollected: "I was always a hero of some kind. Never have I known happier moments than when, sallying forth into the Park, armed with bow and arrows, I pretended to be Robin Hood, Ivanhoe, or Richard Coeur de Lion."[3]

While nursery children played boy games in boy clothes during holidays, working-class girls longed for trousered freedom in public spaces. Two friends in 1908 wanted to "explore London in men's disguise."[4] Charitable worker Flora Freeman was horrified to learn that girls from her club had "dressed up as men and gone to a carnival. They simply regarded it as 'a rare bit of fun,' and were quite unable to see it from [others'] point of view, especially as they had not got drunk."[5]

Dreams of boyhood are hardly unique to the period. Given the cultural valuation of male as better and the visible privileges granted to boys, many girls have envied their brothers. In this period, however, girls' boyishness developed a publicly acceptable face. To an extent, feminism was defined as seeking male privilege. Other "male" traits and activities were, however, recoded: imperial motherhood, for example, would be well served if girls gained health and strength from boys' games. The period was marked by shifts and recuperations in the definition of "girl" and "boy."

The *Oxford English Dictionary*'s entry describing "tomboy" as "a girl who behaves like a spirited or boisterous boy; a wild romping girl; a hoyden" dates the usage from 1592. By the last quarter of the nineteenth century the term had lost its pejorative flavor; the *OED*'s evidence is an 1876 quotation from Charlotte Yonge's *Womankind*: "What I mean by 'tomboyism' is a wholesome delight in rushing about at full speed, playing at active games, climbing trees, rowing boats, making dirt-pies, and the like."

Yonge evidently referred to children. During the following decades, the age limits for permissible tomboy behavior rose. Women's magazines of the 1880s typically let girls "have their pets, their garden, their cricket, their wild games, just the same as their brothers" until they were about twelve.[6] The "Family Doctor" medical series in the next decade said that girls were "no longer young enough to romp and play" after they began to menstruate (which was during "their fourteenth or fifteenth year").[7]

The evidence in popular culture suggests that boy privileges were extended into the teens, through them, perhaps even into the mid-twenties. For some girls, boyhood became the best preparation for adult life rather than a stage to be outgrown. The head girl in the school story *Tom and Some Other Girls* (Jessie Mansergh, 1901)—a wholly admirable person whose manner, stance, glance, stride, pose, handshake, and so forth are continually described as "boyish" or "manly"— grows up, for example, to be principal of Newnham and a model for generations of girls to follow.

Some girls so strongly identified themselves as boys that they were dismayed to realize they would never be men. Mary Toulmin found it "wretched being a girl when one has made no lady-plans and all one's boy plans have crashed." She begged her mother to get her a tutor so she could have "a proper boy's education."[8] Margaret Campbell, a feminist who wrote books as Marjorie Bowen, Joseph Shearing, George R.

Preedy, John Winch, and Robert Paye, describes her own feelings: "I realized, with great regret, that I was a girl and should be, for the rest of my life, a woman. I regretted this miserable fact because it brought with it a sense of deep inferiority, and all whom I admired and on whom I had tried to mould myself were men."[9]

As these quotations reveal, the boy dream had multiple resonances: girls wanted active games, a serious education, and adult rights and responsibilities. Girl artists saw that only men could be painters, and they longed for the freedom to go to galleries whenever they chose.[10] Masculinity provided physical and geographical freedom: nonobstructive clothing, an athletic body, safe passage through public spaces that men made dangerous for those who wore skirts. Boys of the middle and upper classes were trained for the robust assurance and social privilege of imperial rule. The only way to envision and practice becoming a competent and complete adult seemed to lie in boyhood; prevailing gender codes barred the young lady from even imagining independence and risk. The definitions of boyish, however, were under pressure—and certain gendered ideals could be deliberately enlisted to train girls for "manhood" and (ultimately) citizenship.

For middle-class girls the most visible brothers' privileges were education and sports; no wonder fiction's sporty boarding schools rose so prominently in desire. *Girl's Realm* in 1901 suggested a fancy-dress costume to represent the "Girl's Realm" (i.e., not only the magazine but also the domain in which girls should live and rule). Its key symbols were a mortarboard and a tennis racket, hockey stick, and golf club.[11] The *Girl's Own Paper* by the turn of the century also featured athletics—and implicity suggested a reason for women to acquire the courage, responsibility, strength, and discipline that men gain through sports by also presenting a series on army nurses in South Africa.

The obsession with health and physical skill that turned Englishmen of all classes into athletes developed between 1850 and 1880.[12] The cult of team games swept the public schools, the number of individual sports burgeoned, and regulatory bodies arose to codify (and in some cases professionalize) activities from archery to boxing to soccer, Rugby, tennis, golf, cricket, and swimming.

Victorians initially distinguished between games—that is, diversions such as croquet that require little skill and can be played by

"Girls at Hockey." An 1890 article gave instruction in playing the game.
Although the players still wear long skirts, the clothes of the lady spectators
are far more confining.

From *Girl's Own Paper* 12 (1890–1891): 184. Reproduced by permission of the Bodleian
Library, University of Oxford, shelfmark Per. 2537.d.1/12.

women or children—and sports, which were serious, dignified, and
manly.[13] Physically demanding exercise for girls, as opposed to mere
games, was initially linked to feminism. In 1850 Harriet Martineau recommended unladylike activities such as rowing and swimming; Bessie
Rayner Parkes regretted that "people endeavoured to check the physical power of their daughters as much as that of their minds."[14]

By late in the century, the medical awareness that exercise improved
women's health and childbearing capacity contended ambivalently
with fears of masculinization. Men were presumed to prefer girls pale,
frail, and helpless; what use was the capacity to bear healthy children if
gaining it removed one from the game of sexual selection? The issue
was complicated by competing class-based stereotypes. Outdoor sports
were initially the provenance of upper-class women, who were clearly
ladies whatever they did. Emily Lutyens, born in 1874, "joined in all

"Hockey: A capital game for girls." By 1904 the play has become far more vigorous.

From *Girl's Own Paper* 25 (1903–1904): 216. Reproduced by permission of the Bodleian Library, University of Oxford, shelfmark Per. 2537.d.1/1904.

[her] brother's games, being especially fond of cricket. [She] was a fast underhand bowler and captained a side calling itself the Knebworth Bounders."[15] A country-house diarist in her early twenties took part in a ladies' cricket match (September 4, 1886), rode to the hounds, and played ice hockey when it froze.[16] The romping of working-class girls—see, for example, the sledding in Mary Taylor's *Miss Miles* (1890)—was, on the other hand, evidence of the roughness that tainted lower-class women.

A man writing in *Good Words* (a general circulation magazine of wholesome family Sunday reading) in 1879 suggested that women's cowardice—their fear of district visiting, of blood, of thunder, of the sea, of cows, and so forth—arose from their bodily helplessness and would be ended by healthy physical training.[17] The essay is significant in providing an appropriately feminine reason to promote courage through bodily competence. Girls' schools and women's colleges began to adopt the boys' school ethos linking sports, brains, and character. Newnham-Girton tennis matches began in 1878; a silver challenge cup was donated by Charlotte Scott soon after her success in the 1880 mathematics tripos. The colleges proudly associated sports with manly brains. Philippa Fawcett played on the first Newnham hockey team, and its 1892 tennis champion, Florence Stawell, took a first in classics.[18]

In the later 1880s and 1890s, high schools began to appoint games mistresses and acquire playing fields. North London Collegiate overturned the presumption that girls should not exercise while menstruating; its woman medical officer excused only those who suffered unusual pain.[19] At Roedean in the late 1890s, games and exercise took up two hours daily in winter and three in summer. Even Cheltenham Ladies' College was converted to the games ethic when Lilian Faithfull (who had been the first hockey captain at Somerville) succeeded Dorothea Beale as principal.[20] By the 1890s, the medical column in *Girl's Own Paper* urged readers to do exercises that would increase their muscular strength as well as their general health and fitness.

Girls' sports, however, were structured to preserve sexual differences. Rules and equipment were modified; the girl in an Evelyn Sharp novel dreads going to school because her brother Jack has warned her that schoolgirls are sissies who "play cricket with a soft ball."[21] A *Girl's Own Paper* leading article on "A Girls' Cricket Club" has an illustration of players in long skirts and flower-decked garden-party hats.[22] Conservatives enforced gender norms by insisting that girls must not become "*boyish*. . . . Few characters are more despicable than a hoyden, who loses the charms of a young woman, without acquiring the characteristic energy and strength of a young man."[23] A man writing in 1890 insisted that "no game or situation where girl or woman is seen in public should be such that from its nature she is liable to pose therein ungracefully, clumsily, or unbecomingly."[24] Delightfully, however, *grace* had acquired a layered meaning. A *Girl's Own Paper* article about women cricketers in 1905 entitled "Grace at the Wickets" features the mother of Dr. W. G. Grace.[25] (He was cricket's Babe Ruth.)

Girls' fiction also mixed its messages, simultaneously permitting boyishness and ambivalently undercutting it. The tomboy of an 1895 story takes off her skirt, climbs a tree, and rescues a child. She is glad that hardened hands and muscles let her do it—but exhausted by the effort; her last words are: "You may be glad to hear that I have not the slightest wish ever to climb a tree again."[26]

Similar examples can be multiplied. The cover of *A Girl in a Thousand* [1904] shows the heroine indoors weeping—but in the frontispiece she is at the side of the road, with her bicycle, saying to a stranded male motorist: "I will cycle as fast as I can, and will try to get some one to help you out of your trouble."[27] Early in *The Youngest Sister* (Bessie Marchant, 1913) a girl sheds her heavy serge skirt and plunges into a raging torrent to save a drowning man—and is (justifiably, in the author's opinion) ashamed of the sloppy needlework revealed on her underskirt.

Yet the atmosphere changed significantly in the twenty-five years separating two editions of a popular advice manual. The 1869 version of *Girlhood* says that girls must acquire "womanliness" in their later teens: "the hoydenism, the frolic, and the exuberant mirth will now become unseemly."[28] By 1895 the language is softened and a new section added:

> There are very few girls indeed who are kept back by the fear of being called "tomboys." . . . They can become strong and vigorous and yet retain that essential womanliness. . . . So they take their morning bath, and sleep with their windows open; they eat plain food, . . . dress comfortably, and ride on the outside of omnibuses and trams. . . . And when the newspapers call attention to the fact that young women are taller, and young men shorter, than ever, they smile, and are not surprised.[29]

Most women's sports sanctioned in the nineteenth century required money and leisure. The school stories of the workgirls' papers omit hockey, but circus performers and undercover detectives display strength and daring. In *Sweethearts* (which aimed at the romantically inclined and sexually aware)[30] the opening novelette is about a widowed duchess of twenty-four who disguises herself as a stable lad to protect her racehorse. When villains break the jockey's leg she rides (and wins) the crucial race.

Swimming and cycling transcended class lines—and both were also explicitly associated with feminism. The *Englishwoman's Review* charted the progress of women's swim clubs and campaigned for women's hours at public pools. As Kate Chopin would reveal in *The Awakening* (1899), swimming served as a liberating triumph of bodily control and the conquest of fear. In addition, it was the stuff of heroism and therefore a popular locus of athletic daring in workgirls' papers. In one story from an 1898–1899 *Girls' Best Friend* sequence of hospital tales, a probationer is scolded for wearing too many "ornaments." (One suspects that a great many housemaids and shop attendants felt an echo of remembered resentment.) Hers, however, turn out to be swimming medals, and in the story's central incident she dives off Waterloo bridge, rescues a would-be suicide, and is given a hero's welcome when she returns to the hospital.[31] A few months later *Girls' Best Friend* began a series of swimming lessons, with sketches.

Cycling was even more widely transformative. Women's cycles were first manufactured in about 1890. As early as 1891, Gordon Stables, the medical columnist of *Girl's Own Paper*, provided a physician's stamp of approval: "Cycling is, in my opinion, the best of all forms of exercise."[32] The workgirl paper *Forget-Me-Not* asked in 1892, "Should Women Cycle?" and answered yes, yes, yes: for health, for convenience, and for freedom.[33] By mid-decade, cycling was a national passion and one-third of the cycles sold were women's models.[34] The archetypal New Woman image is a healthy young person in dark skirt and white shirt standing beside the bicycle that gave her freedom to travel independently in town or country.

By century's end bicycle prices dropped dramatically; in *Girls' Friend* for 1905, the Mead Cycle Company advertised secondhand cycles for one pound. The halfpenny *Girls' Best Friend* had a "Special Cycling Number" in 1898 with "Hints on Choosing Your Bicycle," instructions on riding, an article about "Famous Beauties Who Cycle," a fashion feature telling how to make a cycling skirt, and a "Love Problems" column on "Cycling as an Aid to Matrimony."

Among middle-class girls' magazines, the most sporting was *Girl's Realm*.[35] Its tone was set in the first volume's "Chat with the Girl of the Period." The editor, Alice Corkran, assertively reclaimed the phrase Eliza Lynn Linton had used to castigate girls of the 1860s:

> The claims that you make are the result of your reaction against the restrictions that hemmed in girls in the days of your grandmothers. . . .
> The modern girl . . . is tired of being taken to see her brother play foot-

ball; she wants to have a kick at it herself.... She has her bicycle, she plays cricket, golf, hockey, lawn tennis. . . . The result is that she has not the appeal of feminine dependence in her deportment; and her carriage suggests that she can hold her own with her kinsmen and masculine friends.[36]

The initial volume of *Girl's Realm* had articles on fencing, bicycling, golf, gymnastics, swimming, riding, lawn tennis, mountaineering, and ice skating as well as installments of two long-running series: "Girls Who Excell in Sports" and "True Stories of Girl Heroines." (Reports of heroism were also featured in the feminist *Englishwoman's Review*, which regularly culled news items on women's courage from papers around the world. It was important that women be demonstrably heroic in order to be fit for man's work in the world.)

By the later Edwardian years it was widely perceived that more exercise and better nutrition made girls "taller, stronger, healthier, more self-assured"[37] than their mothers. Although one would expect women's improved physique to be applauded, especially in view of the period's eugenic fervor, evidence of female strength led to a resurgence of antigames propaganda. Success in sports—like success in examinations—was used to threaten women. There were dark hints of "serious constitutional disturbance having developed itself in young married women from . . . overmuch lawn-tennis."[38] Doctors warned that girls were "more flat-chested" than formerly and that "hairy lips are frequently noticeable."[39]

Yet despite this backlash, the social climate had changed enough so that girls were generally allowed to adore rough play, competition, strength, and physical skill. Some men saw the benefit for themselves of girls' increasing boyishness: "the husband of an athletic girl may take it that his point of view will be understood and appreciated" since "a boy's mother can play his games with him when he is a small boy and talk his games with him when he is a big one."[40] And once these very important adolescent experiences were shared it became more and more possible for athletic girls to imagine themselves as boys.

Other girls indulged their dreams of boyhood primarily through books. Leading boy lives in fantasy let them try on alternate roles, voices, attitudes, and experiences, and enfold boyish traits in their self-image. "Hundreds of girls," as an essayist in *Girl's Realm* put it, would "read their brothers' books and leave their own untouched."[41] The most popular single book in Edward Salmon's poll of girls between eleven and nineteen was Charles Kingsley's brutal adventure of Elizabethan conquest, *Westward Ho!* (1855).[42] Eleanor Lodge (subsequently a noted historian and principal of Westfield College) recounted liking it so much that she "used to recite pages of it" to herself in bed.[43] Lilian Faithfull—in 1883 one of the earliest Somerville students—described the books written for girls as "pabulum."[44] L. T. Meade featured writers such as Rider Haggard and Robert Louis Stevenson in *Atalanta* magazine.

Gertrude Bell at thirteen wrote that she had "been reading a very nice book belonging to Horace called the Tower of London . . . all full of murders and tortures."[45] (Bell was the earliest Oxford woman to take a first in modern history and went on to a noteworthy career as explorer, archaeologist, alpinist, and colonial administrator.) Annabel Grant Duff, at Cheltenham Ladies' College in the mid-1880s, filled her holidays with Charles Lever, Walter Scott, and manly school and college novels such as *Frank Fairleigh* and *Verdant Green.*[46] The four daughters of John Addington Symonds treasured the yearly volumes of *Boy's Own Annual;*[47] one of them grew up to found the Women's Royal Naval Service.

The boys' books that girls liked best were historical novels, empire-adventure tales, and (to a somewhat lesser extent) sea stories. These offered a particular variety of food for girls' mental lives, and all except the sea story were adapted by women authors to feature girl heroes. The feminized versions, however, suggest some of the period's ambiguous shifts in gender roles.

L. T. Meade's *Atalanta* magazine was read by country-house girls and the daughters of merchants and professional men.[48] *Atalanta*'s frequent stories about brave girls were almost always placed in colonial or historical settings, which made it possible to imagine acts inconceivable in contemporary England. "A Golden Silence," for example, by John Strange Winter—the pseudonym of Henrietta Stannard[49]—tells of women's calm capability during the Indian Mutiny. Tottie, the twelve-year-old hero, overhears treachery in progress; one presumes that she has been looked after by an *amah* and understands the dialect better than adults do. Pinned by falling masonry, Tottie lies silent and in pain for four hours, sends her dog home to fetch help, and insists on exposing the conspiracy before her injuries are treated, since she does not want to risk falling into a faint without telling what she knows.[50]

Historical fiction was the boys' reading most generally approved for girls. Although Charlotte Yonge seldom put girl characters into heroic roles in her historical stories, Yonge's androgynous model of Christian boyhood and her characters' wholly asexual life eased the identification between girl readers and active male characters. The early Robert Louis Stevenson stories had much the same advantage, as Claudia Nelson has pointed out. In *The Black Arrow* (1888) a girl character disguised as a boy is an excellent swimmer though suspiciously unmasculine in other ways.[51]

The gender slippage between boyish girls and girlish boys and the disguises of one as the other, which make Stevenson and Haggard and other late-century adventure novelists such interesting fodder for queer theory, is particularly helpful for girl fantasists. Girls, said a writer in *Girl's Realm*, like to read about "heroic friendship between chum and chum."[52] Sea stories, which typically had no female characters but did include very young midshipmen, also had that advantage. *Atalanta*'s fifth volume opens with "A Battle and a Boy,"[53] a Central European tale which eases female readers into the boy's role by its placement next to a reproduction of G. F. Watts's painting "Girl in Armour."

Heroic models for girls found in the collections of women's biographies that had been popular since mid-century were initially Christian, charitable, literary, and royal. In 1879, however, suffragist Ellen Creathorne Clayton produced *Female Warriors: Memorials of Female Valour and Heroism, from the Mythological Ages to the Present Era*, an idea that immediately inspired many imitators. Even *Girl's Own Paper* had an article on "Women Soldiers" with a feminist peroration.[54]

The blood and gore of men's history was generally suppressed in women's military adventures. Even in stories of women who successfully passed as men the emphasis is on caretaking, spying, and delivering messages. Evelyn Everett-Green's *True Stories of Girl Heroines* (originally published in *Girl's Realm*, 1900–1901) includes many whose military heroism is structured so the girl is principally defending her own family. On the other hand, Everett-Green does not define heroism as moral strength or passive endurance, which similar books a generation earlier had done.

Historical novels about girls were far less robust than the more popular boys' fiction. Dorothea Moore's *Captain Nancy: A Story of the 'Forty-Five* (1914) has a heavy dose of caring for youngsters; Nancy fires a gun—but into the air. Girls' historical tales often undercut the adventure by wrapping it in female signifiers: in "A Brave Royalist," for example, fifteen-year-old Barbara carries an essential message concealed in a pat of butter.[55]

By the century's last decade, furthermore, the androgynous Christian manliness that made it easy for girls to identify with boy heroes was, as Claudia Nelson has demonstrated, becoming old-fashioned.[56] Partly because girls' diminishing athletic and educational difference challenged male supremacy, gender codes were in some ways more strongly policed. The changes in boys' books were also affected by middle-class boys' eager consumption of cheap blood-and-thunder fiction and by the perceived imperatives of patriotism. Books for boys veered towards simpler adventures that promoted imperial manliness and stressed action rather than character or emotion. Ironically, girl readers were well served by another aspect of the heightened manliness. Female characters virtually disappeared: no romance, no spoony stuff; sisters and mothers were left behind and forgotten.

G. A. Henty, the leading writer for boys at the turn of the century, was also enormously popular with girls. (The 1909 *Girl's Encyclopedia*, in recommending books, suggests Henty and Verne but does not even mention Charlotte Yonge.[57]) Henty, who had been in the Crimea and knew firsthand about Florence Nightingale, sometimes includes plucky girls. In *A Soldier's Daughter* (1906) he even allows a girl to wield a rifle. More commonly, however, female characters are simply missing. Henty's typical hero is an average boy (not a superhero or nobly born); like the girl hero in school stories, he succeeds through skills a young reader could cultivate rather than because of naturally superior gifts. The Henty hero's averageness made him available for readers' identification[58]—and the absence of women helps girls dream themselves into his stead. No distracting feminine characters remind girl readers of their place in the world, and no romance requires her suddenly to switch from subject to object role.

It's important to recognize that girls used boys' fiction not only for "reading" but also for mental and emotional food. Gwen Raverat remembered her dreams: "I was generally a boy, swimming rivers with a dagger in my mouth, or riding for my life with a message, or shooting my way out of a fray."[59] Eleanor Acland invented extra chapters to put herself into *Masterman Ready* as ship's crew.[60] Fiction stimulates daydreams (which readers with literary inclinations may mask by pretending that they are writing a book). Boys' fiction gave girls not only stories to read but also situations and characters for their private imaginary experience of boyhood.

The authors who tried to create adventure stories explicitly for girls were impeded by cultural "reality." Henty himself contributed "A Frontier Girl" to the 1900–1901 volume of *Girl's Realm*; she shoots, handles a canoe, warns her family of an Indian raid, and has a "wide reputation throughout the district for her courage and coolness."[61] As in this example by the master, a setting outside England is virtually essential. The tales in *Fifty-Two Stories of Courage and Endeavour for Girls* (Alfred H. Miles, [1901]) were largely by American authors. The few set in contemporary Britain have girl characters who demonstrate courage by (for example) letting school friends know mother works for her living.

When an adventurous book is set in contemporary England, its heartily boyish hero is seldom herself English. In *Harum Scarum* (1896), "Toney" Whitburn from Australia has no "accomplishments": "All I know, Aunt Dove, is useful and solid. I can run very well. I could beat most of the boys at running at home, and I shouldn't like to get out of practice." She refuses to wear stays, rides bareback, tames animals with her "magnetic influence,"[62] knows Greek and Latin, pole-vaults in the garden—and also makes friends with the villagers and is kind to Lady Dove's overworked companion. The capstone scenes are not, however, of manly valor but rather revalorize the feminine; Toney heroically nurses a village child through scarlet fever, remaining in isolation with her patient in order to prevent an epidemic. The only real difference between Toney and similar self-sacrificing girls in earlier fiction is that she does not grow gentle after catching the fever herself—she's too healthy to get sick, and she's smart about eating, resting, and disinfecting.

In wilder places, or in wilder times, girls can reveal heroism without qualification—though they may still need gentling at the end. Bushy

Sukolt, a geologist's child raised among men in the Rockies, wears short hair and boy's clothing, rides bareback, out-wrestles two mean boys, points her revolver at a mob to save a man from lynching, digs her father out after an avalanche, shoots a buffalo, rides through a pack of wolves to fetch a surgeon, leads a wagon train across a flooded river, shoots a horse thief, kills three Indians who are scalping a miner, and saves the settlement from an attack by bandits. Oh why, young readers must have asked, after this satisfying fantasy, must she finally be sent east to school to be "educated as a young lady should be"?[63]

The writer who most successfully adapted the adventure tale to put contemporary girls in the central heroic role was Bessie Marchant (1862–1941), often described as "the girls' Henty." Author of well over a hundred books published between 1894 and 1939, Marchant almost always set her tales in the wilds of empire or in exciting foreign places where laws of modesty and decorum did not obtain—though even she generally managed some sort of refeminization at the story's end.

In *Juliette, the Mail Carrier* (1907), for example, Juliette takes on the contract to deliver mail by boat in summer and dogsled in winter when her father—the only substantial resident in a Canadian fishing village—is injured. In fantasy the far-off place erases class and makes Juliette an imaginative persona for both working girls and schoolgirls. Out alone for days at a time in lonely country, with two loaded revolvers in case of an encounter with bear or wolves, Juliette rescues an injured man—in fact, in the course of the book she rescues the same man three times. "I seem fated to have to drag you about, as if you were a bale of goods from a clothing store," she says to him.[64]

In another Marchant story of Canada, Bertha Doyne is the youngest of three orphan sisters; the other two, who work at unpleasant jobs made necessary by their poverty, see her as an incompetent and feckless dreamer, and she (fulfilling their expectations) commits blunders of timidity and thoughtlessness. She is redeemed by physical courage and hard work, although her real trial is heroic housekeeping (alone in a prairie cabin through the winter with five children under six and their mother, who is paralyzed after being thrown from a horse). The situation neatly valorizes a traditional female role; but a pioneering winter of near starvation is, indeed, heroic, and in Marchant's handling, quite moving.[65] And Bertha also rescues a man by diving into a torrent, a settlement by driving a sledge of food through a blizzard, a woman by climbing a rail trestle over a gorge, and a year's crop by beating out a prairie fire.

The plot structure on which Marchant hangs her tales of courage and adventure is usually forgery, embezzlement, smuggling, and detection—the kind of mystery later formulized in girl detective stories. Edward Stratemeyer's Bobbsey Twins and Nancy Drew books also adopt Marchant's strategy of including a good deal of tour-guide information about unfamiliar places. For Marchant, however, the setting is essential to the action: her heroes can ride across country, shoot to kill, travel unprotected among rough men, and swim in their underclothing so long as they are rescuing someone, and are doing it elsewhere than in England. Marchant's books sometimes end with a return to landed leisure in England after independence and courage have made the girl strong and worthy, and (as in some of L. T. Meade's stories) her femininity may be validated by the suggestion of an approaching marriage, though the marriage is typically revealed and simultaneously excluded in an appended afterword.

Like the authors of school stories—and unlike Rosa Carey, Charlotte Yonge, and the authors of girls' domestic fictions—Bessie Marchant is not really willing to let her tomboy heroes grow up. The resistance arises from her ambivalence about women's stories; the new girl has, at least to an extent, found a satisfactory adolescent role but has not yet discovered a way for her boyish virtues to be maintained in a woman's life.

Scouting provides an exemplary case of the interaction between girls' initiative and adult culture. Girls deliberately and on their own imitated boy behavior. Their boy life was subsequently adapted, shaped, and refeminized by adult latecomers, though in the process some "feminine" traits and occupations were channeled into new forms.

Scouting for boys was largely a response to problems revealed by the Boer War. A distressing number of recruits had to be rejected because they were undersized or sickly. In addition, home-front dissatisfactions raised concerns about loyalty in the social class that supplied soldiers and about "effeminization" and "degeneration" among the officer class. Boy Scouts came into being to promote health, discipline, patriotism, and manliness.

Three Girls on a Ranch (1902). In Bessie Marchant's adventure stories, girls who lived in the world's wilder places had courage, strength, and power.

Robert Baden-Powell wrote *Aids to Scouting for N.C.O.'s and Men* (1899) as a war-office manual. Charlotte Mason, who ran a training school for governesses (many of whom taught overseas in military families), was apparently the first person to appreciate its appeal for youngsters. Girl Guide history records that Katharine Loveday, governess for Field Marshall Allenby's children, first informed Baden-Powell about scouting's value in educating boys.[66]

By 1906 Baden-Powell was promoting an organization to improve the health and discipline of (in particular) working-class boys of school-leaving age. After an experimental camp in 1907, the first part of *Scouting for Boys* was published in January 1908. Young men and boys took up the idea with astonishing speed. What was unexpected (and unwelcome) to the founder, however, was scouting's enormous appeal for girls.

Girls who dreamed of being boys were (like their brothers) infected by Edwardian jingo. In spring 1908 a "What to Do With Our Girls" exposition (which supplied career information, promoted girls' organizations, and gave display space to schools) featured a shooting range. Girls were entranced, to the dismay of many adults; Keir Hardie reportedly said that it was "vicious" to encourage girls to kill people.[67] *Girl's Realm* responded with an article emphasizing the importance— to both individuals and the nation—of self-defense. "The Girl and the Rifle" suggests the tensions running up toward the Great War; author Eustace Miles refers to German military power and insists that women in colonies such as South Africa need rifles to protect their children from unspecified dangers that probably include "savages" as well as predatory animals. The article is illustrated with a striking photograph of a resolute girl of about fourteen firing from a prone position—there are no smiles, no girlish cues. At Oxford, St. Hilda's College formed a rifle club in 1909.[68]

The appeal of a military-style girls' organization was shown in another 1908 *Girl's Realm* article. Photographs of the "Girls' Brigade" begun by a former Guardsman show the members in middy blouses, knee-length skirts with braid around the hem, black stockings, and field caps. The Girls' Brigade engaged in physical exercises, military drill, ambulance training, and band practice. Its most thrilling unit was a group of troopers on horseback—given putative sanction by the army's need for nurses who could ride. The Girls' Brigade was designed for working-class neighborhoods, which would have pro-

The Girl and the Rifle.

ARE THEY INCONGRUOUS?

By EUSTACE MILES. Illustrated by HILDA COWHAM.

At the "What to Do With Our Girls" Exhibition, now going on at Prince's Skating Rink, London (open till May 30th), an enormous interest is being taken by girls in the shooting range, which has been put up to provide relief from the more strenuous work of demonstrating all the careers open to intelligent girls. Struck by the eager interest of girls in the use of the rifle, and the remarkable skill developed in the course of the competitions arranged (Lord Roberts having offered one of the prizes), the Editor asked Mr. Eustace Miles to write on the subject.

THE Duke of Argyll, when he was opening the Leeds High School for Girls, was pleased with the arrangements for cooking, but said, on going round the school, he had missed one thing—namely, a shooting gallery, so that the girls of England could l e a r n what Lord Roberts wanted the boys of England to learn.

This is quite wrong, says Mr. Keir Hardie. It is a mistake to make girls military; it is vicious to encourage them to kill people. It breeds the pugnacious spirit.

As a matter of fact, in the case of boxing, the pugnacious man is not, as a rule, the adept boxer; the truculent advocate of battery and bloodshed is the looker-on. If the looker-on were him-

" THEY ARE MEANT MERELY TO DO NEEDLEWORK."

self to learn to box, he would be a better man than he is now, with his talking and his loafing and his drinking.

Then there is quite another aspect. Just as one who can swim need not spend all his time in kicking fish to death, or even in saving himself: for he has been known to save others; so one who can box or shoot need not spend all his time in thrashing or murdering others—which is a poor hobby: he can protect others as well as himself.

I do not think Mr. Keir Hardie and others have at all realised that, as people are to-day (especially the Germans and their unusual Emperor), the best guarantee of peace would not be a

2 V

"The Girl and the Rifle." *Girl's Realm* in 1908 promoted shooting as a serious skill needed by empire-minded girls, and the caption under the small sketch ("They are meant merely to do needlework") reveals the magazine's overtly feminist message.

From *Girl's Realm* 10 (1907–1908): 657. From the author's collection.

THE BEST POSITION FOR GIRLS.

"Our Rifle Club." A *Girl's Own Paper* article about a village rifle club took a
more sporting and ladylike approach.

From *Girl's Own Paper* 29 (1907–1908): 4. Reproduced by permission of the Bodleian
Library, University of Oxford, shelfmark Per. 2537.d.1/29.

vided the majority of military nurses; it was intended to arouse patriotism and discipline as well as providing wholesome activity for adolescent girls.[69]

As for scouting itself, as soon as Baden-Powell's book of instructions, tales, and rituals reached print, girls read its secrets and shared its
pleasures. Girls of all sorts—country-house girls, boarding-school
girls, urban pupil teachers—independently began to play tracking
games, make uniforms, organize patrols, and dream of honorable
national service. By using their initials rather than their given names,

some even managed to obtain official Boy Scout badges, including an entire troop at Lingholt School in Hindhead in 1909.[70]

Some early troops found adult leaders. The First Hampstead company was founded by a "Mrs. Blyth, who was then looking for some work which would help on the cause of women" and who "found a few girls playing scouting games on Hampstead Heath."[71] Notice two important cues here—the sponsor was a feminist, and the girls themselves had independently begun scout activities. Other troops managed to remain in girls' hands. The troop at Abbey School in Malvern carried on for five years under fifteen-year-old scoutmasters until school authorities insisted that they find an adult leader.[72]

Scouting evidently appealed to girls of all classes. Harmsworth's *Girls' Reader* carried a scout serial in July 1909. Presumably echoing the proprietor's philosophy,[73] the editor billed scouting as "a wholly fresh phase of woman's activity" for "healthy, open-air, adventure-loving young women, who go about their work of tracking, spying, signalling and what not with a zeal and intelligence that may well set an example to their male confreres."[74]

"Lieutenant General Sir Robert Baden-Powell" (as he was identified on the title page of scouting manuals) was not pleased by girls' intrusion into the game he had designed to turn boys into men. Girls, he said, needed careful supervision. Boys might commendably take up scouting on their own, but girls should wait for adult guidance.[75] He also felt girls of different classes should be organized separately; boyish comradeship was inappropriate for them. And he particularly disliked girls' appearance in uniform:

> to dress in a conspicuous and clumsy fashion, by way of being *practical*, *very* short skirts, in order to vault gates, is quite unnecessary. . . . Bare brown hands and arms are first rate for flinging sticks and stones for dogs, for digging and what not—but how about nursing sick people, playing the piano or violin, etc.?[76]

But it was precisely these things that excited girls who wanted to be boys: physical freedom, workable clothing, independence, outdoor activity, games played where few of the period's adult women were (as yet) prepared to follow. By 1909 some six thousand girls had already, on their own, become scouts—six thousand girls, without any significant adult organization, resourcefully and eagerly copying boys' activities, following the same rules, and preparing to meet the same challenges of manly, military, active, and honorable life.

Baden-Powell still hoped that girls could be satisfied with an organization that would turn them into cadets for the Red Cross Society.[77] At the first national scout rally at the Crystal Palace in September 1909, however, he was faced with the reality: troops of girls, in uniforms they had made for themselves, invited him to inspect them.[78] He and his sister Agnes reluctantly published a pair of pamphlets that tried to undo some of the damage by proposing a separate organization with a separate name. Girls would become "Guides" rather than "Scouts." (The word *scout* in its military sense perhaps too clearly denoted danger, daring, and independence.) Their organization would respond to the threat of moral and physical "decadence," which Baden-Powell blamed on the "ignorance or supineness of mothers who have never been taught themselves."[79]

Tim Jeal's recent authoritative biography of Robert Baden-Powell casts doubt on his "revulsion" against girls "using the sacred word 'Scout.'"[80] His opposition, however, is described in an official Girl Guide history published while he was still active, although (as a further complication) the history's author—Rose Kerr, Chair of the Guides' World Committee—had, when she was young Rose Gough, rejected a proposal of marriage from the middle-aged bachelor General Baden-Powell.[81]

The 1909 pamphlets that shaped the girls' movement used the empire to valorize household duties: "in a Colony, a woman must know how to do many things which she finds done for her at home in civilization."[82] Yet Baden-Powell did recognize that militarism was largely responsible for his movement's appeal. Girls therefore could suitably be prepared to help the wounded. They might also learn foreign languages—as well as doing household chores in preparation for a rougher life in the Colonies.

The 1912 *Handbook for Girl Guides* (with the alternate title *How Girls Can Help Build the Empire*) was organized to put the more adventurous activities first, with sections headed: "Finding the Injured" (woodcraft, open-air pursuits, tracking); "Tending the Injured" (first aid, hospital duties); "Frontier Life" (camping, seafaring, self-defense); "Home

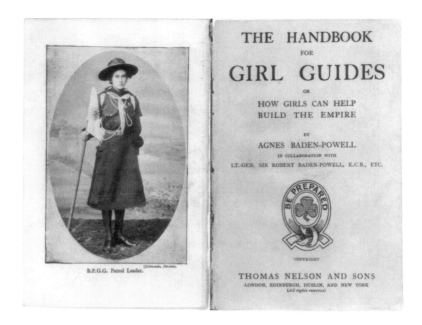

THE HANDBOOK
FOR
GIRL GUIDES
OR
HOW GIRLS CAN HELP
BUILD THE EMPIRE

BY

AGNES BADEN-POWELL

IN COLLABORATION WITH

LT.-GEN. SIR ROBERT BADEN-POWELL, K.C.B., ETC.

BE PREPARED

COPYRIGHT

THOMAS NELSON AND SONS
LONDON, EDINBURGH, DUBLIN, AND NEW YORK
(All rights reserved)

B.P.G.G. Patrol Leader.

Title page and frontispiece of the 1912 Girl Guides handbook.

Reproduced by permission of the Bodleian Library, University of Oxford, shelfmark 38483.f9.

Life" (sanitation, cookery); "Health" (care of children, physical fitness); and "Patriotism" (chivalry, self-discipline, self-improvement, the empire, citizenship).[83] The original Guides handbook has many stories about famous women and far fewer of the homecraft badges that are in later editions; it is significantly more bracing, boyish, and scoutish.

By 1912 patriotism and service loomed significantly in the nation's consciousness. *Terry the Girl-Guide*, written by Guide commissioner Dorothea Moore, functions rather like Robert Baden-Powell's campfire yarns in the Boy Scout handbook, providing fictionalized idols to emulate (though I suspect some gentle mockery of Baden-Powell in the poem on "Nashonall Decadence" that one of the girls produces). Terry hears about her school's old girl Mary Mainwaring, who married a major, nursed the garrison through a fever, and picked up a rifle to

defend the hospital. This exemplum neatly embeds the important signifiers of female heroism: Mary as a girl competed on male preserves
by winning a Somerville scholarship and taking a double first, but as a
woman she exhibits her valor as wife and nurse, using a weapon only to
defend helpless patients.

Girl Guides preserved the Boy Scouts' class and denominational
inclusiveness. In some areas, of course, residential patterns imposed
class segregation; and for girls over fourteen the school troops and
those organized in factories drew on entirely separate populations. In
other areas, however, individual troops were fairly inclusive. Guiding
proved quite popular among working girls.

As it came broadly into girls' culture, the guiding/scouting ethos
was very much like the boyish school mores already enshrined in girls'
books. To be a Guide, in the words of an Elsie Oxenham character,

> You must be smart [i.e., tidy] like a soldier. And you must play up, and
> keep the law, and do your good turns, and never complain or get
> whiney, and be jolly altogether. And you must always keep your word,
> and let people know they can trust you.[84]

Despite some co-option and watering down, scouting was in its
early years a signal success through which girls demonstrated their
demand to be like boys and achieved public recognition of the extent to
which they shared boys' skills, ideals, goals, and character. In the
mature form represented in the 1918 handbooks of the two organizations, there was (aside from the naming and the gender of pronouns)
only one difference between the Guide Law and the Scout Law:

1. A Guide's honour is to be trusted.
2. A Guide is loyal to the King and her officers, and to her
   parents, her country, and her employers or employees.
3. A Guide's duty is to be useful and to help others.
4. A Guide is a friend to all, and a sister to every other Guide,
   no matter to what social class the other belongs.
5. A Guide is courteous.
6. A Guide is a friend to animals.
7. A Guide obeys orders of her parents, patrol leader, or
   Captain without question.
8. A Guide smiles and sings under all difficulties.

9. A Guide is thrifty.

10. A Guide is clean in thought, word, and deed.

The difference? A Scout, unlike a Guide, "smiles and *whistles*" under difficulties.[85]

Since the army and the empire drove scouting's conception and its dramatic spread in the half-decade before war came, even Robert Baden-Powell used the lure of combat to inspire girls. His 1909 Guides pamphlet begins: "Girls! imagine that a battle has taken place in and around your town or village. . . . Are you going to sit down, and wring your hands, and cry? Or are you going to be plucky and do something to help your brothers and fathers who are fighting and falling in your behalf?"[86]

Military imagery pervades the period. A homesick girl at school in a Katharine Tynan novel is buoyed by a letter asking, "Are you being brave? You've got to be a soldier, you know, and stick to your post."[87] The omnipresent Edwardian patriotism undoubtedly spurred girls' hunger to wear uniforms and join boys' military games; so, if only subliminally, did the antisuffrage contention that persons who could not defend the law had no right to share in its making.

Another popular source of mental food for girls who craved power and glory was found in swashbuckling novels. Anthony Hope's *The Prisoner of Zenda* (1894) took third place in Florence Low's 1905 survey of secondary schoolgirls' favorite books.[88] Others cherished by adolescents were Baroness Orczy's *The Scarlet Pimpernel* (1905) and the Graustark series begun in 1901 by American George Barr McCutcheon. *The Three Musketeers* (Alexandre Dumas, 1844) must be given classic standing for the frequency with which it appears in memoirs. Eleanor Farjeon records one complex and transgressive response to Dumas:

> I am Porthos. I love him. I love him more than anyone I am. I love boasting like him, and being vain like him, and stupid like him, and making love like him, and having an enormous appetite like him, and being the third-best fencer in the world, and the very strongest man.[89]

Swashbuckling novels provide combat in its most sanitized form. Their self-evident unreality makes for enemies who need not be imagined as suffering human beings. All conflicts are essentially personal;

orders come from a glamorous sovereign rather than an all-too-human drill sergeant. The military adventures in these books do not require a girl reader to imagine joining up, being trained, living in barracks, or bivouacking in uncivilized places. The romantic costumes—plumed hats, flowing sleeves, jeweled swords—are fancy dress, and the heterosexual love story (if any) is generally so extraordinarily pure that it easily leaves intact the girl reader's projection into a putatively male body.

The Scarlet Pimpernel travels disguised as a woman as well as a fop on his missions to rescue aristocrats from the guillotine. Although it was Anthony Hope's *The Prisoner of Zenda* that brought the principality of "Ruritania" into linguistic currency, the popular writer Ouida had been since the 1870s creating romantic adventures set in imaginary places with frequently disguised heroes of transparently ambiguous gender. The high-strung and intermittently disabled hero of *The Gadfly* (written in 1897 by Ethel Voynich)[90] is another of the class.

Frances Hodgson Burnett's *The Lost Prince* (1915) is a romantic royalist fantasy for young readers; though both adventurers are boys, one is a cripple who has made himself strong through physical exercise. Bessie Marchant did a girl-centered version in *A Princess of Servia* (1912). The central character has Marchant's typical independent/feminist credentials—she has lived in Canada and been to college—and is distressed, when returning to her native Servia, to find how restricted women's lives are. Soon, however, like Anthony Hope's hero, she must masquerade as royalty and, in a typical Ruritanian fantasy of "swords jangling and horses snorting in frantic chases across the snow, . . . Mary meets every challenge . . . 'with a dauntless air and flashing eyes.' "[91]

The war books written for girls in the immediate aftermath of August 1914 had a similar romantic and personal quality. In May Wynne's *An English Girl in Serbia* [1916], a sixteen-year-old making her way back to England after war breaks out is captured by a Bulgarian enemy who is far more of a brigand than a military officer, and she is rescued by gypsies. Winding up at a hospital, she is put to work not because she has any training but because nursing skill is natural to attractive females. "The sight of your bonnie face will be as good as a tonic," she is told[92]—a long-lived fancy soon to crumble in the face of actual wartime field hospitals.

Many scenes in *An English Girl in Serbia* come straight from a scouting manual: finding one's way in the woods, identifying wild fruit and nuts to eat, building a fire for protection against wolves. The book is illustrated with a photograph of "A Young Serbian Heroine who fought gallantly in the 'Great Retreat.'" She is the same size as a boy of perhaps fourteen who is also in the photo; she's barefoot and wears ragged trousers, coat, and padded vest. The only clue to gender is her head scarf. This, however, is a real Serbian girl used to give photographic "authenticity" to a very imaginary story allowing English girls to insert themselves into the great patriotic war.

(In an 1899 advice book, May Wynne had worried that athletic competition was "threatening to rob us of the tender womanly woman."[93] I cannot discover whether her about-face was personal or market driven. In either case, there is an enormous difference between the effeminate activities and attitudes she recommends in 1899 and the adventurous girl protagonists in her fiction little more than a decade later.)

Another book about an English girl marooned on the continent when war breaks out turns international affairs into a two-suitors romance. Gill (a high-school girl and an officer's orphan) has a holiday job providing companionship and English conversation to a Ruritanian grand duchess who is courted both by an English officer and by the Kaiser's son. Inspired by her own chaste chivalric love for the grand duchess, Gill takes to spying and to lurking about in secret passages. When she and the officer escape through German lines, the man is wounded, captured, and tortured while Gill hides and watches; finally she flashes an S.O.S. with her flashlight (the book is by Guides commissioner Dorothea Moore) and the British army comes to the rescue.[94] A splendid illustration shows Gill in a spotlessly clean white coat after crawling through a tunnel, binding up wounds, and concealing herself in a woodpile.

Significantly, Dorothea Moore displaces the principal events in *Wanted, an English Girl*. The romance at the center of the book is not the protagonist's—she and the man chivalrously work together to rescue the woman he (they) love(s). The girl's viewpoint usual in girls' books has been damaged—probably unconsciously—by the reality of war; Moore needs the male figure for heroic and romantic scenes, while the double/persona hides in the closet or woodpile looking on.

"Standing on a tottering first floor, she flashed out that 'Save Our Souls' again and again." Wartime heroism was imagined in Dorothea Moore's *Wanted, an English Girl* (1916).

Reproduced by permission of the Bodleian Library, University of Oxford, shelfmark 2537.e.1678.

Much the same had been true of May Wynne's *An English Girl in Serbia*—Nancy the English girl has a boy twin, to whom the more masculine and heroic parts of the adventure take place while she watches or listens. The war was a shock to girls' boy nature. Girl Guides who had dreamed of "tracking out the wounded, and of carrying messages between the lines" were bitterly disappointed, according to the Guides' historian, "to find that they were allowed to do nothing more than knit socks and collect waste paper."[95]

In another early wartime book, Edith C. Kenyon's *Pickles: A Red Cross Heroine* [1916], Joan—"Pickles"—is, at seventeen, "lithe, strong, yet somewhat small in figure, with a quantity of red-gold hair,"[96] rides well, and has passed examinations in nursing. A flyer friend of the family who needs an observer takes Pickles along to France. Camouflaged in her missing brother's flying gear, she lights bombs and tosses them out of the plane; she also has a splint in her suitcase so that when the pilot is wounded she can bind up his arm and help him land the plane. Once again, the story is a fantasy of war as individual combat. As an unofficial volunteer, Pickles is not under anyone's command but roams the countryside fighting and nursing at will. In the climactic incident, she rescues an abandoned child from a burning house and also frees her father from the Germans who have taken him prisoner. Thus Pickles takes a principal L. T. Meade fantasy one step further: she not only wins her father's respect but also courageously saves his life.

Soon after this book was in readers' hands, more than 400,000 British soldiers had become casualties on the Somme, and the realities of conscription and mass warfare annihilated ideals of choice and chivalry. The books of girls' heroism had prepared them for war as badly as the verses of male comradeship had served their brothers.

I will come back to the wartime changes in gender ideals in the concluding chapter. Before that, let's summarize girls' craving for boy life. What did girls themselves perceive about the meaning of the gender codes? What feminine traits did they reject? What manly characteristics did they want?

First was appearance. *Blackwood's* in 1890 described the "universal custom of civilized communities" that "the gentler sex must on all occasions consult appearances in a special manner not demanded of men."[97] But in girls' fiction of the Edwardian years, neat, clean, gentle, and obedient girls are not often likeable. When the initial description mentions a girl's untidiness and careless dress, readers knew at once that she would be jolly, wholesome, and active. A generation earlier the same terms had served as warning of a moral flaw.

Second was the question of female emotional fragility. The tomboy in *The Human Girl* despises her new roommate on sight because she's a "horrid, sniffy, pink and white sort of girl who talked through her nose, and what was worse, she began to cry."[98] Tears in real life are often an irrepressible response to frustration and helplessness; fiction's tomboys despise tears as an illicit strategy to elicit chivalric rescue. The *Royal Annual* for 1913 instructs Girl Guides "to restrain their tears" since crying harms one's brain and eyesight. Girls should emulate the (male) Chief Scout: "Sir Robert Baden-Powell, even as a baby, was never known to cry in his life."[99]

In the 1890s magazines often complained about girls' masculine ways. The *Girl's Own Paper* blamed competitive schooling and athletics for inducing "a deplorable degree of roughness, and puerile imitation of the off-hand manners of young men."[100] College girls were especially suspect. Prime Minister Gladstone's daughter Helen, a student at Newnham, "was the most breezy, boisterous creature possible. . . . She had a habit of picking her friends up and running with them the length of the corridors."[101] Much of the objection to girls' "roughness," however, arose in pure reaction. As Ellen Clayton had pointed out in the introduction to *Female Warriors*:

> Popular Prejudice, having decided that woman is a poor, weak creature, credulous, easily influenced, holds that she is of necessity timid, that if she were allowed as much as a voice in the government of her native country, she would stand appalled if war were even hinted at. If it be proved by hard facts that woman is not a poor, weak creature, then she must be reprimanded as being masculine.[102]

Because valor was so strongly associated with manliness and both were seen as essential to public life, girls' magazines, feminist periodicals, and the halfpenny press all took notice of women's courage. The tabloid *Girls' Best Friend* on February 26, 1898, made Grace Darling the first in a series of "Women to Copy." *Girl's Favourite* in September

1898 began running "True Tales of Brave Women." *Girl's Realm* articles by T. C. Bridges in 1906–1907 praised physical courage as shown in rescuing people from fires and other disasters of ordinary life.

The good boyish girl in fiction was admired for (as one author put it) "strength and rectitude, honour, and physical courage."[103] Moral courage was also seen as distinctive in the new girl. It followed, in the novelists' reasoning, from physical competence; the "old" girl's weakness made her afraid of trouble and easily intimidated.

In girls' culture, the admirable boyish characteristics include loyalty to one's own sex—in other words, it is generally (if not overtly) associated with a variety of feminism. In a *Girl's Own Paper* essay competition on "My Favorite Heroine from Shakespeare," over one-third of the entrants wrote about Portia, and the examiner complained about the number who used her merely as an excuse to construct an essay on women's rights.[104]

Fiction placed strict limits on girls' aggression. Peggy, in Angela Brazil's *A Terrible Tomboy* (1915), beats up a boy who is bullying her brother—but the scene is very unusual, though a fist fight in defense of an underdog is virtually essential in boys' school stories. Girls in historical tales may not fire weapons unless the circumstances are extraordinary; in Dorothea Moore's *Captain Nancy* (1914), for example, it is to protect twenty schoolchildren. The archetypal military scene is the one that opens an 1899 series of "Dramatic Real-Life Stories" in the *Girl's Favourite*: nurses take fallen men's place at the guns to protect the wounded soldiers in a tent hospital.

Perhaps authors had trouble imagining situations that would require female aggression even in self-defense, particularly since rape had not yet reentered the syntax of visibility. Yet there is also a question of value systems. Sensationalist boys' fiction depicts battles among bands of "brigands" or "pirates" or the conquest of "savage" native peoples in the name of empire, but women authors, even when writing for boys, generally avoided these incidents. Charlotte Yonge's memorable scenes of heroism, for example, involve male self-sacrifice.

The ascription of male vices to girls was also rare, although the Girl Guide handbook did mention smoking and alcohol in feminized (indeed sexualized) terms: "foolish girls get into the way of taking wine or alcohol when they are not well." The 1912 Guide handbook also tells girls that "secret bad habits" will "lead to hysteria and lunatic asylums ... blindness, paralysis, and loss of memory,"[105] though it doesn't provide even a clue as to what these "secret bad habits" might be. (The parallel passage in the boys' version refers to the "secret vice" of "beastliness" and suggests that it can be overcome by "bathing at once in cold water" or "exercising the upper part of the body by arm exercises, boxing, etc." when the desire arises.[106])

Having imagined girls with manly virtues and manly roles, girls' culture also explored the reverse. Leslie Farquhar's father wishes that she (and not her brother) were the boy: "so fearless and active, so endlessly cheerful and contented, so shrewd when summoned for consultation in the business-room."[107] Role reversals take place in many of Bessie Marchant's frontier adventures. In *Juliette, the Mail Carrier*, for instance, the protagonist's invalid father darns the stockings and her injured half brother does the cooking while Juliette is gone with the mails. In *Three Girls on a Ranch* (Bessie Marchant, 1901)—which actually has six girls: George, Clem, Hen, Flossy, Dossy, and Peter—the three eldest farm while their father looks after his invalid wife and educates the three younger girls.

Some of the real girls who wanted to be boys may merely have craved comfortable clothes or minor privileges their brothers had. Yet even in trivial forms, their desire encoded girls' recognition of their oppression. A women's magazine columnist advised in 1889 that girls and boys should have essentially the same education and training, at least until puberty, so that a little girl would not feel too soon "the burden of her sex."[108]

In girls' imagination, being a boy meant adventure, fun, and freedom from constraining clothes. When the new girl in an Elsie Oxenham story encounters the school's Guide troop she longs for the "big, square, business-like pockets" of their uniform.[109] Mary Toulmin envied her young uncles:

> I want to be one of them, to exchange my silly frock and socks for breeches and gaiters, to have my hair cut short, to feel my face hard and rough, to throw my leg across a horse to ride and ride and ride. As nothing is impossible for God, I pray with all my might to be turned into a boy.[110]

Boys' clothes signified freedom of movement in a larger sense as well: the law of clothes blended almost imperceptibly into the law of chaperonage. When dressed to attract male attention and impede their strength, girls may well need protection. An advertisement published in the in *Forget-Me-Not* for March 24, 1906 read:

"I Wish I Were a Man"

Does a girl really wish she were a man when she says so, or is it merely a desire to see herself in a sleek black dress-suit, with a vast expanse of shirt-front, and a high collar? And, in addition, to be the possessor of a latchkey, to visit music-halls, roam about unchaperoned, and enjoy life in what is supposed to be the good old bachelor style?[111]

A passage in "Handsome Harry" begins with clothing and swiftly moves to an expression of its significance. When "Handsome Harry" was Harriet,

in her modest frock, with her long hair curled into a graceful knot, lace at her neck and wrists . . . what a hard-working, dull, listless little nobody she was then! Just a poorly-paid working girl! A typewriting slave, at the mercy of a bullying manager. What a contrast between the days then and now! Ruled by the harsh conventions of womankind, she was bound to the tyranny of hairpins, of being always gloved, of taking her modest lunch at the ladies' table in a teashop.

And now she stood there, a lithe, well-groomed figure, her long tresses gone, and a smart peaked cap taking the place of the big, floppy hat, riddled with hatpin punctures. Who would have known her again in that garb—the big uniform coat, collar and tie, and smart driving-gloves! And blessed with a man's freedom![112]

It was not, of course, terribly rare for girls or women to assume male dress, usually temporarily, for economic reasons, personal causes, safety, or adventure. There was also an extremely popular Victorian stage tradition of breeches roles for leading actresses, girls as principal boy in pantomime, and music-hall male impersonators. Some "Pleasure Gardens" in working-class neighborhoods provided men's clothing that women could rent when they wanted to smoke, drink at the bar, and enjoy the freedom of an evening out.[113] When war came, working-class women suggested to recruiters that the appeal of a military uniform for oneself was a powerful draw to enlistment in the WAAC.[114]

Girls of more privileged classes wore boys' clothes for play. Beryl Booker writes, "I realised half my ambition towards becoming a boy by having my hair cut short"; she was "on special occasions . . . allowed to dress up in Arthur's sailor suit."[115] Mary, Countess of Mento, wore her cousin's clothes during the holidays.[116] In fiction, a character laments that "after Tommy went to Osborne and there was nobody to change clothes with, it was very dull."[117]

Having male relatives at home was often a girl's only opportunity to lead an unsupervised outdoor life. In an Evelyn Everett-Green novel, a girl of twenty-one laments that "boys can do such a lot of things. Girls do have such a dull time."[118] When her brother is home from Oxford, however, she has liberty to roam with him. Rosa Carey is able to produce a tale of mystery and adventure in *Aunt Diana* (1888)[119] by having Alison accompany her brother Roger to catch a thief and save their father's business.

Brothers might also be a (temporary) passport to education. When they went away to school, girls who had shared their governess might well lose not only outdoor sports but also some lessons; Eleanor Acland and her sister, for example, were no longer taught Latin and algebra once the boys went to school.[120] Historian Mary Prior has suggested to me that—for these reasons—girls of that generation were closer to their brothers than any before or since. For a decade or two it was acceptable for girls to behave like boys when in their brothers' company; after 1920 single-sex schooling was nearly universal and adolescent gender roles were reimposed. The chivalry, manliness, and naive patriotism of the golden boys and girls thus become especially touching in the ironic glare of hindsight, and the brothers' loss in 1916 especially poignant.

But a boy's freedom of movement did not comprise merely playtime pleasures. In 1885, at seventeen, Gertrude Bell yearned to go to the National Gallery but lamented that there was no one to take her. "If I were a boy," she exclaims, "I should go to that incomparable place every week."[121] Masculinity meant vocational opportunities and education; most essentially, it represented the freedom to make choices. Lynn Linton thought the chief danger of cycling was "the intoxication which comes with unfettered liberty."[122]

The boy dreams in girls' fiction open a vision of male privilege. Girls' rebellion may be distanced through humor, yet the depth of their discontent is barely concealed. Pauline Riverstone, in Emma Marshall's *Eastward Ho!* (1890), is miserable at home: "If I had only been a boy," she complains, "it would have been all right. I could go to Eton and have fun. I could play cricket in earnest—not sham cricket, with a soft ball."[123] But the title *Eastward Ho!* is a wry allusion to Charles Kingsley's stirring novel of imperial adventure; in her novel Marshall—who was a suffragist—lets Pauline Riverstone find her own adventure doing social welfare work in the East End.

Grown-up tomboys pushed at the barriers that kept them from the man's life boyhood prepared them for. Katherine Symonds not only wished she were a boy but also knew her parents had wanted a son; her father's autobiography does not even mention her birth as a disappointing fourth daughter. After a childhood of outdoor play, *Tom Sawyer*, and *The Last of the Mohicans*,[124] she managed to spend most of her adult life in uniform: she founded both the Women's Royal Naval Service and the VAD (Voluntary Aid Detachment, which provided nursing services to supplement the regular army's medical corps). After the war she became assistant chief commissioner of the Girl Guides. Margaret Nevinson, an only daughter with five brothers who "hated being a girl and felt, that clearly at [her] birth someone had blundered,"[125] became a social worker, Poor Law guardian, suffragist, tax resister, and—once women finally achieved citizenship—a justice of the peace.

Other women took a post-Freudian look back at their boyhood and perceived sexual revulsion. Phyllis Bottome, born in 1882, suddenly became a tomboy after her mother told her of "the pains of childbirth—the greater physical strength of men—their far from greater moral strength—the white slave traffic."[126] Conversely, boyish behavior could serve dawning heterosexual interest, since it provided male companionship (in actuality or in imagination). Mary Butts—yet another girl who used *The Three Musketeers* as a basis for her own fantasies—imagined herself into the story as a youth and made Athos a "friend to be comforted."[127]

The *Girls' Home* story of "Handsome Harry" encloses most of these signals. Harriet undertakes the masquerade after losing her job as a typist for resisting sexual harassment. In trousers she can run to rescue a child; valor earns her a responsible job. As a trolley driver she wears a handsome uniform and masters a big machine. She also works out in a gym and learns self-defense; girl readers surely smiled at the double-entendre of "Very soon she would have nothing to fear on the score of holding her own in any fracas among men. And it was to prove very useful in the future."[128]

The reader's doubled recognition of gender and sexuality gives the story a fizz of erotic energy. Harry's good looks and sensitive feelings attract adoring girls. "He" also meets (in the gym) a man with strength, physical attractiveness, and consideration to win her own heart. Since she has been his male buddy, she is positioned to become a desirable romantic partner when she again becomes female. The erotics are complicated, however, since Harriet wins love as a man in both cases; somehow one suspects that conventional "girls" have no appeal except for sleazy poachers like the harassing boss.

Like Harry/Harriet, the typical new girl can be seen as using a short passage through boyhood to establish improved existence as a woman. Both Claudia Nelson and Kimberley Reynolds have argued that boys' fiction became more manly at the turn of century. So, in my opinion, did popular fiction for girls. Tomboys grow more thoughtful and steady when they mature, but they need not abandon all of their boyish ways. Bessie Marchant's empire adventures altered significantly between 1900 and 1915. In the earliest books girls listened and watched while men acted. In Marchant's later books girls have adventures and courageously rescue men, while their fathers and brothers act as helpers and housekeepers.

At the same time, however, the period framed a significant gender anxiety. The language of degeneration, of effeminacy (in men) and masculinization (of women), the labeling of "homosexual" as person rather than act and the "consequent" urgency of policing "normal" masculine development in boys—all of these are a part of the complex discourse of sexuality that marks a major social transition. A girl's boyishness might express her dawning heterosexual interest—or it might suggest a male identification that could become desire for women as lovers. Boyishness might (as writers in the nineties often worried) destroy a woman's appeal for men in search of romance, or it could (alternately) prove a strong element of sexual attraction.

In the social (rather than the sexual) realm, a girl's desire for male privilege (adventure, money, freedom of movement) seemed less innocent to men when women really began to have the education, training, and opportunity to compete in the marketplace. Tomboys could be cute when it was only a stage; a backlash arose when the accumulating evidence of real equality threatened centuries of comfortable male dominance. The new girl's mental life as a boy—fed by fiction, fantasy, games, and education—provided training in strength, independence, self-sufficiency, and personal responsibility.

six

Reading Feelings

PERPLEXED AS WE ARE WHEN TRYING TO RECOLLECT THE INTENSE
and shifting emotions of our own adolescence, it is probably not possible to apprehend the shape of girls' inner lives a century ago. Yet culture supplies images, narratives, situations, and cues that focus girls' feelings and give them ways to name and dwell on the powerful emotions that sweep through their interior lives. Culture also lays down explicit and implicit rules about what girls are permitted to feel. The experiences and questions and sensations that may not be mentioned (and may perhaps therefore remain unperceived) provide potent fuel for the workings of fantasy and imagination. Although certain emotional states may be universal to adolescence (at least as experienced in postindustrial European-American families), their mode of expression has a historical dimension. In addition, other interior drives may become more or less significant as patterns of upbringing change or standards of public discussion alter the nature of material that must be repressed and therefore stocks the unconscious with its problematic energy.

Caroline Timings, who became a pupil teacher in 1890, at sixteen, remembered the emotional indulgence of reading *Little Lord Fauntleroy*, *Little Women*, *Jo's Boys*, and *Eric; or, Little by Little*: "We were brought up in a spartan way and hid our feelings. . . . In our home there was no demonstration of affection; to show your love was to be softy."[1] Another girl, who spent her fifteenth year at home between school and pupil teaching, wrote: "Do I want friends? Perhaps—of the pattern

139

supplied by Lyndall in *The Story of an African Farm*, by Hawkeye and Uncas in *The Last of the Mohicans*, by other proud and free spirits who look at me from the world of print. Reading is becoming a drug."[2]

The concept of books as compensation—a source of desired experiences and feelings missing in daily life—is often used to explain reading pleasure. When discussing books for young people, however, critics generally emphasize instruction. Nineteenth-century moralists feared that penny novels would "directly encourage a desire to go on the stage, to wear jewellery and dress smartly, and to seek a wealthy and brilliant marriage."[3] Another writer advised girls to concentrate on "*Female* Biography . . . the biographies of good wives, good sisters, good mothers, good daughters."[4] Judith Rowbotham's recent book on girls' fiction focuses on plots that encourage readers to seek conventional feminine roles.

Critical emphasis on direct instruction, however, ignores the ways in which emotion operates: the almost inescapable conservatism, for example, of women writers whose own emotional responses were shaped by images absorbed in their formative years, or the working girl's perfectly understandable craving for money and attention. The Religious Tract Society's *Jessica's First Prayer* (Hesba Stretton, 1866) is always treated, in the twentieth century, as a prime example of evangelical moralizing; its readers are portrayed as passive receptors brainwashed by Christian morals and gender texts. Yet from the vivid circumstantial and sensory memories with which autobiographers thirty or forty years later recalled their avid absorption when reading the book it is clear that something far more active and engaging had taken place.

This chapter speculates about readers' feelings rather than authors' messages. I am not concerned with arguments about whether novels have an influence on people's behavior. The girl who worried that reading was "almost a drug" reported what her culture had taught her about the danger of emotional self-indulgence, but the phrase also accurately describes fiction's power and sustenance for some adolescents. By looking at the books girls chose to read—often secretly because they feared others would laugh—we can perhaps glimpse their interior world.

The syrupy advice about "*Female* Biography" exposes the (probably male) writer's own anxieties by recommending accounts of women in families, although the collections actually published during the period are more apt to supply heroic and extrafamilial models.[5] Not many advice books are so full of twaddle as *Girls and Their Ways*, but only a few admit that family life is not always ideal. In the face of such silencing, girls may well have had a powerful need for fiction's codes to express their unhappiness, tension, anxiety, and fear.

Fiction helps to shape acceptable images, determine what can be imagined, and envisage concrete situations that express formless emotions or unconscious desires. Let us take the common adolescent mood of overwhelming sadness and self-pity. Fiction lets readers of a particular era know what it is all right to feel sad about, creates some scenes that arouse tears—and may (forever after) moisten a woman's eyes when she recalls that scene, even though in her adult and intellectual mode she calls it "cheap sentiment" and laughs at herself.

Indubitably people read identical books for diverse reasons, and any one person reads for different purposes at sundry times. Girls read about people somewhat older than themselves to anticipate as-yet-unknown experiences and discover information that they suspect no one is telling them. They read romances hoping to find out what it feels like to be in love. They read about unexpected disasters and (in recent generations) about mental illness because they faintly distrust adults who are teaching them that people who work hard and behave well will inevitably prosper. Readers may be drawn to the supernatural when religious belief declines. Girls also read simply to pass the time. They read for companionship, for a grown-up version of early childhood's imaginary playmates. Once she discovered *The Story of an African Farm*, Helen Corke (who as a young teacher in Croyden in 1909–1910 became colleague of a young man still then known as David Lawrence) "felt no longer alone."[6] In this chapter, however, I am interested in a special kind of reading—reading that touches the springs of feeling and provides signs of its relationship to a particular interior world.

In one of her talks to girls, headmistress Lucy Soulsby gave advice about how to recognize topics that should not be discussed:

> There are many things which it is not wholesome to talk about among yourselves . . . this includes everything which makes you feel at all hot, with a sense of something not quite nice;—everything in books which it would make you hot to read out loud (an excellent test);—and *I*

include all uncanny things such as ghosts and palmistry and fortune-telling:—these are not safe things to talk about.[7]

The physiological clues point to a particular kind of emotional content that—note carefully—need not necessarily be sexual or erotic. Avid absorption in a book combined with a sense of secrecy or a dislike of revealing its contents to someone else suggests that reading is somehow touching repressed fantasies. The fiction is not providing some new and unwholesome information but rather revealing something the reader already knows but is unable or unwilling to bring to consciousness.

Among the books vividly recalled decades later—books that were read repeatedly and that prompted girls' own extended fantasies—a particular cluster of titles stands out. When the young domestic servants of the Girls' Friendly Society were asked in the 1890s what book they'd most like to own, *John Halifax Gentleman*, *The Wide, Wide World*, and *Uncle Tom's Cabin* were on the top of their lists. All three have central characters who are outcast, oppressed, misunderstood; complex family ruptures and reconstitutions; multiple scenes of pain, suffering, and death; and (at least as understood within the book's context) a putative rebellion against social law. Other tearful books beloved by Girls' Friendly Society members were *A Peep Behind the Scenes*, *Stepping Heavenward*, *Misunderstood*, *East Lynne*, and several of Hesba Stretton's "city arab" stories.[8] The lending records of a free library in the East End used by poor and working-class women in the 1890s show the most popular writers to have been Edna Lyall, Susan Warner, Hesba Stretton, and Mrs. Henry Wood.[9]

Fifteen years later the middle-class readers of *Girl's Realm* were asked for essays on their favorite books. One (in the condescending self-knowledge of middle adolescence) remarked that she used to love the "appealing pathos" of Mrs. O. F. Walton and Hesba Stretton. Many other girls mentioned the equally pathetic but less overtly religious titles by American Gene Stratton Porter: *Freckles* (1904) and *Girl of the Limberlost* (1909). Another girl wrote, "Perhaps my favourite book of all—I forget how many times I have read it—is 'The Gadfly' by E. L. Voynich." The same reader listed two other classics of pain, victimization, and lengthy dying: Rudyard Kipling's *The Light That Failed* (1890) and George Du Maurier's *Trilby* (1894).[10] E. E. Constance

Jones, who grew up to write a treatise on logic and served as Mistress of Girton from 1903 to 1916, recollected the engrossing power of *Black Beauty*.[11]

The books most frequently mentioned by those who read them as girls are *Little Women, Jane Eyre, Jessica's First Prayer, A Peep Behind the Scenes, Christie's Old Organ, The Wide, Wide World*, and *The Story of an African Farm*. Other similar and beloved titles include *The Lamplighter, The Secret Garden, Donovan, Black Beauty, Uncle Tom's Cabin, East Lynne, The Gadfly*, and three by Charlotte Yonge: *The Heir of Redclyffe, The Daisy Chain*, and *Heartsease*.

There are multiple explanations for the popularity of some of these books. Aside from the pain and tears, readers often recalled their joy in discovering a "realistic" portrait of active girl life in Louisa May Alcott. *The Story of an African Farm* contained forbidden knowledge about feminism, atheism, cruelty, and sexuality.[12] Some readers consumed *Jane Eyre* primarily as a love story, though others in their initial readings put the book down soon after Rochester appeared; they were intensely drawn to the unhappy child but not yet emotionally ready to be interested in the rest of the story. Louisa May Alcott and Charlotte Yonge supplied the companionship of large happy families that some lonely readers recollect craving.

I do not therefore mean to imply any simple single theory of reading. The same material has multiple uses for different readers, for the same reader at different times, and for the same reader simultaneously when the book serves overlapping and conflicting functions. The complexity and multiplicity of interpretations make these texts interesting, even though many critics even in their own day—to say nothing of the twentieth century—reject most of them as simplistic sentimental moral tales.

This chapter will analyze some of these books and motifs, though I still have more questions than answers. I wish, for example, that I had a way to get a grip on fiction's role in shaping girls' emotional responses as they in turn become a generation of adult women. I suspect that the themes and codes and cues of many women's fantasy life become set between eleven and fourteen. Half a dozen authors of girls' books trace one or more of their own novels to daydreams that preoccupied them at puberty. But is this because the images and themes crystalized as "literary devices" subsequently determine the shape of emotional experience? Or is it that the fantasies appearing at puberty encode individual psychologies; the needs don't change significantly thereafter, so the emotional cues continue to work? Finally, do books in any way create the fantasies, the needs, the desires that women will strive to satisfy? Or is it rather that readers seek the books that supply usable codes for their own existing psychological tensions?

In the most benign interpretation, books might provide a safety valve that protects (rather than controls) individual choices. Let us take, for example, a girl reader addicted to the kind of love story in which Prince Charming rescues the heroine from her difficulties and carries her off to a life of ease. Does this "teach" the reader to look for male rescue and all-fulfilling love, to be unhappy if it doesn't come her way, and perhaps to do stupid things in her search for it? Or does this reading and fantasy satisfy some inner need for that kind of love, so she doesn't have to let it muck up her real life?

Reading's relationship to the unconscious is simultaneously suggested and complicated in the intermediate stage of daydream. The mental stories we tell ourselves are at least partly under voluntary control. They may deal with recognized (though unsatisfied) desires rather than with materials more deeply repressed. The codes of daydreams may be more transparent than those of many (night) dreams, although their very plausibility may succeed in misdirecting not only the daydreamer but also (when daydreams are translated into fiction) the reader and critic.

Freud explained literary skill as the author's ability to disguise daydreams so they can be enjoyed without shame. With popular fiction, the relationship may be quite visible. A continuous thread connects the daydreams of some girls who grew up to become authors, the fictions they wrote (as adults) for a new generation of girls to read, and the (subsequent) daydreams that provided expressive codes for the new girls as they grew to womanhood.

Charlotte Yonge, a solitary child, daydreamed of "ten boys and eleven girls living in an arbour in the garden. . . . Somebody was always being wounded in the Peninsular war and coming back with his arm in a sling."[13] In her early teens she composed adventures about her imaginary sisters as a French exercise. Next they became the Mohuns of

"A maiden's dream."

Illustration from *Girl's Own Paper* 5 (1883–1884): facing page 556. Reproduced by permission of the Bodleian Library, University of Oxford, shelfmark Per. 2537.d.1/5.

Scenes and Characters (1847), published when she was twenty-four, and of its sequels, the last of which was her final book, *Modern Broods* (1900). Meanwhile, for other lonely children—or even not-so-lonely children whose siblings were less helpful and interesting than the day-dream families of Charlotte Yonge—the Mohuns and the Mays and the Underwoods became a part of some readers' own individual mental life. The loose, ongoing plots of Yonge's family stories made it easy for a daydreaming girl to insert herself as an additional sister, cousin, neighbor, friend, or ward of the May or Mohun family.[14] Rosa Carey wrote that *Nellie's Memories* (1868) grew out of a story she made up as a child which "took possession of" her imagination. "The characters," she remembered, "lived with me so long that they had become almost my personal friends."[15]

The unspoken theory behind these daylight explanations of day-dream (and authorship) is essentially based on compensation: only children dream of large families, unrooted children of stability, and those bored in rural isolation of exotic adventures, while those whose families are inexpressive seek the stimulus of strong emotions. Writing in her diary in 1904, a twenty-year-old working girl suspected that she was unhappy and bitter because her vision of home life was so idealized that reality was bound to be disappointing. Yet even though her intellect understood the delusion, she continued to find sustenance and pleasure in Rosa Carey's novels: "They are so refreshing, and full of sweet simple home life."[16]

Critics have been far less generous in seeing healthy compensation at work in the reading of working-class youngsters. One nineteenth-century social welfare worker, complaining about sensational fiction, did notice that a girl with wages of £10 a year who spent nearly one-tenth of her income on serials "had to spend every evening alone in a kitchen that swarmed with black beetles."[17] Is it any wonder that such a girl might choose an aristocratic romance with brightly lit ballrooms and tasty midnight suppers in preference to an earnest evangelical tale of domestic life? Servants seem to have consumed more fiction than factory girls. Factory and shop workers had more stimulation and companionship; servants (especially those in single places) not only craved excitement and romance to fill their lonely hours but also enjoyed the imaginary friends supplied by the letters and advice columns in cheap papers.

Compensation theories, however, only partially explain the consuming power of certain fantasies. Margaret Haig remembered her vivid adolescent daydreams as an addiction as compelling as drink or drugs.[18] The avid, "hot" attention headmistress Lucy Soulsby feared suggests that the fiction/daydream is tapping highly significant repressed material in the author's unconscious and perhaps communicating it directly to the reader's unconscious without either becoming aware of the transaction. The novels with the most intense shimmering appeal are often those written (as was *Jane Eyre*) at great speed and virtually in a trance.

Charlotte Yonge's stories reveal another characteristic typical of daydreams. J. S. Bratton calls it Yonge's "inclination to allow the characters to run away with her, to outgrow the story and then the book and reappear in other tales."[19] When characters continue to live though the plot may be ended, they presumably encode some important element of the dreamer's persona or enact situations that must be compulsively repeated. These characters (or very closely analogous characters) reappear in subsequent books; key situations are told and retold so they can be experienced yet again. Many popular writers were inundated by letters asking for sequels. Readers of an imaginative turn do the "sequel writing" on their own, reshaping the characters and modeling new plots to fit the outlines demanded by their own needs.

Many girls dreamed of becoming authors. The largest number of entrants in a 1900 *Girl's Realm* competition on "My Ambition" wanted to be "famous writers."[20] The secretary of the Authors' Society was "inundated" with verse and fiction written by "young ladies in their teens."[21] Writing was, of course, a way to earn money without leaving home or losing social caste, yet it's also evident that the line between daydreaming and writing is blurred. When they do not mechanically imitate commonplace plots, beginning writers often create scenes that have heavy emotional content but fail to link together as a narrative. Traces of such writing are evident in Olive Schreiner (whose great novel had been virtually completed before she was twenty-one). Ethel Voynich was unable to let go of the character whose story she told in *The Gadfly* (1897) though she ended the book with his death; a second, fragmentized collection of other incidents and alternate versions of Felix's history appeared as *An Interrupted Friendship* (1910).[22] Stories written under these circumstances often vibrate with resonance: the author's emotion speaks to the reader's emotion and provides codes that the reader can use.

One upper-class girl who began writing fiction to enter a *Girl's Realm* competition and discovered that she could sell to magazines found an enormous release for tensions she could not otherwise face: "My typewriter was never still, and each story I wrote seemed to lift a burden from my soul, as if I had rid myself of an emotion or a thought that had been weighing on me."[23] Other authors flippantly defend their own egos through writer-characters. In *The Poet and the Pierrot* (1905) a spinster whose serials support her younger sister wipes tears from her eyes while creating scenes of hopeless love.[24] Fiction and daydreams help girls bring into consciousness material they are not—or not yet—able to name and understand. A daughter born in 1900 to fashionable people— "sometimes King Edward (Kingy) came to tea with Mamma"[25]—was writing "novels" at age thirteen or fourteen:

> The continents of Asia and Europe divided the heroines, but a similar theme of rape pursued them both, dug up out of the abyss of my subconscious. Lately, and surreptitiously, I had taken to reading novelettes wherein love scenes figured largely, yet my actual knowledge of the facts of life was nil.[26]

Elaborate disguises may be needed to cope with threatening material. Often the most compelling narratives take place in another place and time, or center on a poverty-stricken waif, or a crippled man, or (especially in the working-class papers) an extremely privileged titled character rather than a person who shares the reader's age, class, and gender. *Black Beauty*, we might notice, is a story of injustice, abuse, oppression, alcoholism, family rupture, and violent masculine stupidity in which the centrally empathic character is a horse.

Anne Mozley wrote in *Blackwood's* in 1870 about fiction's potency:

> What a passionate necessity to unravel the plot. . . . What a craving for the next volume, stronger than any bodily appetite. . . . What pity and tears in the tragic moments; what shame in these tears—the shame that attends all strong emotions—as they are detected by unsympathising, quizzing observers: shame leading to indignant, protesting, pertinacious denials, haunting the conscience still, and deceiving no one![27]

This passage is a fine summary of symptoms suggesting the implication of psychologically intimate yet deeply inarticulate drives. The reader feels flushed, almost as if sexually aroused; so avidly engrossed that recognition of the outside world temporarily slips away; and personally exposed: it would be humiliating to show the book to someone else although—in any objective sense—there's nothing "wrong" or "shameful" about it. The capacity to be deeply engaged by a book may be strongest at adolescence. Is it that the feelings are new, strong, confusing? That repressions and defenses have not yet been constructed to suppress the awareness of what one does feel and know? That social constraints are making one deny essential impulses and culture teaching one to rename and misname what was once known?

Parents and teachers—and girls—for a hundred years or more have recognized girls' heightened emotional tension and even psychological risk at the onset of adolescence.[28] Girls' anxiety and sadness are revealed in their taste for tragedy. The *Monthly Packet* reported on its 1890 story competition that most of the entries were "extremely melancholy. We have sat by the deathbeds of so many innocent children, and have seen marble crosses erected over so many broken-hearted widows and deserted lovers, that we have hardly spirits to continue the magazine."[29] L. T. Meade advised young authors to "avoid *morbid* writing."[30] Ethel Heddle, editing *Young Woman* in 1900–1901, asked why girl writers "always revel in tragedy?"[31] E. M Delafield described a story she wrote at eleven (in 1901):

> There were six Hamiltons, young and beautiful, and they had an unkind stepmother, and sooner or later they all died, excepting one called Marjory, who went to the bad in some unspecified way and lived in London; but I feel sure that if I had ever finished the book she would have died too.[32]

A girl who had dancing lessons at Windsor Castle with Queen Victoria's grandchildren remembered a "morbid period" in her middle teens and speculated that she had been suffering from "a form of suppression, the most deadly menace for girls whose lives are not sufficiently filled."[33] Yet the same luxurious sadness was enjoyed by working-class girls. Kathleen Woodward recalled loving to cry while singing melancholy songs.[34] Charlotte Yonge thought that Dinah

Craik's *A Noble Life* was "exceedingly relished" by servants because they like stories "with what more educated persons think rather an over-amount of pathos."[35] Amy Cruse remembered

> being set to read *Little Lord Fauntleroy* aloud to a sewing class of about fifty girls, aged twelve to fifteen. The girls listened with absorbed interest, and when the false heir was introduced and Cedric's inheritance was in danger they held their breath; at the little boy's artless and noble reception of the news they sobbed aloud, while the reader—aged eighteen—quite broke down, the teacher—aged perhaps forty—caught the infection, and all wept comfortably together.[36]

While depression may be characteristic of female adolescence (in the last two centuries in the West, at least), the particular cues that dependably made late-Victorian and Edwardian girls cry suggest cultural specifics. The Amy Cruse recollection identifies one such motif: noble silence or acquiescence while suffering a great wrong. Did girls sense, somehow, that their own situation was implicated in the scene? An 1890 book opens with the fourteen-year-old narrator, semiconscious in an illness following her father's death, hearing the nurse say that because of his debts she's no better off than a workhouse child. But she is scolded for asking questions: "Little girls have to do as they are told. Something will be arranged for you and you will be informed of it in due time."[37] This is a concrete, if exaggerated, version of the way many girls must have felt: baffled, silenced, shut out, and (in practical terms) made helpless.

Many beloved books provide situations that justify feelings girls were taught to suppress as unacceptable or wrong (or nonexistent). *Cousin Geoffrey and I* even manages to make it work for the adolescent's dissatisfaction with her physical appearance. Mabel is untaught, unloved, brave, miserable, misunderstood, abused, and shut up in her room: "I am very ugly. . . . And Mrs. Grey loves pretty people. I have often heard her say so. If only I were beautiful like Geoffrey perhaps she would care for me a little. It is hard to be made ugly and to have just the same heart as those who are pretty."[38]

Another common trope is the secret wound; the character conceals an injury or ailment, and no one notices until there is a collapse. Especially noteworthy (among many examples) are Charlotte Yonge's

The Clever Woman of the Family (1865), Florence Montgomery's *Misunderstood* (1869), Maud Carew's *Little King Richard* [1899], and Ethel Voynich's *The Gadfly* (1897). The emotional response is typically complicated—and intensified—by a certain ambivalence in identification; the reader is both onlooker and participant, and the suffering character is simultaneously victim and victor. The "message" would seem to be that concealing pain is admirable, but a luxurious outpouring of warmth comes in consequence, when the damaged person is admired, comforted, praised, and taken care of.

Family stories provide touching scenes of reconciliation. Emma Marshall—later a suffragist and a writer for girls—remembered crying especially over *Heir of Redclyffe*, *Heartsease*, and *Daisy Chain*.[39] Evelyn Everett-Green's *The Head of the House* (1886) contains deaths, illnesses, injuries, and tearful reconciliations between brother and sister. The reader weeps because her own family is not so warm and close as the culture tells her families are; the ideal may seldom, in fact, exist, but the overwhelming ideological pretense makes girls ache for what they are "missing."

Another primary fantasy might be named "virtuous but friendless and bereft." Serials in halfpenny papers repeatedly use "Outcast" or "Alone" in the titles. Sarah Doudney's *Michaelmas Daisy* (1882), a staple of recommended reading lists, is about a fragile girl emotionally abused in her rich uncle's house; she's unfailingly good and kind, therefore arousing the dislike of the self-centered and socially ambitious people who surround her. The *Girls' Friend* favorite Mabel St. John (as impersonated by Henry Cooper) gently pokes fun at "that sort of feeling that it would be nice to die and have everyone who had been unkind and unfeeling towards me standing round my pallid corpse, undergoing agonies of remorse."[40]

The most often mentioned and avidly remembered sad books fall into two categories, neither of which seems evidently intended for the readers who were so consumed by them. The "city arab" tales written by Hesba Stretton and her followers for the Religious Tract Society were purportedly for and about poor children (cheap editions were given away in great numbers as Sunday school prizes) but remembered with extraordinary vividness by many girls of the respectable working class and the middle class. And a group of bestselling adult novels (often American in origin) from earlier in the nineteenth century had a long second life as girls' fiction.

Susan Warner's *The Wide, Wide World* (1850) was the best-loved in the latter category. Ellen Montgomery is ten when it begins. Her ailing mother sends her to live with an unsympathetic aunt. Ellen is helpless to change her circumstances: her home, her duties, her associates, and her studies are imposed on her by others and constantly disrupted. Adults demand not only physical obedience but also mental compliance. Ellen learns that anything she asks for will be denied; she can get what is rightfully hers only if she quells her desires and hides her feelings. After four years of struggle, she gains control of her emotions and learns voluntary submission. By ceasing to feel anger and grief, Ellen perfects her humility—and earns material rewards. The reader's tears are for the lonely child within, who (like Ellen) is misunderstood, craves mothering, and feels melancholy. The reader weeps also for the tension and sadness of girls silenced by the culture's voice before they are able to hear and articulate their own.

Some psychoanalysts view the losses of adolescence as structural and essential: "withdrawal from the parents, necessary though it may be, is . . . not achieved without considerable sadness and pain."[41] Fiction makes the "loss of parents" manifest. The reader's sadness is both a mourning over the enactment of her own end-of-childhood losses and a function of her repressed guilt for wanting to be free of parental control.

Contemporary reading specialists assume that adolescents want to identify with the central character in books they read. Teachers look for realistic situations and diverse representation—and they expect strong gender divisions. In the nineteenth century, girls adored *Little Women* and the Charlotte Yonge family stories because they were delighted with the recognizable—if idealized—versions of themselves. *The Wide, Wide World* depicts girls' own inner life: Ellen Montgomery's exaggerated troubles justify feelings they experienced. Twentieth-century adolescents may no longer share Susan Warner's religious motives, but girls still learn that giving things up—things such as exposing their feelings, telling certain truths, and following their own interests—makes other people happy. They learn to ignore inner demands because they want to be liked by others.

Since girls lack the analytic resources to engage in a cost-benefit assessment of these transactions, they are left with the sadness of denying or repressing what they feel. And (additionally) they become expert at reading subtexts and understanding what must not be said. This helps to explain the puzzle of other books emotionally meaningful to girls that seem to have no character with whom the young reader could "identify."

A case in point is the premier "city arab" tale, written by Hesba Stretton (her real name was Sarah Smith) for the Religious Tract Society. *Jessica's First Prayer*, first published in *Sunday at Home* in 1866, subsequently appeared in innumerable editions at all prices, was set to music as a children's "service in song," became a film (1906), and was mentioned by autobiographers of all classes as a favorite book.

The impoverished child of a drunken actress, Jessica (during the course of the story) enters a church for the first time, learns to pray, falls ill, and inspires adults to become better Christians. Yet girl readers are doubly distanced from Jessica by the narrative technique. The book's opening presents an elderly man (Daniel) who keeps a coffee stall; the ragged waif Jessica is seen through Daniel's eyes. There is, in addition, a narrator who observes and explains Daniel and who has the self-assured gaze of civil authority: implicitly patriarchal and overtly sentimental in looking at picturesque poverty rather than sharing its experience. The appeal of this book is at first rather difficult to perceive, though its technique did break new ground as a storybook for insecure readers: it told of interesting events in short sentences with strong words, and it never preached to Jessica or scolded her.

But why did it fascinate so many girls? As the reader's persona— and given a distance that supplies deniability—Jessica is ignorant but innocent, abused but never naughty. She is wholly independent (her drunken mother never appears); she lives on her own; she is cool, self-possessed, forward, independent; and she is also the visibly bruised victim of abuse. Almost at once the book provides a glimpse of one central fact that girls knew but culture's voice denied: mothers were not always loving; families could be the site of violence and pain. The knowledge is made safe by locating it in an outcast class; readers may therefore pretend to be looking from outside, feeling sorry for Jessica, and moved by acceptable charitable motives.

The congregation began to arrive quickly. She heard the rustling of silk dresses, and she could see the gentlemen and ladies pass by the niche between the door and the post. Once she ventured

W.J.Morgan

Jessica's exclusion is vividly expressed in an illustration by W. J. Morgan for *Jessica's First Prayer*, by Hesba Stretton [1867].

From the author's collection.

The book's primary emotion is Jessica's internalized sadness. Her sense of exile is framed not as envy or self-pity but, very quietly, as knowledge of her exclusion. One sharp visual image makes Jessica's status concrete: she is crouched behind a church door, watching people arrive for the service, and touched by bewildered wonder. Outside are cold, dark, abuse, and a policeman who is "one of her natural enemies";[42] inside are warmth, beauty, light, music, and some mysterious glory. Jessica knows that she has no idea what the mystery is. The few short sentences of simple words create a primal image of vast power: separation, loss, the child's not-understanding, not-sharing, not-being-visible. The nonverbal nature of the image suggests pre-oedipal roots: exclusion from mother's breast, from the room where others talk while one is abandoned in a crib or basket.

Exclusion and loss also have a specifically female aspect. The impression that men must know something special in order to have such an imbalanced portion of the world's power and goods occurs to many girls and women, who are mystified by not having even a clue as to the nature or content of male "secret knowledge." The core image of exclusion from love and light in *Jessica's First Prayer* is the image of *Jane Eyre* behind the curtains, of *A Little Princess* (1905) looking in windows, of dozens of enormously powerful visual moments in fiction that lives for girls.

According to J. S. Bratton, the emotional resonance of *Jessica's First Prayer* is drawn from a period when Sarah Smith "had felt herself on the brink of social extinction, living in squalid lodgings, with no settled income." She and her sister "regularly attended a chapel for over a year before anyone there condescended to speak to them."[43] The author's own experience is crystalized in an image that can then be filled up with whatever exclusions the reader feels.

In another powerful scene (and screen[44]), Jessica hears that God is her father. The knowledge is transforming because she has no human father. For readers, however, the screen is further elaborated: Daniel, who has become her pseudofather, leads a thoroughly righteous life of duty, work, and saving. When Jessica is near death, Daniel weeps because he had ignored his daughter to spend his time at work. The antimaterialistic message is presumably directed at the middle class rather than the poor—but it is also a wonderful self-justification for daughters made to feel that their demands on fathers' attention are illicit and inappropriate.

J. S. Bratton asserts that the importance of the "reward fiction" lies in its "explicitly didactic intention to teach certain moral and social attitudes, which were not even necessarily general truths, but which were specific to the age, sex and social standing of a very precisely defined reader."[45] But whatever the publishers' intent, the disjunction among implied reader, moral, and the tales' function for thousands of girls is more layered than one would think possible from their simple texts.

In *Jessica's First Prayer*, the implied reader appears to be the character through whose eyes Jessica is first seen: an unemotional mature man. Insofar as the book is didactic, its moral lesson seems directed to that reader. Why then did the story so impress and fascinate and haunt girls? Is it possible that a man—an older, hard-working, steady, upright, churchly, sober, clean, conscientious, righteous man—needs scolding? Needs instruction? That something about his behavior needs alteration? Is it possible that a girl of twelve or so should be the one to open his eyes and change his ways? The book validates a girl's inner sadness and also makes her powerful: through her this good, distant, unemotional man learns a lesson. We can read this as the cultural prescription for a daughter's behavior—to provide a safe expressive medium of love for overworked and anxious fathers—but its emotional urgency surely had powerful resonance for daughters who felt excluded from the masculine and desirable world.

The public face of the patriarchal family in the Victorian and Edwardian years reflected an ideal that many girls knew was a lie. Amy Barnard's 1912 advice book, for example, has ten rosy pages on girls' relationship with their fathers and then, in one paragraph, recognizes that sometimes a girl "has to decide how far, when she arrives at years of discretion, she is justified in sacrificing herself for the poor broken reed or the overbearing tyrant."[46] The workgirls' paper *Girls' Home* revealed the dark side of family life in an advertisement (for a story that was, however, much tamer than the teaser suggests): "Are you hard done by at home? Then you will be interested in 'A Rod of Iron' starting in next Thursday's 'Girls' Home.'"[47]

For thoughtful girls by the century's last quarter, another unspoken secret lay in religion itself, which further complicated the issue of patriarchal rule. Helen Corke remembered (in an incident of which the selected details may be significant):

> Two only of the books in the house are forbidden to me, Eugene Sue's *Mysteries of Paris* and Olive Schreiner's *The Story of an African Farm*. There is a copy of the latter in the drawer of a chiffonier I have to dust weekly. Opening the book first at random, I happen upon the account of the team-driver's cruelty to his ox—a vivid, terrible incident which cannot be isolated from the rest of the story. When Papa notices I have the book, he tells me to put it away; this prohibition is in itself so unusual that my curiosity is aroused, and the chiffonier drawer exerts a fascination I cannot always resist. Very real becomes the boy Waldo— I understand how he feels and thinks—many of his thoughts are mine. And the writer of the book *knows* how confusing is religion, and how impossible it is to believe the incredible and love the unlovable. The badly printed, pirated American copy of *The Story of an African Farm* becomes the hiding place of intimate friends.[48]

The religious tales most memorable to girls were all examples of melodramatized realism rather than the fantasy and allegory used in mid-century by A.L.O.E. and her imitators.[49] Melodrama, however, not only presents a fantasy of an "ideal" world, in which the good are (defined and) rewarded and the bad punished, but (also) educates the feelings, so that readers are habituated to feel anger, or fear, or the reward of a warm and positive glow, in response to certain specific stimuli. "Moral" fiction preaches outright, speaking directly to the reader ("Have you ever fallen into such a sin?"); it appeals to intelligence or conscience in explaining what acts are wrong, how one may be led wrong, and what the consequences are. Melodramatic fiction, on the other hand, teaches through feelings.

The avid response to *Jessica's First Prayer* created a school of "city arab" fiction about poor, outcast waifs. Part of the fascination surely lay in the exposure of secrets about drink, poverty, unhappiness, and family dysfunction, topics unmentionable even among girls who experienced them. Fiction about the downtrodden also appealed to charitable motives and thus permitted even the minimally comfortable to feel superior. Most essentially (I would argue) it allowed readers to cry, and thus to express their own unnamed and inexplicable sadness while also projecting themselves into child heroes powerful enough to make adults realize their errors and change their ways.

Among the best-loved "city arab" tales was Mrs. O. F. Walton's *A Peep Behind the Scenes* (1877). Twelve-year-old Rosalie is a caravan-dwelling actress in a fairgrounds theater. Her alcoholic father is clearly abusive; in one thinly veiled scene of transference he brutally beats his horse. Rosalie—like Jessica—stands outside and looks: on one occasion into a house, and later into a church. A long account of her mother's past, distanced and condemned in the mother's narrative voice, reveals that she was ruined by novel reading and eloped with an actor. As far as there is a moral in *A Peep Behind the Scenes*, it would have to be expressed as "don't dream of stage glamour; it's a wretched life." But the misery of theatrical performance is a very minor part of the book. The stage (and even more appealing, the horse-drawn van that takes the traveling theater around to fairs) provides an attractive come-on; the real terror is the behavior of Rosalie's father. I suspect that even the writers of Sunday school tracts realized that emotionally distant, abusive, and alcoholic fathers were not necessarily restricted to the lower classes or to "wicked" professions.

A Peep Behind the Scenes is longer than most of the comparable tracts; it is novelized by added incidents and interpolated echo narratives that repeat the themes and double the images of exclusion and longing. The lengthy dying of Rosalie's perfect mother (which takes up nearly a third of the book) and the introduction of a wicked stepmother provide a metaphor for the experience of a girl at thirteen, when conflict becomes virtually a necessity in order to accomplish the independence from maternal bonds that is as frightening as it is essential. In addition, *A Peep Behind the Scenes* is less male-dependent than most of the tracts. Except for the wicked stepmother, its women provide a network of help and support. Even the religious instruction is supplied by mother; the book's clergyman appears only offstage.

A Peep Behind the Scenes had a very long life: my undated edition has a colored frontispiece in which Rosalie is dressed in fashions from the 1920s. Of the books in its class it may be the best story (as literature) because the fantasies are well disguised and thoroughly elaborated. It might also be the best tract (as lesson) because the emotions are captured in a narrative whose moral is appropriate to the Sunday school

Tract fiction about poor and abused children exposed topics that were not mentioned in a middle-class context.

From *Cassy*, by Hesba Stretton [1874]. From the author's collection.

reader: don't run away to go on stage. Many of the theater and circus stories in the Harmsworth papers are versions of the same tale, though theatrical life is presented with slightly more glamour, the escape is accomplished with less pain, and the ending is a return to home and a new good mother. As a feminist, however, I rather dislike *A Peep Behind the Scenes* because it teaches girls to forswear ambition and despise the "wide, wide world"—unlike the nicely subversive message in *Jessica's First Prayer* (Daddy may be wrong; you have to trust your own knowing).

Let me suggest once more that it is the double messages, the suppressions, and the partially revealed subversions that give books of this sort their puzzling emotional vitality. In another Stretton tale, *An Acrobat's Girlhood* (1889), Trixie—who once more has a drunken father and a deceased mother—is fond of "romping and doing things a boy would do."[50] She is "adopted" by a couple who train her as an acrobat. Trixie loves the crowds and lights and applause, but she is always strained and tired; by the book's end she dies. This is a tract for adults; the moral is "performance by children should be outlawed because they are exploited by the exhibitors." For girl readers, however, it's a splendid emotional mix: athletic success, glory, excitement, oppression, and tears.

The power of ambivalence is made evident by stories that don't "work." Evelyn Everett-Green's *The Secret of the Old House* (1890) is an earlier, less compelling, and less popular assemblage of the situations and images that were later to prove so potent in *The Secret Garden* (1911). Dinah Meredith, a self-sufficient, middle-class, capable girl of fifteen, is sent with her brother to stay with her grandmother while recovering from typhoid. Exploring the neighborhood's "haunted" house, they discover locked rooms inhabited by a boy who is deformed, orphaned, and ill in mind and body. They become his friends and get him to plant a garden. The book lacks *The Secret Garden*'s energy partly because various adults have conspired to get Dinah and her brother to play in the house and tempt the sufferer back to life, partly because religion obtrudes with messages of goodness and forgiveness, partly because adult medicine plays a major role in the cure, and, finally, because of the moral drawn by the poor sufferer: "If my mother hadn't been so very, very kind to me always, and given me my own way in everything . . . I should have been better and stronger in mind and body than I was."[51] Very few child readers are able to believe (consciously or unconsciously) that mother is too kind. Thus although Everett-Green has many of the right ingredients, she exerts an adult narrative moralizing that prevents them from touching the reader's secret desires.

One of the most common tropes of nineteenth-century fiction is the use of illness to bring about the resolution. In women's novels from the earlier and middle part of the century, an attack of fever or brain fever softens the woman and frightens the man into realizing his love. Women writers also use illness to feminize—or humanize—the leading man, making him aware of interdependence and of his need for care.[52] And again and again in stories about girls, illness marks the transition to womanhood, softens the rebel or the tomboy,[53] and induces demonstrations of love from other characters as a delicious reward of subjugation.

Female helplessness also schools men. In *Jessica's First Prayer*, Jessica's illness softens Daniel and makes him generous. The power of weakness lies in eliciting tenderness from others; the child hero of the most popular tracts is not reformed or converted by illness but rather is, although ignorant, innocently good from the outset of the book. Illness matters for its impact on others. This may be another unconscious echo of babyhood: if I were helpless I would be loved and cared for.

Most evidently, in dozens of novels and stories, infirmity intervenes as a gendering event between rebellious girlhood and feminized womanhood. Injury or illness quells girls' impetuous activity and their ambition; they become gentle women, lovable and ready for marriage. The trope is so omnipresent that its absence is more noticeable than its presence. It is particularly disappointing in a book such as M. H. Cornwall Legh's *An Incorrigible Girl* [1899], in which both the "incorrigible" poor girl and the young lady who befriends her were fine and attractive girls (defiant, empathetic, self-confident) but come to womanhood through illness, suffering, submission, and endurance.

Is the wound of adolescence—the illness and suffering that turns a girl into a woman—a code for the onset of menstruation? And does the scene of martyrdom (often vivid, touching, and tearful) communicate the author's awareness that adulthood literally cripples women?

Essentialist Victorian physicians believed that feminine timidity, modesty, and dependence arose "directly and inevitably from the physical manifestations of puberty."[54] Although the illness/injury plot so common in girls' fiction embodies this cultural belief, I do not believe it (often) does so deliberately. Like a Jungian archetype, the narrative was embedded so deeply in the culture that it sprang "naturally" to authors' minds as a device to gather the threads of plot and lead to an emotionally layered conclusion. Some writers who used the scenario were explicitly trying not to encourage women's passivity—but the archetypal elements, familiar through long use, perhaps satisfied their own emotional needs.

In the twentieth century, physiologically based psychological research has suggested that girls' sexual fantasies actually diminish at puberty but that themes of abasement and self-damage increase. This is generally read as a response to the blood and pain of menarche as a physical event and also to the stress and anxiety associated with sexual maturity.[55] In a book such as Rosa Carey's *No Friend Like a Sister* (1906), pain and anxiety follow from any exercise of female assertion. Whenever the young woman takes any direct action she becomes "so worn out that she is trembling from head to foot with exhaustion"[56] and must be put to bed, coaxed to eat, and tended lovingly by sisters and friends.

The wound of adolescence is not, however, merely bleeding and fragility. The way in which adolescence disables female power is figured with outright violence in book after book: injury, dire illness, pain, or the death of loved ones gentles girls into suppression. Though authors may paint the scenes with tender and brimming sentiments, a stormy undertow of grief and anger remains. The anger, masochism, struggle, and pain are visible in Charlotte Yonge's *The Heir of Redclyffe* (1853)—a novel of heroic masculine self-sacrifice (and Tractarian Christianity) that appealed to men as well as women when it was published in 1853 but became thereafter a transformative book for many girls. Three male characters in this book supply screens for the projection of girls' adolescent wound. Passionate Guy struggles mightily to repress his temper and his anger; invalid Charles uses his weakness to manipulate others' emotions; and self-righteous Philip is conquered by Guy's sacrifice. The book throughout is suffused with scenes of suffering, death, and self-pity consciously transformed to self-sacrificing piety.

Evangelical religion in the nineteenth century was a compelling sanction for the construction of nurture and service as women's appropriate glory. Girls learned to project their anger and self-pity onto others, and were taught that female power was manifested as care for those who were weaker, poorer, or younger. Gwen Raverat remembered a fantasy play she called "Being Kind to Poor Pamela" in which she would get out of bed and lie on the cold floor, pretending that she was "Pamela," a child she disliked, and that she had been cast out into the snow by her cruel parents. Then, turning again into herself, she would rescue Pamela, bring her into her own warm bed, comfort her, and enjoy the good and tender feelings thus inspired.[57] As Flora Thompson said of the "city arab" tales she borrowed from the Sunday school lending library, "saddening as it was to read about the poor things, it was also enjoyable, for it gave one a cheering sense of superiority."[58]

Lady Sybil Lubbock's *The Child in the Crystal* refers to "the Marcella period," in which serious girls are devoted to good works.[59] The name alludes to Mary Arnold Ward's popular novel of 1894, which tells of a young woman's sometimes-mistaken practice of social work. Notably, however, Marcella is also rebellious and misunderstood; the book contains many scenes of men's violence toward women. The letters of Eva Slawson and Ruth Slate show the desire for "noble unselfish work," "heroic deeds," and "lives of service" that formed an essential emotional fuel in the energy and ambition of two young, nonconformist working women.[60] Service and rescue are the appropriately female modes of heroism—though the heroic dream may be so blatant that adult women, remembering, seek the distance of laughter. Margaret Haig (who eventually became a militant suffragette) recorded a daydream from age fifteen or sixteen:

> Dressed in a strikingly beautiful frock—usually white—having come out first in the Cambridge Tripos, [I] rescued large portions of my family from a burning house. The frock remained as immaculate at the end of the rescue as it had been when the story started—indeed, the *finale* of the affair, which partook of a general recognition of all my qualities, was really the frock's great hour.[61]

It is evident that a complicated range of unacknowledged sexual emotions could enter girls' mental lives cast as a religious impulse to service, as a longing to nurture, as heterosexual love, or as friendship. Readers in a post-Freudian world are tempted to interpret all of the codes through which girls experienced tender-yearning-melting feelings as suppressed or sublimated unrecognized erotic desires. Twentieth-century developmental psychology assumes that the "main task of the adolescent" is the "attainment of genital primacy and the definitive completion of the process of non-incestuous object finding."[62] For literary critic Patricia Meyer Spacks adolescence "designates the time of life when the individual has developed full sexual capacity but has not yet assumed a full adult role in society. . . . Real and imagined sexual energy, crucial in the mythology of the teen-age years, accounts for much of the imaginative power implicit in the idea of adolescence."[63]

Is it, however, in fact the twentieth century that sees sex everywhere? The (repressed) power of eroticism may conceivably be buried in nineteenth-century texts of girlhood, but the rhetoric of sexuality is "visible" primarily when its absence attracts the attention of sex-mad twentieth-century critics. And though others (such as Rowbotham) emphasize fiction's plots as training for good wives, there is a great deal more love and marriage in books for today's teenagers than there was a hundred years ago.

The Victorians generally assumed that young people were asexual, and that (through care, caution, and choice) latency could be extended. Romantic novels were objected to because "the descriptions of love-scenes, of thrilling, romantic episodes, find an echo in the girl's physical system" that leads not only to masturbation but also to premature menstruation.[64] Proponents of women's education argued, in its favor, that brain-work postponed sexual interest. Dr. Elizabeth Garrett Anderson, for example, writes:

> From the purely physiological point of view, it is difficult to believe that study much more serious than that usually pursued by young men would do a girl's health as much harm as a life directly calculated to over-stimulate the emotional and sexual instincts. . . . The stimulus found in novel-reading, in the theatre and ball-room, the excitement which attends a premature entry into society, the competition of vanity and frivolity, these involve far more real dangers to the health of young

women than the competition for literary knowledge, or for scientific or literary honours.[65]

If prolonging asexuality and chastity postponed maturity and its problems, time would be gained for self-development and for vocational, mental, emotional, and intellectual independence. Romantic love is necessarily dependent on another person; for girls, it is generally the point of reinsertion into patriarchal structures. In addition to the religious yearning to do good (and be admired) that—perhaps—sublimates the wish for attachment, scenes with primacy in girls' pseudoromantic imagination are found in mothering, in loving admiration for girls or women, in narratives of pain and comfort (often between men), and in other examples of complex androgynous role switching.

The lonely child's fantasy of a large happy family, for example, blends almost seamlessly into a dream of motherhood. Margaret Haig wanted to marry early and have "a very large family to play with—twelve at least."[66] Margaret Campbell (Marjorie Bowen) recalled that she wanted "passionately and desperately . . . to look after a large family of children," going on to say, "I did not at that time think of a husband or a lover."[67]

Campbell (who was later to write children's fiction) had been very poor, raised in lodgings by an ambitious and self-occupied mother. Her fantasy was certainly—at least to an extent—a way of mothering herself: transforming herself into the good mother she had not had. The permeable boundary between mothers and daughters blurs: wishing to be a beloved child, wishing for child playmates, reproducing—improving—mothering by becoming simultaneously daughter and mother in imagination. The blending of mothering, being mothered, and marriage extends to some stories that end with romance. The only embrace in Evelyn Everett-Green's *Dorothy's Vocation* (1890), for example, is Dorothy's postproposal hug from her suitor's mother.

Sexual feelings and maternal longing also perhaps mingled in a girl's crush on an older woman. Recollecting her experience at fifteen, when she was a poor pupil teacher living with her dying father and young stepmother, Leonora Eyles wrote:

> I suppose nothing in after life approaches the agony, the glory and the wild fantastic beauty of a girl's first falling in love with a mistress. I

have been in love many times since but it was nothing like this first aching self-immolation. I wanted her house to be set on fire so that I could climb a ladder and rescue her (very difficult since I was about half her size). I wanted a poisonous serpent to bite her and I die sucking the poison away.[68]

Other scholars have discussed nineteenth-century attitudes toward girls' loving friendships and the shifting definition of various points along a continuum of erotic desire. Because the labels now available to us were under construction at the turn of the century, it is extremely difficult to recapture the meaning of girls' feelings; autobiographers, looking backward, reinterpret their own experience in terms they learned subsequently. Some fiction strikes us as touchingly innocent. Handsome Harry, for example, gently tells Bertha (who is very fond of "Harry" as a man) that "he" has a "sister":

"I shall love her!" whispered Bertha. "Stan says he believes I am capable of loving girls more than men, because I was so fond of Alice Trench, the friend I spoke of to you. He says if I had a sister to love, he knows I should be an old maid, as he is sure I should never want anyone else."[69]

A student at Newnham just after the turn of the century recollected that she was "blankly ignorant about sex and its manifestations, even the most normal ones. . . . Looking back . . . certain pairs of friends loom up as attached by bonds so close that, nowadays, they would have roused suspicion. . . . Not only had we no suspicions; we should not have understood what anyone was talking about who expressed such."[70] In the emotionally powerful climactic scene of L. T. Meade's *A Sweet Girl Graduate* (1891), awkward Priscilla Peele gains the courage to perform stunningly in the male lead of the college dramatic society production of *The Princess* because she catches sight of the man who loves Maggie (cast as the Princess) in the audience. Priscilla becomes "Hammond pleading his own cause"—yet she is also at last able passionately and safely to express "the sensations which animated her own breast."[71]

Many a girl focused her unrecognized sexual desires in a crush on an actor—then, as now, distance provided safety and the pleasant ache of impossibility enhanced her feelings. The public admiration and attention mentally enacted in such fantasies, furthermore, is a strategy of resistance: it transgresses the retiring privacy and self-suppression culturally mandated for women.

Books about manly friendship and male bonding also supplied girls with images that ex/suppressed ardent emotion. At fifteen Helen Corke lived intensely "with Uncas and Chingachgook and Hawkeye"; she was completely uninterested in the officer and the girls.[72] Stories of male friendship disguised a girl reader's erotic interest and also disguised its object. Was she identifying with a man so she could be unchaperoned in male company? Was she using a double gender shift to elide her own "homosexual" love for girls? Or was she simply—as well as simultaneously—adopting a male role to live a more active and interesting life in fantasy? The ideal "husband" in a great many of the bachelor girl novels is a socially active doctor or a muckraking journalist or a reforming M.P.; often, in fact, he is clearly the man the girl herself would like to be. In L. T. Meade's *A Princess of the Gutter* (1895), Joan Prinsep studies at Girton, inherits £3,000 a year, and spends her time rebuilding slum properties and running girls' clubs; she does not marry. This is one of several books in which the phrase "Eastward Ho!" is used with a sort of ironic nudge to transform Kingsley's gory masculine imperialism into a woman's adventure of power through social reform.

A good deal of adult literature responds to the period's gender anxiety by exaggerating the masterfulness of the man who finally wins the New Woman's love and submission. Boys' fiction also created less androgynous images of boyhood. The romantic heroes in girls' favorite books, however, are far less stereotypically masculine. The tomboy Leslie Farquhar, for example, is attracted to Malise Ogilvy, who has "a hint of womanliness" in his "tenderness, unselfishness, sympathy, and moral fortitude."[73] Later, from Italy, Malise writes enthusiastic letters about Sir Arthur Egerton, whose secretary he has become. I certainly understand Malise to be gay, though I can't decide whether or not the book's author does.

The frailty of the romantic hero is strikingly identified in the memoir of a girl who constructed an extended fantasy based on *The Three Musketeers*. She made of Athos

a friend to be comforted, not only for his high mysterious griefs, but because again he appeared sometimes as part of a pattern, with the

Bluebird Prince (not Maeterlinck's but out of Andrew Lang). With other heroes also, and . . . with Hector whom Achilles killed . . . when should I meet him alive, the Wounded Prince?[74]

Again and again girls realize their love when the boy who has been their neighbor, buddy, or workmate is injured or rescued from drowning or thought to be dying. Flipping through *Forget-Me-Not* for 1901, I am struck by the number of illustrations of men in bed: granted, it's a wartime year, but nevertheless this seems to be the pictorial image of love's dawn.

In its simplest interpretation, illness or injury provides an acceptable way to imagine a man in bed and a girl close by. The frail or injured man elicits the tenderness appropriately associated with infants—thus the girl can express love in the form she has learned acceptable, and along which it flows. In the tenderness and caretaking there is an erotic thrill. Additionally, however, the damaged man is "safe." His physical weakness protects a girl from the (unspoken) threat of assault as well as suggesting some social or symbolic equality between man and woman. Furthermore, the man often has quite overt "feminine" characteristics to match with her "masculine" ones; together, the pair of androgynes make a couple with as full a complement of "male" and "female" as would a pair of opposites. In *Dorothy's Vocation* (1890), for example, Evelyn Everett-Green provides an appealing mix of tenderness and role reversal. The man is nurturing, willing to make and pour tea, and also a certified athletic hero. Since he's "under doctor's orders" after rescuing five children from a burning house, Dorothy—a tennis champion at their club—does the heavy work when they are partnered for mixed doubles.

The last of the "Pixie O'Shaughnessy" books was published after the outbreak of war. Pixie, we recollect, is noteworthy for articulating—behind the mask of humor—many of girlhood's forbidden secrets. In *The Love Affairs of Pixie* (1915) she jokes about her imaginary love affairs with characters from books or attractive men she passes on the street. Urged by her married sister to stop putting off potential suitors, Pixie answers, "When I meet a man who needs me I'll find my own happiness in helping *him*!"[75] The man she marries is lame from an accident in youth; they fall in love while they are (together) tenderly nursing Pixie's brother Pat through a case of pneumonia.

Ultimately (because of the insecurity arising from his disability) Pixie has to do the proposing.

In addition, Pixie's evaluation of her beloved can serve as a description for woman's situation: "His heart is not crippled, nor his mind, nor his will, and fancy, me dear, going on being patient, day after day, year after year, while your body held you back."[76] This complex androgynous ambiguity provides the burning energy of several intensely beloved books. Is a recurrently disabled but admirably heroic man such as "The Gadfly" a persona for the girl dreamer, an object for her romantic interest, and/or both? Charles in *The Heir of Redclyffe* (1853) articulates many a girl's silent cry to her brother:

> "And now you are going to Oxford. You will take your place among the men of your day. You will hear and be heard of. You will be somebody. And I!—I know I have what they call talent—I could be something. They think me an idle dog; but what's the good of doing anything? I only know if I was not—not condemned to—to this—this life."[77]

The very breakdown of language exposes the strength of feeling—and the difficulty of suppressing it.

Edna Lyall's *Donovan* (1882), a book very popular among older girls for two or three decades after being published in 1882 as a novel for adults,[78] demonstrates the interaction of tears, fantasies, and gender questions with other material that is culturally specific. The novel opens with a scene of martyrdom in which Donovan Farrant, a "tall slight fellow of nearly eighteen" with "extraordinary eyes,"[79] is, after a miserable lonely childhood, expelled from school for honorably confessing to his own card playing while refusing to snitch on others. Donovan is consumed by the shame and sorrow of disappointing his father, who had been absent in India since Donovan's infancy. Before father and son have a chance to reveal their love to one another the father dies in an attack of illness "caused" by Donovan's disgrace.

The book progresses through an extraordinary accumulation of martyrdom, masochism, self-pity, and isolation. Donovan, a self-professed agnostic, is done out of his inheritance by a stepfather, socially outcast among the neighbors, and unthanked even when he rescues a girl from drowning. Meanwhile he tenderly nurses his invalid sister, a small dog, and a half-drowned cat. His sister dies; Donovan is homeless, goes hungry, nearly sinks in a bog (he's rescued by a different dog). He is several times ill to dying; nobly gives up the girl he loves; is misjudged, misunderstood, blamed, selfless. At last he has a David-and-Jonathan friendship with a fellow medical student who is a true Christian and they tenderly nurse one another through various further illnesses. After training as a surgeon, Donovan regains his faith and his property and returns to his destined life as country squire. The chief emotional display of the proposal scene at the book's end is a warm embrace from his future wife's good mother.

Although girls' sadness at adolescence may be "universal" (at least in the postindustrial Anglo-American middle class), the codes that allow them to express this sadness acceptably—that elicit tears without (much) laughter—are, to an extent, culturally specific. The energy of engrossing fiction arises from its ability to satisfy unconscious desires, some of which linger from infancy while others are formed from material strongly repressed by culture. Thus Donovan's agnosticism made him a figure of dangerous and shimmering attraction in the 1890s; it appealed to the unvoicable religious doubts of conventional middle-class girls and lent him an empathetic, pitiable erotic appeal. That appeal is no longer widely available; Donovan can no longer draw energy from powerful unconscious sources, and the book pales.

Donovan as character serves as both an object of love and a mask for girl readers. Culture's gendering acts become evident in its sequel, *We Two* (1884). Edna Lyall tells the same story of secularism, exile, sorrow, death, illness, persecution, and conversion with a girl as hero. Erica is first seen as a high-school student of sixteen whose father is Luke Raeburn, the atheist lecturer of *Donovan*. The book also features Brian Osmond (Donovan's good Christian friend from medical studies); Donovan and his bride appear in minor roles late in the book, much as Freckles and Angel were to do in *Girl of the Limberlost* (1909). Sequels that allow a new set of characters to encounter the same emotions and same situations reenact the manner in which daydreamers insert themselves into a story and make its events and feelings their own. A further emotional bonus lets the reader/fantasist get "close" to a "famous person" without damaging the written story that already exists.

Edna Lyall (and the culture that shaped her creative imagination) devised some significant differences in the female and male versions of the story. Erica has much more family love and support than Donovan; she is soon motherless but has good fathers in profusion. Donovan recovers fully from his many brushes with death; Erica's illness permanently softens and gentles her. She becomes Christian by mid-book. The repressed attraction of atheism is watered down by exhibiting a set of truly awful churchgoers (mean, rude, hypocritical, angry, vindictive, selfish, uncaring) but opposing them with a fine set of true Christians.

The social compact in any period demands repression or nonexpression of some inner impulses. At the period of adolescence, when feelings are especially strong and adult reticence must be achieved, the fiction most emotionally appealing to girls thus serves both to internalize society's codes and to express rebellion against them. Through fiction, girls struggle with the conflict between their own inner voice and the idealizations necessary to domestic and civil harmony. The raw emotion and overdetermined situations that may seem silly or objectionable to the adult critic draw their energy from the contradictions experienced by girls seeking a new way of being in the adult world.

seven

Conclusion: Time and Change

BY THE TWENTIETH CENTURY'S SECOND DECADE, THE PATTERN "girl" was not at all the same person she had been thirty or forty years earlier. "A generation ago," wrote the author of a popular advice manual published in 1913, "few girls thought of asking themselves, at fifteen or sixteen years of age, what they were going to do with their lives."[1] Now, she instructs her readers, it is no longer enough—or appropriate—for girls to be docile, obedient, self-sacrificing, and kind. "Let it be your ambition," she writes, "to be an all-around girl, good at games and good at lessons, able to cook a dinner or make a speech if at any moment you should be called upon to do so."[2]

Sports, academic education, and the mere idea of speaking in public (and of having opinions and causes to speak about) were all new for girls in the last third of the nineteenth century. Physician Elizabeth Sloan Chesser, the author of this advice manual, recollected elsewhere that in her youth she had been "rebellious of the life girls were supposed to live"—and that she had smoked cigarettes in secret and had been advised by her brothers not to "tell the chaps that you are taking your cases in midwifery" because "there is something indecent about a girl studying in midwifery."[3] Her suggestion that a girl should be prepared to cook dinner with her own hands reveals that by 1913 concepts of class as well as occupation had changed. Middle-class girls were less confined by rules about gentility, and daughters of the working class

172

had come to be included among the conceptual "girls" for whom conduct manuals were written.

By the end of the First World War, however, the girls' culture I have been describing in this study was breaking up. Young people's lives grew more regulated with the extension of compulsory schooling, an increasingly uniform curriculum, and widespread age grading of classrooms. Schoolgirl fiction settled into a mold suited for children between nine and twelve: the characters were younger, and the fantasies more utterly located in a world where adult life was as yet invisible. In addition to the regularization of school life, activities such as Girl Guides also became much more centralized, uniform, rule bound, and under adult control.

An increasingly commercial popular and material culture became available to older girls. Films and records provided mass entertainment that was (unlike music hall) seen as respectable—and girls' new freedom gave them access to it. This nonprint mass culture, however, was controlled by men and meant for an audience mixed in age and gender. In films, girls and women were the objects of an adult male gaze; girls' periodicals and series novels, although generated by adults, could attain commercial success only by satisfying girls' own tastes and desires.

Finally, as I will argue, the length of the free space that new girls had occupied diminished. Adolescent girls were sexualized (or regendered)—which has the consequence of promoting their interest in men and diminishing their centrality in their own lives. The age range once occupied by "girls" was divided and sequenced: schoolgirl, teenager, woman. Marriage once again became paramount in the formulation of adult expectation. The liminal fluidity and wide possibilities of the (imaginative) new girl vanished.

It seems curious that wider access to an institutional girls' culture had the effect of narrowing the girl's world. Possibilities were perhaps more open when girls entered communal life only through imagination. Yet the newness in girls' culture had always aroused anxiety; the internal tensions account for much of its interest.

Real change and contemporary ambivalence are nicely exemplified in another popular advice manual, Amy Barnard's *A Girl's Book About Herself* (1912). Barnard insists that women, like men, must have "work in some form—real, honest, honourable work" and instructs girls in self-interest and class values: "Be fair to yourself as well as to your

VOL. XXIX.—No. 1473.]   MARCH 21, 1908.   [PRICE ONE PENNY.

THE MODERN TRAVELLER AT EASTERTIDE—WITH CYCLE AND MOTOR.

"The modern traveller at Eastertide—with cycle and motor." Both wealthy women and working girls are active and independent, though the division between them is evident.

employer, and do not, through dread of not finding other work, let unfair advantage be taken of your willingness."[4] Describing the ideal girl's character, Barnard creates a boyish list of qualities: keeping cool in an emergency, having the courage of one's opinions, demonstrating a sense of justice, having the "strength of will" that "ensures self-control."[5] Although girls "should be peace-lovers rather than fighters," she says, "yet there are times when struggle is inevitable, when right must be upheld and evil put down, when, if a girl lacks courage, a life may be maimed or lost, a character smirched, or an animal cruelly injured."[6] Almost as if the very excellence she promotes makes her nervous, however, Barnard sometimes undercuts her own message:

> Girls are far more self-controlled than they used to be, and less self-conscious. How often do you see a girl faint nowadays? The modern girl's school training has changed all that. But, while gaining self-control and self-management, it would be a pity if, at the same time, that nice sensibility and tenderness of feeling we associate with the right type of girlhood should be roughened and hardened. I believe there is a danger of this with girls who have to fight their own way through life.[7]

Echoing the assorted characters typically found in schoolgirl and college novels, Amy Barnard no longer requires that girls be cut from a uniform pattern. She praises "the home girl, the athletic girl, the musical girl, the teacher, the artist, the student, the writer, the society girl, the business girl."[8] "The popular girl"—held up as a particularly attractive model—is a student at Girton, "not extraordinarily beautiful, . . . not even particularly clever, and certainly not possessed of much pocket-money." She is enthusiastic, open, natural, strong, and healthy.[9] The "home girl" is not self-evidently superior; she must be valorized by revealing that she is the type most needed in Australia, Canada, and the outposts of empire: "We cannot build up a settlement, a township, a province or a country without you."[10]

Is there a problem, however, when the Girton girl is "not particularly clever"? Barnard's celebration of change is mixed with anxiety; deep-seated feelings are at odds with her own conscious intelligence. True equality may be subliminally terrifying. While emphatically promoting girls' education, Barnard worries about "the danger some girls run by excessive devotion to books at a time of rapid growth" when "the brain needs less, rather than more, to do."[11] Her equivocation is hazardous for girls, since really serious study generally begins at the "time of rapid growth" when choices must be made and the foundations laid for advanced work. Furthermore, with the spurt in mental integration that typically follows puberty, it is the time at which girls are most likely to do better than boys (who mature more slowly) on intellectual tasks of all sorts.

In locating Barnard's internal conflict, however, we need to remind ourselves how rapid and major a shift had taken place in public assumptions about girls' education and mental capacity. *The School and the World*, written forty years earlier by a man who asserts his masculine authority by supporting his argument with untranslated quotations from the Greek, may have been already somewhat reactionary when it was published: by 1872 the reform of girls' secondary education was under way and women had taken up residence at Girton. While that was happening, however, the author of *The School and the World* proclaimed that girls' schools of any sort were "altogether objectionable." Girls should be kept entirely at home so they would depend "upon their brothers . . . for what they know." Thus they would be properly prepared for life: "As the ivy clings to the oak, so should the woman cling to the man, and be wholly dependent upon him; first upon her brother, then upon her father, then upon her husband, and, last of all, upon her children."[12]

In that context, it is no wonder that new girls made women of an older generation feel anxious as well as proud. "During the last twenty years or so," Amy Barnard asserted, "social and economic changes have been altering not only woman's position, but her very self. Her brain is becoming more logical, her will firmer. She is less emotional, distinctly more intellectual, more courageous." Not surprisingly, Barnard continues the sentence thus: "while at the same time she retains her more feminine characteristics—love of home and children, quick practicality, adaptability and intuition."[13]

Frightened, perhaps, by the implications of change, Barnard—in common with growing numbers of declared feminists in the century's second decade—reserves her most purple prose for the maternal imperative, which recasts biology as female destiny and woman's power:

> But the hour is coming; the dawn is quite certainly breaking. Surely, we
> may say the Joy of Understanding is welcoming Eugenics, and will

176

only rest satisfied when she is united to her sister Joys, for in the day when that comes to pass all shadows will vanish in a flood of brilliant light. Maternal Love may then hope that no cripples, no idiots, no moral imbeciles, no degenerates will be born into the world. What can surpass the pure joy of motherhood in the heart of a good woman?[14]

A contemporary feminist can hardly help being disappointed if the new girl merely turns into a new and improved version of the Victorian ideal mother. Yet the apparent diminuendo in girls' culture was not simply a resurgence of conservatism. There were also demographic and societal changes, as well as widely felt shifts in the public consciousness. In 1910 the brief Edwardian era ended; with George V on the throne the Victorian age receded one generation further into the background.

The women who had created the most popular literature of the new girl were also passing from the scene. L. T. Meade died just after the outbreak of war, in October 1914. Mary Bramston, among the earliest writers to feature attractive business girls, had died in 1912. Rosa Nouchette Carey—whose feminism was extraordinarily timid, but who had (both in *Girl's Own Paper* and in novels) brought girls at least temporarily out of the house to earn their own way in some post other than governess or companion—died in 1909; Hesba Stretton (*Jessica's First Prayer*) in 1911; Jessie Mansergh of *Girl's Own Paper* and Pixie O'Shaughnessy in 1917; Frances Marshall, who wrote the "Alan St. Aubyn" college-girl novels, in 1920. Alice Corkran, the editor who gave *Girl's Realm* its distinction, left the magazine in 1911 and died in 1916.

For twenty or twenty-five years, girls' papers and magazines had played a major role on creating a community of interest from readers who were geographically scattered. The publishers' commercial motive—to create a set of loyal subscribers—led them to institute a variety of strategies that encouraged girls to identify with "their" magazine and its culture. Prizes for readers' stories and essays helped to discover readers' tastes (as well as filling space at a cheap rate). Advice columns answered readers' questions about health, beauty, careers, and personal problems. Most magazines ran regular competitions in art, needlework, photography, and crafts. The workgirls' papers had picture-puzzle contests and invited readers to submit samples of their handwriting or their hair for character analysis. At various times almost all of the papers and magazines offered free space for readers to seek pen pals or offer to trade books or postcards. In addition, most of the girls' periodicals had some kind of charitable "guild of service." There were typically regional meetings or newsnotes mentioning the names of members, and regular contests for dressing a doll or knitting mittens (all entries—whether winners or losers—would be given to a hospital or children's home). Activities of this sort had fueled an important sense of community—but imaginative community presumably became less vital as the number of daughters at home and isolated young servants began to diminish, and as real communities of school, workplace, and clubs absorbed girls' energy and emotions.

In the public world of law and politics, new measures for the protection of children suggest a growing recognition of the difference between "immaturity" and "maturity," which—for all the vaunted Victorian sentimentality about childhood—had not really been extended to working-class youngsters much before the end of the nineteenth century. In the early years of the twentieth there were free school meals for poor children, an improved system of juvenile courts and reformatories that meant those under sixteen were no longer sent to prison, a new law to protect girls against paternal incest, an almost annual revision of codes that regulated young workers' hours, occupations, and working conditions, a tightening of school inspection and school attendance policies, and growing numbers of secular as well as church-based organizations and recreations for young people. Occupational patterns were also changing. The number of domestic servants relative to the number of households had begun to diminish in the 1890s and those in service grew older. By 1913 the membership of the Girls' Friendly Society began to shrink.[15]

Girls' periodicals scrambled, in the face of these changes, to redefine their readership. With volume 30 (1908–1909), *Girl's Own Paper* added *and Women's Magazine* to its title. Edited for the first time by a woman —Charles Peters, who ran the magazine for twenty-eight years, had died in December 1907—it was evidently feeling the competition from other recreations and from a diminished breadth in its pool of readers. Those who remained loyal were retained with more and more features for "grown-up girls." The new combined periodical had recipes, knitting patterns, and a fashion page. By the early wartime years, *Girl's Own Paper and Women's Magazine* had become distinctly more pure and religious in character, perhaps in hopes of encouraging mothers to buy the paper for their daughters but perhaps also to carve out a segment of loyal tradition-alists disturbed by the increasingly relaxed tone of other popular journals.

Girl's Realm began to print articles on homecraft and decorating and fashion. Its advertising—as has become so utterly typical of women's magazines in the twentieth century—became explicitly tied to its edito-rial contents. (When there is a health article on exercise and corsets, for example, a full-page advertisement from the Royal Worcester Corset Company and Peter Robinson's Stores features the very styles promoted by the "article.") By 1912 the publisher's notice in the *Newspaper Press Directory* described *Girl's Realm* as "an ideal home magazine appealing to the girl who will do the shopping and housekeeping of the future." Even the pictorial covers were transformed. No longer did they feature an athletic body in motion (playing hockey, riding a bicycle, carrying a tennis racquet); instead there are head shots: softened, glamorized, with a focus on the girl's pretty face rather than on her activity. In November 1915 *Girl's Realm* also merged with an adult magazine, *Woman at Home*, under the pressure—or excuse—of wartime paper shortages.

The breezier and more adventurous workgirls' papers published by Alfred Harmsworth and his rivals were not, apparently, the crucial source of competition, for they also changed, ultimately vanishing when paper grew scarce and expensive. The war, I believe, was only partly responsible; as in so many other spheres, it accentuated trends that had already begun. Harmsworth's weeklies were first reduced from sixteen pages to eight and then began combining; by April 27, 1918, features drawn from *Forget-Me-Not*, *Girls' Friend*, and *Our Girls* were all appearing in a single journal. There had already been a scram-ble for new readers; the fiction in *Girls' Friend*, for example, came to feature much younger characters.

Most of the titles that vanished during wartime did not reappear when paper was once more available. With the demographic and insti-tutional realignments, age lines and common interests shifted; in the postwar reconstitution of the periodical audience, new arrangements and new segmentations of readership came into being.

It seems likely that older girls and young women were largely drawn into the adult (or quasi-adult) media culture. One wartime analyst sug-gested that "abnormally high" wages provided girls with the money to indulge in entertainment and luxuries.[16] Another contributor to the same volume pointed out that boring, tiring, and repetitive work created in the working girl a craving to let "others amuse her" during her leisure time.[17] Both clerical and factory girls during the war were paid at a rate that made it possible to work away from home and live in a shared flat; older teens found it possible to be really (and not purely in imagination) independent of parental supervision.

Simultaneously, the 1918 education act finally abolished the part-time system and the exceptions for need, thus making full-time schooling to age fourteen compulsory for everyone and creating a large and stable audience of older schoolchildren that had not existed in the 1890s. A new generation of magazines established in the years after the war catered explicitly to them: *School Friend* (1919), *Schoolgirls' Own* (1921), *Schoolgirls' Weekly* (1922), and *Schooldays* (1928). These twopenny papers with endlessly running serials and wide readership among schoolgirls of all classes—all of them edited and chiefly written by men—had very little appeal for anyone past the age of twelve or thirteen.

Books about schoolgirls also grew distinctively younger. The generation of writers who gave school stories their formulaic nature in the interwar years had found their voice just prior to the war. The vintage Angela Brazil style begins with *A Fourth Form Friendship* (1911). Elsie Oxenham's first Abbey Girls book was *Girls of the Hamlet Club*, published in 1914. Schoolgirl heroines of the 1920–1940 years were usually in the fourth form rather than their final years of schooling. Angela Brazil believed that the happiest years of a girl's life were thirteen and fourteen, when she had a certain amount of freedom but was not yet consumed by exams and careers.[18]

As I have suggested in chapter 4, the perpetual youth of schoolgirls had a certain psychological value for escapist fiction. At the same time, however, it foreclosed the extension of girl possibilities into the years of early adulthood, and it also eliminated the seriousness and feminism of earlier school stories, in which girls worked hard to achieve an ambitious objective and appreciated the ways in which their own lives would advance beyond their mothers' lives.

Thus a division between girls and adults was more strongly established. Not only was girls' literature increasingly youthful, but the novel became more adult: tougher topics, less emotion, no character a

A Fourth Form Friendship. The dust-jacket of Angela Brazil's 1914 novel, which established her as the leading writer of formulaic school stories for young teens.

Reproduced by permission of the Bodleian Library, University of Oxford, shelfmark 2537.e.1456.

girl could identify with. Libraries began to provide special collections for young people, which were separate from both the children's room and the adult section.[19] Modernist literary fiction was usually too intellectual and unemotional to attract girls, while women's popular fiction was increasingly devoted to romance (which also tends to bore adolescents who have other concepts of ambition and adventure).

It may be that the very growth of the girls' reading audience encouraged its disintegration. *Girl's Own Paper*, which always outsold *Boy's Own Paper*, actually reached the peak of its popularity in 1890.[20] By that time there were enough girl readers to allow for successful competition from two directions: the cheap workgirls' weeklies on the one hand and the more expensive, middle-class, and proto-feminist *Atalanta* and *Girl's Realm* on the other. The size (and commercial potential) of the audience began the process of segmentation that led toward a weakening of girls' culture.

The other significant change (in addition to economics and demographics) that broke up the old unity of girls' culture during the period spanning the First World War was the sexualizing—and consequent regendering—of young women, which turned the girl into the adolescent. Women in general had more sexual knowledge than had been available to them in the mid-Victorian years, and even the most careful parents found it more difficult to keep daughters in a state of ignorant innocence. Girls at school could talk with other girls; girls going to and fro on city streets observed people and newspapers; girls' culture promoted their freedom. Cheap editions and halfpenny papers, pointed out an advice book of 1907, had made it "almost impossible for parents or guardians, however careful, to regulate the reading of their girls."[21] By the middle of the following decade, Freud's writings were available in English and reductive versions of his theories about the importance of libido at all stages of life began seeping into public awareness. Marie Stopes's *Married Love* (1918) promoted the recognition of women's erotic desires and made their right to sexual fulfillment at least privately thinkable.

The creeping sexualization of girlhood began in the years before the war, with the sudden emergence of the "flapper." In her first incarnation, the flapper was not the cigarette-smoking, gin-drinking, short-skirted flirt of the 1920s but rather a much younger version, poised on the border between girlhood and womanhood. The women's magazine *Home Notes*—which was also designated as "The Official Organ of the B-P Girl Guides"—carried "A Page For Flappers" in 1911:

> Who and what is a flapper? How does she "flap" and why? Who christened her, and why has the name stuck to every girl between the ages of fourteen and seventeen? . . . "Flapper" is now the accepted nomencla-

ture of every girl whose hair is not yet up, and whose skirts have just been let down.[22]

The significance here is that the term designates a very specific portion of girlhood and marks it as quasi-mature: erotically attractive but not yet marriageable. The word carried definite sexual connotations; according to the *Oxford English Dictionary*, it had been used during the 1890s for a very young prostitute. In the immediate prewar years, "flapper" identified a new stage of life. It described girls who were interested in looks and fashions, boy-conscious, flirtatious, teasing—but cute, rather than fast. *Our Girls* and *Girls' Reader* began to show clothes and hairstyles for the "big schoolgirl" or the "young business girl" or the "girl who is almost old enough to do up her hair." The hairdo, in particular, nicely signifies the flapper's transitional state; the front is styled in a fashion current for women (usually high curls or an elaborate fringe) but the back hair, instead of being "up," is pulled into a club or braid and decorated with a large bow. The flapper, according to costume historian Elizabeth Ewing, "wore her skirts enticingly shorter than adults" and had "large upstanding taffeta ribbon bows" on her hair. "The big bows, the twinkling legs and ankles, the new gaiety, confidence and youthful fun were all bound up with the name. . . . She created a sensation and enjoyed shocking her elders."[23]

The emergence of the teenaged flapper weakened the earlier assumption that girls were not interested in romance and could therefore mix freely with young men at play or college or work. (Of course some Victorian men were sexually attracted by girls, but the presumption of innocence had allowed Ruskin blamelessly to court Rose La Touche and Lewis Carroll to photograph his naked darlings.) New assumptions about girls' erotic potential coincided with a strong movement toward the reification of gender roles that took place at the outbreak of war. In November 1914 the editor of *Girl's Realm* had reaffirmed her emphasis on careers for girls. Loss of life among men would, she explained, make marriage impossible for many women; in addition, women would necessarily be doing men's work both temporarily and permanently. It was thus even more essential for girls to give deliberate and careful thought to the choice of a career and to qualify for a profession or for skilled work instead of simply taking a job as stopgap between school and marriage.[24]

ROUND AND ROUND SHE WENT, FASTER AND FASTER, WHILE

An early version of the flapper as an object of male interest in the frontispiece to *About Peggy Saville* by Jessie Mansergh [1900].

From the author's collection.

But as Susan Kingsley Kent has demonstrated, even feminists began to modify their insistence on equality and their understanding of gender during the war years. Nationally, one immediate response to the outbreak of war, in the writing of politicians and others whose words carried cultural authority, was an emphasis on difference and the reestablishment of separate spheres. War would rescue men from Edwardian luxury and decadence and affirm the strength and honor of English manhood. Propagandists emphasized men's chivalry and warrior nature—and urged women to do their duty by taking care to look as attractive as possible. Additionally (and perhaps even biologically), the threat of death and destruction aroused widespread yearning for home, babies, and nurture.[25]

Those who wrote for girls were not immune to these impulses. The girls' annuals, for example, began almost at once to feature a new—if fairly thin—variety of love story along with their usual offering of school fiction and first-person narratives by women golf and tennis champions. As in some of the early wartime adventure novels discussed in chapter 5, the focus shifts to men. In a typical 1915 story, "A Prince from the Skies," very little happens except that a girl waits for the missing airman to whom she is engaged; he returns in a "paean of triumph" in the end.[26] In March 1915 a correspondent to *Girl's Realm* wrote: "I do not think that women have any right to refuse marriage—i.e., a suitable marriage—in favour of a career. It is our proud duty to produce the future sons of England."[27]

The wartime urge toward love and motherhood played into the maternal feminist arguments about women's eugenic power that had already become part of the sex education provided for modern girls. After explaining about "mother and father flowers": ("Down the tiny passage leading to the ovary the pollen passes, carrying the life force to the seeds"),[28] physician Elizabeth Sloan Chesser recuperates the virtues girls learned in their passage through boyhood by turning them into preparation for maternity. Remember, she instructs her readers, that you must "grow up strong and brave" because you are the "possible mother of a long line of men and women stretching hundreds of years into the future."[29]

As the war lengthened and more and more women moved into jobs formerly held by men, concern about the consequences grew wide-

Illustration for "A Prince from the Skies." A wartime story published in a
1915 girls' annual shifts focus: the girl is no longer the center of her own
imagination, but is pictured as the object of a male gaze.

From *Empire Annual for Girls*, 1915. From the author's collection.

spread. The "reestablishment of sexual difference" came to be seen as one essential means of recreating "a semblance of order" at war's end.[30] As would happen again toward the close of the Second World War, the government and the unions both found it expedient to get women back home as quickly as possible so that returned soldiers would be able to find jobs. Even Newnham College experienced a wave of mild antifeminism; its debating society in 1917 passed the motion "That Woman's sphere is the home."[31]

The Girl Guide handbook demonstrates the way in which institutionalized girls' culture thoroughly mixed its messages about young people's sexuality. In 1918, Baden-Powell is asserting that "if she is to be equally efficient with her brothers for work in the world a girl must be given equal chances with him; equal chances for picking up character and skill, discipline and bodily health, and equal chances for using these when she has got them."[32] Simultaneously, however, he uses anti-tomboy language to make available a proper gender role for girls—and to look forward to their future as married women.

> Now I shall be told that I am trying to make girls into tomboys. Not a bit of it—quite the opposite; but girls don't want to be dolls, they have an ambition above that; and also men do not desire to have dolls as their wives—they want comrades.[33]

Even Baden-Powell began to promote heterosexual interests in later adolescence. The 1918 Guides policy statement for the first time suggests that joint recreational events might be held for Guides and Scouts.[34] And the regendering of girls clearly marks the end of their period of equality: "however independent and self-reliant she may have felt in her time there comes a joy in snuggling down under the care of a strong and loving right arm" of a "pal and protector."[35] Social-work handbooks also began to recommend mixed clubs and joint recreation for working girls and boys in their teens.[36] Sexual rules were relaxed at the women's colleges; chaperonage became extinct at Newnham, for example, in 1917.[37]

In the years after the war there was a slow but steady decline in women's age at first marriage. Women were closed out of some medical colleges that had eagerly trained them during the period when doctors were desperately needed. The census of 1921 showed fewer women gainfully employed than there had been in 1911. Oxford University opened its degrees to women—and then set a limit on the number of students that women's colleges were allowed to admit.

All of these influences were part of the change in atmosphere that fragmented the new girl culture. It is not essential to see a conspiracy: times change. On the other hand, one way to contain the girl who has learned to imagine her future as a healthy, strong, well-educated professional is to teach her that romance is at the core of life; that without erotic satisfaction—without eliciting male desire—she will be forever unfulfilled. The man, rather than the self, becomes the focus of her interest in the strong and active years when she might be developing her own potential. The romance that had been just beyond the last page of books by L. T. Meade and Bessie Marchant or sketched lightly in Alan St. Aubyn and even Edna Lyall became increasingly central to the stories—and the mental lives—of girls past puberty; the free space in which they had room for other imaginings diminished.

Fiction that moves readers forward—that can perhaps even move an entire cultural group of readers forward—creates new emotional satisfactions by giving shape to formless longings or providing new images to satisfy inner drives. Truly effective images and narratives work on the unconscious and absorb intense affective charges. The college and school and career stories that combined the manly rituals of team, house, ambition, and work with a happy circle of supportive friends who satisfy a girl's needs for caring and love ultimately threaten the primacy of patriarchal ways.

The girls' culture that emerged after 1920 was less open, less fluid, less promising than the new culture of the nineteenth century's final decades. The boundaries between life stages were more fixed, adults were more in control of cultural institutions, working girls (of whatever age or class) were sexualized, and schoolgirls had become distinctively children. Girls' culture, no longer new, lacked the range and promise and daring agency of its first generation.

notes

one   *Girls and Their Culture: The Case of L. T. Meade*

1. Mary Ann Broome, *Colonial Memories* (London: Smith, Elder, 1904), pp. 293, 295, 300.
2. Beryl Lee Booker, *Yesterday's Child, 1890–1909* (London: John Long, 1937), p. 73.
3. Eugenius, "The Decline of Marriage," *Westminster Review* 135 (1891): 20.
4. Kirsten Drotner, *English Children and Their Magazines, 1751–1945* (New Haven: Yale University Press, 1988), p. 45.
5. Elizabeth Roberts, *A Woman's Place: An Oral History of Working-Class Women, 1890–1940* (Oxford: Basil Blackwell, 1985), p. 39.
6. Maude Stanley, *Clubs for Working Girls* (London: Macmillan, 1890), p. 5.
7. Stanley, *Clubs*, p. 235.
8. Stanley, *Clubs*, p. 242.
9. Helen C. Black, "Mrs. L. T. Meade," in *Pen, Pencil, Baton, and Mask: Biographical Sketches* (London: Spottiswoode, 1896), pp. 226–27.
10. L. T. Meade, "How I Began," *Girl's Realm* 3 (1900): 58.
11. Hulda Friedrichs, "A Peep at the Pioneer Club," *Young Woman* 4 (1895–1896): 304. See also Dora M. Jones, "The Ladies' Clubs of London," *Young Woman* 7 (1898–1899): 409–13.
12. "City arab" or "street arab" tales were instructional stories about poor (often homeless) children. Although generally written by evangelical authors and printed by publishing houses that specialized in religious

titles, the genre was popular enough that many other children's writers got their start by producing a few "city arab" tales.

13. *The Cleverest Woman in England* (1898) is described in publishers' advertisements with the phrase quoted. *Wages* (1900) and *The Way of a Woman* (1897) are about drug taking; *Victory* (1906) opposes vivisection. The brief annotations in Janet Grimes and Diva Daims, *Novels in English by Women, 1891–1920: A Preliminary Checklist* (New York: Garland, 1981), are useful for suggesting the topics of Meade's novels, although one must use judgment in evaluating the notes, since they are drawn from contemporary reviews.

14. Jessica Mann, *Deadlier Than the Male: An Investigation Into Feminine Crime Writing* (Newton Abbot: David & Charles, 1981), p. 32. The novel in which Madame Koluchy appears is *The Brotherhood of the Seven Kings* (1899).

15. The stories, which ran intermittently in the *Strand* between August 1893 (vol. 6) and February 1897 (vol. 13), were published in book form as *Stories from the Diary of a Doctor*, first series (1894) and second series (1896). A further sequence in *Harmsworth Magazine* in 1899–1900 also had a medical narrator; the actual detective is a woman, Florence Cusak. One of the Florence Cusak stories is reprinted in Michele B. Slung, *Crime on Her Mind* (New York: Pantheon, 1975).

16. Dorothy L. Sayers, introduction to *The Omnibus of Crime*, reprinted in *The Art of the Mystery Story*, ed. Howard Haycraft (New York: Simon and Schuster, 1946), pp. 93–94. The identity of Meade's medical informants is discussed in Trevor H. Hall, *Dorothy L. Sayers: Nine Literary Studies* (Hamden, Conn.: Archon, 1980), pp. 71–96.

17. Kate Flint, *The Woman Reader, 1837–1914* (New York: Oxford University Press, 1993), p. 173.

18. See *Atalanta* 3 (1889–1890): 642–44, and also the unpaged supplement to the volume.

19. *Atalanta* 3 (1889–1890): 113.

20. Dorothea Beale, "Schools of To-Day," *Atalanta* 3 (1889–1890): 317.

21. Florence B. Low, "The Reading of the Modern Girl," *Nineteenth Century* 59 (1906): 278–87.

22. Letter to Vita Sackville-West, 1920, quoted in Gill Frith, " 'The Time of Your Life': The Meaning of the School Story," in *Language, Gender, and Childhood*, ed. Carolyn Steedman, Cathy Urwin, and Valerie Walkerdine (London: Routledge & Kegan Paul, 1985), pp. 123–24.

23. Mary E. S. Root, "Not to Be Circulated," *Wilson Bulletin* 3 (1929): 446.

24. See, for example, Humphrey Carpenter and Mari Prichard, *The Oxford Companion to Children's Literature* (New York: Oxford University Press, 1984), p. 470.

25. Gillian Avery, *Childhood's Pattern: A Study of the Heroes and Heroines of Children's Fiction, 1770–1950* (London: Hodder & Stoughton, 1975), p. 212.

26. L. T. Meade, "Story Writing for Girls," *Academy and Literature* 65 (1903): 499.

27. John G. Cawelti, *Adventure, Mystery, and Romance: Formula Stories as Art and Popular Culture* (Chicago: University of Chicago Press, 1976), pp. 10–36.

28. Sarah Stickney Ellis's *The Women of England* (London: Fisher, 1838) and its sequels, which were perhaps the most popular conduct manuals for women of the middle classes, advise women and girls to accept their sphere, deny their feelings, conceal their talents, and always put the needs of others first.

29. Isabel Quigley, *The Heirs of Tom Brown: The English School Story* (London: Chatto & Windus, 1982), pp. 83–84.

30. As Rachel DuPlessis reminded me.

31. *Atalanta* 1 (1887–1888): unpaged supplement.

32. Carroll Smith-Rosenberg, "The Female World of Love and Ritual," in *Disorderly Conduct: Visions of Gender in Victorian America* (New York: Oxford University Press, 1985), pp. 65–66.

33. Meade, "Story Writing for Girls," 499.

34. Black, "Mrs. L. T. Meade," 223.

35. L. T. Meade, "Girls' Schools of To-day. II.: St. Leonards and Great Harrowden Hall," *Strand* 9 (1895): 463.

two   *At Work*

1. May Wynne, *Life's Object; or, Some Thoughts for Young Girls* (London: James Nisbet, 1899), p. 19.

2. "Between School and Marriage," *Girl's Own Paper* 7 (1885–1886): 769.

3. Elizabeth Sloan Chesser, *From Girlhood to Womanhood* (London: Cassell & Company, 1913), p. 132.

4. Mrs. George Curnock, *A Girl in Her Teens, and What She Ought to Know* (London: Cassell, 1907), p. 110.

5. Evelyn Everett-Green, *Adventurous Anne* (London: Stanley Paul, 1916), p. 52.

6. Phillis Browne [Sarah Sharp Hamer], *What Girls Can Do* (London: Cassell, [1880]), p. 307.

7. *Factory acts* is a generic term used to describe legislation passed by Parliament (from 1802 on) to regulate the hours and conditions of work. The *Englishwoman's Year Book* (annual, 1881–1916) provides convenient and regularly updated summaries of employment laws that affected women, children, and "young persons" during the period under discussion.

8. Chesser, *From Girlhood to Womanhood*, pp. 48, 55, 58, 54.

9. Jessie Boucherett, *Hints on Self Help: A Book for Young Women* (London: S. W. Partridge, 1863), p. 50.

10. Evelyn March-Phillips, "Women's Industrial Life," *Monthly Packet*, n.s., 13 (1897): 502.

11. Dorothy Constance Peel, *Life's Enchanted Cup: An Autobiography (1872–33)* (London: Bodley Head, 1933), p. 62, quoted in June Purvis, *Hard Lessons: The Lives and Education of Working-Class Women in Nineteenth-Century England* (Cambridge: Polity, 1989), p. 60.

12. March-Phillips, "Women's Industrial Life," 503.

13. "Editor's Chat," *Girl's Realm* 3 (1900–1901): 655.

14. Jessie Mansergh, *Tom and Some Other Girls: A Public School Story* (London: Cassell & Co., 1901), 146–47.

15. Margaret Bateson, "A Pound a Week; Why Girls Should Earn It," *Girl's Own Paper* 18 (1896–1897): 14.

16. Clementina Black, "Typewriting and Journalism for Women," in *Our Boys and Girls and What to Do with Them*, ed. John Watson (London: Ward Lock, 1892), p. 45.

17. Florence Hodgkinson, "The Adventures of Joan," *Girl's Realm* 10 (1907–1908): 639.

18. "The Girls of To-Day, by One of Them," *Girl's Own Paper* 21 (1899–1900): 131.

19. Their names are listed in *Englishwoman's Review* 20 (1889): 65–69.

20. Mrs. M. A. Maxwell, "Medicine for Women," in *Our Boys and Girls*, ed. Watson, p. 113.

21. Edward Salmon, *Juvenile Literature as It Is* (London: Drane, 1888), p. 22.

22. Florence Hodgkinson, "The Adventures of Joan," *Girl's Realm* 10 (1907–1908): 638.

23. "Businesses for Girls," *Girls' Best Friend* 1 (1898–1899): 142.

24. "Queen of the Ring," *Girls' Best Friend* 1 (1898–1899): 142.

25. M. H. Cornwall Legh, *An Incorrigible Girl* (London: Religious Tract Society, [1899]), p. 124.

26. Meade, "Story Writing for Girls," 499.

27. See, for example, Flora Freeman, *Polly: A Study of Girl Life* (Oxford: A. R. Mowbray, 1904).

28. Amy Beatrice Barnard, *The Girl's Encyclopedia* (London: Pilgrim Press, [1909]), p. 172.

29. March-Phillips, "Women's Industrial Life," 162.

30. March-Phillips, "Women's Industrial Life," 279–80.

31. March-Phillips, "Women's Industrial Life," 279.

32. Emily Pfeiffer, *Woman and Work: An Essay Treating on the Realtions to Health and Physical Development, of the Higher Education of Girls* (London: Trübner & Co., 1888), p. 8.

33. "Women's Work: Its Value and Possibilities," *Girl's Own Paper* 16 (1894–1895): 51.

34. "The Type-Writer and Type-Writing," *Girl's Own Paper* 9 (1887–1888): 745. Although gendered characteristics are often ascribed rather than real, women's superiority at fine motor skills is indeed validated by contemporary research. Society, however, continues to assign sometimes-irrational meaning to differences in ability. As psychologist Luci Paul reminds me, the female advantage of "nimble fingers" is so overwhelming that it ought to be unthinkable for men to enter fields such as brain surgery.

35. Mercy Grogan, *How Women May Earn a Living*, rev. ed. (London: Cassell, 1883), p. 84.

36. *Girl's Own Paper* 1 (1880): 74–75.

37. Girls' Friendly Society, *Report on the Conference of the Department for Members in Professions and Business* (London: Girls' Friendly Society, 1886), p. 11.

38. Leonora Eyles, *The Ram Escapes: The Story of a Victorian Childhood* (London: Peter Nevill, 1953), p. 152.

39. "The Girls of To-Day," 131.

40. Katherine Tynan, *Kitty Aubrey* (London: J. Nisbet, 1909), p. 135.

41. Marianne Farningham [Mary Anne Hearne], *Girlhood* (London: J. Clarke, 1869), p. 108.

42. Peter N. Stearns, "Working-Class Women in Britain, 1890–1914," in *Suffer and Be Still*, ed. Martha Vicinus (Bloomington: Indiana University Press, 1972), pp. 109–10.

43. Christina V. Butler, *Domestic Service: An Inquiry by the Women's Industrial Council* (London: G. Bell, 1916), p. 13.

44. Amelia Young and Rachel Trent, *A Home Ruler: A Story for Girls* (London: W. H. Allen, 1881), p. 160.

45. L. T. Meade, *Engaged to Be Married: A Tale of To-Day* (London: Simkin, Marshall, 1890), p. 66.

46. *Englishwoman's Year Book*, 1899 (London: F. Kirby, 1899), p. 177.

47. *Forget-Me-Not*, January 21, 1911, p. 321.

48. *Forget-Me-Not*, April 6, 1901, p. 481.

49. Maxwell, "Medicine for Women," 123.

50. *Leng's Careers for Girls: How to Train and Where to Train* (Dundee: John Leng, 1911), p. 17.

51. Lee Holcombe, *Victorian Ladies at Work* (Hamden, Conn.: Archon Books, 1973), p. 34.

52. *Leng's Careers for Girls*, p. 53.

53. Holcombe, *Ladies at Work*, p. 34.

54. O. P. V., "The Lady Clerk: What She Ought to Know and What She Has to Do," *Young Woman* 1 (1892–1893): 262. Emphasis in the original.

55. Gregory Anderson, *Victorian Clerks* (Manchester: Manchester University Press, 1976), pp. 43ff.

56. Holcombe, *Ladies at Work*, p. 216. In 1881 87.4 percent of employed women were in working-class occupations and 12.6 percent in middle-class occupations. By 1911 the latter figure had nearly doubled: 23.7 percent of employed women were working in occupations described as middle-class.

57. Bateson, "A Pound a Week," 14–15.

58. Black, "Typewriting and Journalism for Women," 42.

three   *College, and a Hero*

1. Quoted in "Paragraphs," *Englishwoman's Review* 21 (1890): 335.

2. Walter William Rouse Ball, M.A., a fellow of Trinity College, was subsequently author of a history of mathematics at Cambridge.

3. Geoffrey Thomas Bennet, Sc.D., F.R.S., became lecturer and fellow in mathematics at Emmanuel College, Cambridge.

4. Millicent Garrett Fawcett, *What I Remember* (London: T. Fisher Unwin, 1924), p. 143.

5. Fawcett, *What I Remember*, p. 143.

6. Fawcett, *What I Remember*, p. 142.

7. Ray Strachey, *The Cause: A Short History of the Women's Movement in Great Britain* (1928; reprint London: Virago, 1978), p. 160.

8. Letter from Evelyn, Lady Portsmouth, quoted in Fawcett, *What I Remember*, p. 142.

9. "Phillippa Garrett Fawcett," *Education* 1 (1890): 151.

10. Fawcett, *What I Remember*, 141. Henry Fawcett stood in seventh place on the tripos list in his year; see "Millicent Garrett Fawcett and Her Daughter," *Review of Reviews* 2 (1890): 20.

11. "Philippa Garrett Fawcett," 148.

12. "University Successes of June, 1890," *Englishwoman's Review* 21 (1890): 289. The full list of women ranked in Cambridge, London, and Victoria University examinations is printed on pp. 290–93.

13. "Philippa Garrett Fawcett," 151.

14. Strachey, *The Cause*, p. 260.

15. Constance L. Maynard, "From Early Victorian Schoolroom to University: Some Personal Experiences," *Nineteenth Century* 76 (1914): 1060.

16. The bibliography in Barbara Kanner, *Women in English Social History, 1800–1914: A Guide to Research*, vol. 1 (New York: Garland, 1990), pp. 737–55, supplies handy dated evidence.

17. *Girl's Own Paper* 3 (1881–1882): facing p. 682.

18. M. P. S., "The Disadvantages of Higher Education," *Girl's Own Paper* 3 (1881–1882): 333.

19. *Girl's Own Paper* 3 (1881–1882): 444.

20. David Rubenstein, *A Different World for Women: The Life of Millicent Garrett Fawcett* (Columbus: Ohio State University Press, 1991), p. 118.

21. May Baldwin, *Golden Square High School* (London: W & R Chambers, 1908), p. 292.

22. Quoted words are from Helen Dawes Brown, *Two College Girls* (Boston: Ticknor & Co., 1886), p. 226. The book was also published in London by Trübner & Co. (1886) and praised in *Englishwoman's Review* 17 (1886): 212–14 by H. Stanton Blatch, who suggested that its heroines would become "the bosom companions of the rising generation."

23. The accident is described in Ann Phillips, ed., *A Newnham Anthology* (Cambridge: Cambridge University Press, 1979), pp. 73–74; one fictional representation is in Jessie Mansergh (as Mrs. George de Horne Vaizey), *A College Girl* (London: RTS, 1913).

24. Gertrude Margaret Bell, *The Earlier Letters of Gertrude Bell*, ed. Elsa Richmond (London: Ernest Benn, 1937), p. 73.

25. *Atalanta* 5 (1891–1892): 302.

26. Evelyn Sharp, *Unfinished Adventure* (London: John Lane, 1933), p. 40.

27. Maynard, "Schoolroom to University," 1066.

28. Vera Brittain, *The Women at Oxford: A Fragment of History* (London: George G. Harrap, 1960), p. 119.

29. Emily Davies, "Home and the Higher Education" (address given at the annual meeting of the Birmingham Higher Education Association,

February 21, 1878), in *Thoughts on Some Questions Relating to Women, 1860–1908* (1910; reprint New York: Kraus Reprint Co., 1971), p. 149.

30. Helena Maria Swanwick, *I Have Been Young* (London: Victor Gollancz, 1935), p. 118.

31. *Girls at Home* (Oxford: A. R. Mowbray, 1903), p. 42.

32. Eleanor C. Lodge, *Terms and Vacations*, ed. Janet Spens (London: Oxford University Press, 1938), p. 41. A historian and the first woman to be recognized by a D.Litt. from Oxford, Lodge became vice-principal of Lady Margaret Hall and subsequently principal of Westfield College.

33. Catherine B. Firth, *Constance Louisa Maynard, Mistress of Westfield College* (London: Allen & Unwin, 1949), p. 105.

34. Sibyl Oldfield, *Spinsters of This Parish: The Life and Times of F. M. Mayor and Mary Sheepshanks* (London: Virago, 1984), p. 32.

35. [Eliza T. Minturn?], "An Interior View of Girton College, Cambridge" (1876), in *The Education Papers*, ed. Dale Spender (New York: Routledge & Kegan Paul, 1987), p. 281. The piece is signed "E. T. M."; the only pre-1876 student on the *Girton College Register* with the appropriate initials is Eliza Theodora Minturn.

36. L. T. Meade, *The Chesterton Girl Graduates* (London: W & R Chambers, 1913), p. 32.

37. Jane Ellen Harrison, *Reminiscences of a Student Life* (London: Hogarth Press, 1925), p. 36.

38. [Eliza T. Minturn?], "Interior View," in Spender, *Education Papers*, pp. 281–82.

39. Janet E. Courtney, *Recollected in Tranquility* (London: Heinemann, 1926), p. 100.

40. Quoted in Brittain, *Women at Oxford*, p. 39. Another Ruskin anecdote was reported by Jane Harrison who, at Newnham in the middle 1870s, showed the distinguished visitor around the library: "He looked at it with disapproving eyes. 'Each book,' he said gravely, 'that a young girl touches should be bound in white vellum.'" See Harrison, *Reminiscences*, p. 44.

41. Eva Knatchbull-Hugessen, "Oxford and Cambridge Colleges for Women," *Atalanta* 3 (1889–1890): 422. Knatchbull-Hugessen herself was at Newnham 1883–1886 and passed the Cambridge classical tripos in 1886.

42. "Philippa Garrett Fawcett," 151.

43. Harriet Martineau, "The Young Lady in Town and Country: Her Health," *Once a Week* 2 (February 25, 1860): 191–92.

44. [Eliza T. Minturn?], "Interior View," in Spender, *Education Papers*, p. 280.

45. A health book for girls alludes to the "danger some girls run by excessive devotion to books at a time of rapid growth" when "the brain needs

less, rather than more, to do." See Amy B. Barnard, *A Girl's Book About Herself* (London: Cassell, 1912), pp. 21–22.

46. Frances Marshall [Alan St. Aubyn, pseud.], *The Junior Dean*, new ed. (London: Chatto & Windus, 1892), p. 82.

47. Emily Davies, "Some account of a proposed new College for women" (paper read at the annual meeting of the National Association for the Promotion of Social Science, 1868), in *Thoughts*, p. 96.

48. As Martha Vicinus points out, professional men who had themselves risen through education and qualifying examinations saw the value of giving their daughters similar advantages; see Martha Vicinus, *Independent Women: Work and Community for Single Women, 1850–1920* Chicago: University of Chicago Press, 1985), p. 122.

49. Mary Hannah Krout, *A Looker-On in London* (London: B. F. Stevens and Brown, 1899), p. 105.

50. Brittain, *Women at Oxford*, p. 52.

51. Lady Bellairs, *Gossips with Girls and Maidens, Betrothed and Free* (London: Blackwood, 1887), pp. 147–48. According to the *Englishwoman's Year Book* for 1901, Girton charged £35 for each of the year's three terms for board, lodging, and instruction and Newnham either £30 or £35, depending on course. There was more variety at the Oxford colleges, depending on the quality of room and the courses pursued, but the range was similar.

52. About half of the students in the early years were on the reduced terms; see Phillips, *A Newnham Anthology*, p. 5.

53. *Englishwoman's Review* 12 (1881): 80.

54. Joyce Senders Pedersen, *The Reform of Girls' Secondary and Higher Education in Victorian England: A Study of Elites and Educational Change* (New York: Garland, 1987), p. 306. One Oxford High School pupil recalled, however, that as a result of the rule forbidding girls to walk together they "walked just behind" one another.

55. Barry Turner, *Equality for Some: The Story of Girls' Education* (London: Ward Lock Educational, 1974), p. 128.

56. Alice Stronach, *A Newnham Friendship* (London: Blackie & Son, 1901), p. 9. Stronach was at Newnham apparently for one year in 1887–1888.

57. *Sisters* 1 (1895–1896): 445. Italics in the original.

58. See also Gill Frith's discussion in "'The Time of Your Life': The Meaning of the School Story," in *Language, Gender, and Childhood*, ed. Carolyn Steedman, Cathy Urwin, and Valerie Walkerdine (London: Routledge and Kegan Paul, 1985), p. 128.

59. Anne Jemima Clough, "Women's Progress in Scholarship" (1890), in Spender, *Education Papers*, p. 300. The Mistress of Girton made much the same point in an interview reported in a girls' magazine; see L. T. Meade, "Girton College," *Atalanta* 7 (1893–1894): 331.

60. Quoted in Strachey, *The Cause*, p. 147.

61. Charlotte Yonge, *Modern Broods; or, Developments Unlooked For* (London: Macmillan, 1900), p. 83. The first principal of St. Hugh's, in 1886, was Charlotte Yonge's goddaughter, Charlotte Anne Elizabeth Moberly, a daughter of the late Bishop of Salisbury; see Brittain, *Women at Oxford*, pp. 78–79.

62. Mary Agnes Hamilton, *Remembering My Good Friends* (London: Jonathan Cape, 1944), pp. 46–47.

63. Joan N. Burstyn, *Victorian Education and the Ideal of Womanhood* (New Brunswick: Rutgers University Press, 1984), pp. 42–89.

64. Frances Power Cobbe, "The Education of Women, and How It Would Be Affected by University Examinations" (1862), in Spender, *Education Papers*, p. 41.

65. *Times*, January 4, 1880, quoted in *Englishwoman's Review* 11 (1880): 69.

66. *Englishwoman's Review* 16 (1885): 415.

67. Frances Marshall [Alan St. Aubyn, pseud.], *A Proctor's Wooing* (London: F. B. White, 1897), p. 78.

68. Catharine St. John Conway, "University Degrees for Women: Their History and Value," *Girl's Own Paper* 16 (1894–1895): 565.

69. Frances Marshall [Alan St. Aubyn, pseud.], *The Master of St. Benedict's* (London: Chatto & Windus, 1893), pp. 26–27.

70. Marshall, *The Junior Dean*, p. 82.

71. Brittain, *Women at Oxford*, p. 18. Annie Rogers took honors in Latin and Greek at the special women's exams that Oxford offered in 1877 and eventually became a tutor in classics at St. Hugh's.

72. Quoted in Deborah Gorham, *The Victorian Girl and the Feminine Ideal* (Bloomington: Indiana University Press, 1982), p. 172.

73. Katharine Tynan, *Heart O'Gold; or, The Little Princess* (London: S. W. Partridge, 1912), p. 165.

74. Frances Marshall [Alan St. Aubyn, pseud.], *Fortune's Gate* (London: Chatto & Windus, 1898), p. 35.

75. E. Nesbit, "The Girton Girl," *Atalanta* 8 (1895): 755–59.

76. Yonge, *Modern Broods*, p. 149.

77. Emily Davies, "The Influence of University Degrees on the Education of Women," *Victoria Magazine* 1 (1863): 263.

78. "Some Girl-Graduates: A Few Sketches by One of Them," *Girl's Own Paper* 16 (1894–1895): 131–32, 219–21.
79. Maynard, "Schoolroom to University," 1071–72.
80. Marshall, *The Junior Dean*, pp. 34–35.
81. "Is College Life Desirable for Girls?," *Sisters* 1 (1895–1896): 114.
82. Nesbit, "The Girton Girl," 755.
83. Eliza Lynn Linton, "The Higher Education of Women," *Fortnightly Review* 40 (1886): 501.
84. Eva Knatchbull-Hugessen, "Oxford and Cambridge Colleges for Women," *Atalanta* 3 (1889–1890): 421.
85. "The Child: How Will She Develop," *Girl's Own Paper* 16 (1894–1895): 12–13.
86. "Higher Education of Women," *Westminster Review* 129 (1888): 152–62. In the following decade a mainstream magazine printed a glowing article on "Famous Bachelor Women" by Sarah Tooley; see *Woman at Home* 7 (1899): 685–96.
87. Cobbe, "Education of Women," 38. Italics in the original.
88. Nesbit, "The Girton Girl," 755.
89. Eugenius, "The Decline of Marriage," *Westminster Review* 135 (1891): 13, 20.
90. "Thoughts on the Higher Education of Women, by a Man," *Girl's Own Paper* 12 (1890–1891): 713–14.
91. Rita McWilliams-Tullberg, *Women at Cambridge: A Men's University—Though of a Mixed Type* (London: Victor Gollancz, 1975), pp. 42–43.
92. M. C. Bradbrook, *"That Infidel Place": A Short History of Girton College, 1869–1969* (London: Chatto & Windus, 1969), p. 96.
93. Florence Ada Keynes, *Gathering Up the Threads: A Study in Family Biography* (Cambridge: W. Heffer & Sons, 1950), p. 37. Florence Brown Keynes was later a justice of the peace, alderman, and mayor of Cambridge as well as the mother of economist Maynard Keynes.
94. Mary Paley Marshall, *What I Remember* (Cambridge: University Press, 1947), p. 22.
95. Linton, "Higher Education," 508.
96. Eleanor Mildred Sidgwick, *Health Statistics of Women Students of Cambridge and Oxford and of Their Sisters* (Cambridge: University Press, 1890), pp. 20, 67. Sidgwick did not, however, apparently consider the possibility that some sisters might have been purposely kept home because of delicate health.
97. McWilliams-Tullberg, *Women at Cambridge*, pp. 103–4.

98. Marshall, *A Proctor's Wooing*, p. 37.

99. Alice M. Gordon, "The After-Careers of University-Educated Women," *Nineteenth Century* 37 (June 1895): 957, 960.

100. McWilliams-Tullberg, *Women at Cambridge*, p. 114.

101. See Vicinus, *Independent Women*.

102. Elizabeth Wordsworth, "Colleges for Women," *Monthly Packet*, n.s., 1 (1891): 248.

103. Stronach, *A Newnham Friendship*, p. 285. Ellipses in original; the syntax suggests Stronach's troubled ambivalence.

104. Negley Harte, *The University of London, 1836–1986* (London: Athlone Press, 1986), p. 128.

105. Rita McWilliams-Tullberg, "Women and Degrees at Cambridge University, 1862–1897," in *A Widening Sphere*, ed. Martha Vicinus (Bloomington: Indiana University Press, 1977), pp. 141, 298 n.63.

106. P. Gardner, "Women at Oxford and Cambridge," *Quarterly Review* 186 (1897): 551.

107. Margaret L. Woods, *The Invader* (London: William Heinemann, 1907).

108. Tynan, *Heart O'Gold*, p. 188.

109. Mansergh, *A College Girl*, p. 204.

110. Marshall, *The Junior Dean*, p. 105.

111. Stronach, *A Newnham Friendship*, p. 201.

112. Stronach, *A Newnham Friendship*, p. 201.

113. Meade, *A Sweet Girl Graduate*, p. 310.

114. John Sutherland, *The Stanford Companion to Victorian Fiction* (Stanford: Stanford University Press, 1989), p. 549. Although Frances Marshall is described in *Who Was Who* as "educated at Cambridge," no discernible form of her name appears on the registers of Girton or Newnham. There were, however, teachers' training colleges, girls' schools, and other educational institutions in the city.

115. Virginia Woolf, *A Room of One's Own* (1929; reprint London: Hogarth Press, 1967), p. 53.

116. Marshall, *A Proctor's Wooing*, p. 312.

117. Elizabeth Champney, *Three Vassar Girls in England* (Boston: Estes & Lauriat, 1884), pp. 224–27.

118. *Times* (London), June 12, 1948, p. 6.

four   *Schoolgirls, School Stories, and Schoolgirl Culture*

1. Mary V. Jackson, *Engines of Instruction, Mischief, and Magic: Children's Literature in England from Its Beginnings to 1839* (Lincoln: University of

Nebraska Press, 1989), p. 146. Jackson notes that the "flaw" of unlady-like conduct was corrected when Mary Sherwood issued her revised edition in 1820—a reminder of the influence of adult didacticism on children's fiction.

2. Isabel Quigley, *The Heirs of Tom Brown: The English School Story* (London: Chatto & Windus), pp. 212–13. Although many boys' school stories fetch collectors' prices, schoolgirl books by L. T. Meade, Angela Brazil, May Wynne, and so forth could still be found quite recently for twenty-five or fifty pence.

3. The vocational education available to working-class and lower-middle-class girls through apprenticeship and other training has as yet had very little attention from historians.

4. Carol Dyhouse, *Girls Growing Up in Late Victorian and Edwardian England* (London: Routledge & Kegan Paul, 1981), p. 41.

5. Dyhouse, *Girls Growing Up*, pp. 41–42. James Bryce gave evidence about middle-class girls' education to the Schools Inquiry Commission; see the summary in Joyce Senders Pedersen, *Reform of Girls' Secondary and Higher Education in Victorian England: A Study of Elites and Educational Change* (New York: Garland, 1987), pp. 46–47.

6. Josephine Kamm, *Hope Deferred: Girls' Education in English History* (London: Methuen, 1965), p. 214.

7. Fiction and memoirs, however, reveal that girls were also sent to board with a relative or a woman who ran a private boardinghouse when no school was available in their own neighborhood.

8. *Englishwoman's Year Book*, 1899, p. 70.

9. For an interesting view of Cheltenham by a writer very popular among girls, see L. T. Meade, "Girls' Schools of To-day. I.: Cheltenham College," *Strand* 9 (1895): 283–88.

10. Dyhouse, *Girls Growing Up*, pp. 46–50.

11. Edward W. Ellsworth, *Liberators of the Female Mind: The Shirreff Sisters, Educational Reform, and the Women's Movement* (Westport, Conn.: Greenwood Press, 1979), p. 165.

12. See, for example, Sara Annie Burstall, *English High Schools for Girls: Their Aims, Organization, and Management* (London: Longmans, 1907).

13. "The ordinary English subjects" are, I think, literature, history, grammar, and composition.

14. *Englishwoman's Year Book*, 1899, p. 70.

15. See Dyhouse, *Girls Growing Up*, p. 58; and Lilian M. Faithfull, *In the House of My Pilgrimage* (London: Chatto & Windus, 1924), pp. 79–80.

16. Alfred W. Pollard, "Fees, Work, and Wages in Girls' High Schools," *Murray's Magazine* 10 (1891): 577.

17. *Englishwoman's Year Book*, 1899, p. 71.

18. *Englishwoman's Year Book*, 1899, p. 70.

19. Kamm, *Hope Deferred*, p. 223.

20. *Englishwoman's Year Book*, 1911, pp. 4–5.

21. *Englishwoman's Year Book*, 1899, pp. 74.

22. *Englishwoman's Year Book*, 1916, p. 4.

23. Josephine Kamm, *Indicative Past: A Hundred Years of the Girls' Public Day School Trust* (London: George Allen and Unwin, 1971), p. 113.

24. One of the more openly subversive of the high-school novelists is May Baldwin—about whom I have been unable to discover any biographical information. In *Golden Square High School* (1908) the girls do a pageant of women's part in English history from Boadicea onward, and in the 1917 *"Miss Peter"* an innocent girl child asks, "Why is it wicked for the Germans to kill us, and not wicked for us to kill the Germans?" (55).

25. Sarah Doudney, *Monksbury College: A Tale of Schoolgirl Life* (London: Sunday School Union, [1878]), p. 21.

26. Kamm, *Indicative Past*, pp. 47–48.

27. Kamm, *Indicative Past*, p. 55.

28. Helena Maria Swanwick, *I Have Been Young* (London: Victor Gollancz, 1935), p. 75.

29. Kamm, *Indicative Past*, pp. 57–58. Another Kensington pupil was Eleanor Rathbone, one of the earliest women members of Parliament; see Pedersen, *Reform of Girls' Education*, p. 348.

30. M. V. Hughes, *A London Girl of the 1880s*, new ed. (Oxford: Oxford University Press, 1978), p. 40.

31. "Lena," *Our Magazine* 2 (1876): 98.

32. Alice Stronach, *A Newnham Friendship* (London: Blackie & Son), p. 28.

33. Swanwick, *I Have Been Young*, p. 73.

34. May Baldwin, *Dora: A High School Girl* (London: W & R Chambers, 1906), p. 53.

35. As Amy Key she earned a University of London B.A. in 1887 and a M.A. in 1888; she was also at Newnham for one year, 1875–1876. A teacher for several years at Plymouth High School for Girls, Clarke was among the educators who signed the petition in favor of women's suffrage printed in *Fortnightly Review* in July 1887.

36. Amy Clarke, *A Clever Daughter* (London: The Sunday School Union, [1896]), p. 51.

37. Clarke, *A Clever Daughter*, p. 88.

38. Elizabeth M. Sewell, *Note-Book of an Elderly Lady* (London: Walter Smith, 1881), pp. 17, 128–29.

39. Janet E. Hogarth, "The Higher Education of Women," in *The Woman's Library*, vol. 1 (London: Chapman and Hall, 1903), p. 21.

40. Janet E. Courtney, *Recollected in Tranquility* (London: Heinemann, 1926), p. 129.

41. According to the British Library accession stamp; the copyright date of *The Fortunes of Philippa* is 1907.

42. Quoted in Gillian Avery, *Childhood's Pattern: A Study of the Heroes and Heroines of Children's Fiction, 1770–1950* (London: Hodder & Staughton), p. 207.

43. Burstall, *English High Schools for Girls*, p. 161.

44. At the school run by Elizabeth Sewell and her sisters, for example, girls called the teachers "Aunt Ellen" and "Aunt Elizabeth"; see Pedersen, *Reform of Girls' Education*, p. 121.

45. J. G. Fitch, "The Education of Women," *Victoria Magazine* 2 (1863–1864): 432–36.

46. Jessie Mansergh, *Tom and Some Other Girls: A Public School Story* (London: Cassell & Co., 1901), p. 14.

47. Mansergh, *Tom and Some Other Girls*, p. 83.

48. Burstall, *English High Schools for Girls*, pp. 141–42.

49. Graham Moore, *The Human Girl* (London: Elliot Stock, [1909]), p. 110.

50. *Englishwoman's Review* 41 (1910): 146.

51. Evelyn Everett-Green, *Adventurous Anne* (London: Stanley Paul, 1916), p. 19.

52. Martha Vicinus, *Independent Women: Work and Community for Single Women, 1850–1920* (Chicago: University of Chicago Press, 1985), p. 165.

53. Dorothy Owen, *Letters to School-Girls* (London: Skeffington, 1908), pp. 100–101. Shifting attitudes to boarding-school friendships are discussed in Martha Vicinus, "Distance and Desire: English Boarding-School Friendships," *Signs* 9 (1984): 600–22.

54. *School Girls All the World Over* (London: Routledge & Sons, 1884), pp. 280–81.

55. Quoted in Kathleen E. McCrone, *Sport and the Physical Emancipation of English Women, 1870–1914* (London: Routledge, 1988), p. 227.

56. Barry Turner, *Equality for Some: The Story of Girls' Education* (London: Ward Lock Educational, 1974), p. 151.

57. Jane Frances Dove, "Cultivation of the Body," in Dorothea Beale, Lucy H. M. Soulsby, and Jane Frances Dove, *Work and Play in Girls' Schools* (London: Longmans, 1898), p. 398. Dove was the second headmistress

of St. Leonard's and subsequently the founder of Wycombe Abbey School.

58. Dove, "Cultivation of the Body," pp. 400–401.

59. Baldwin, *Golden Square High School*, p. 51.

60. Dorothea Moore, *A Plucky School-Girl* (London: James Nisbet, 1908), p. 205. Sir Henry Newbolt's "Vitaï Lampada"—with its transition from cricket in the close to desert sands sodden red and its refrain of "Play up! play up! and play the game!"—was the archetypal poem linking English sport to imperial militarism. Dorothea Moore subsequently became a Girl Guides commissioner, and memorizing Newbolt's poem was one of the skills required to qualify for the Guides' sportswoman badge; see Girl Guides Association, *The Girl Guides: Rules, Policy, and Organisation* (London: Girl Guides Association, 1920), p. 62.

61. Jessie Mansergh, *Sisters Three* (London: Cassell & Co., 1903), p. 14.

62. Dorothy Scannell, *Mother Knew Best: An East End Childhood* (London: Macmillan, 1974), p. 83.

63. Kirsten Drotner, *English Children and Their Magazines, 1751–1945* (New Haven: Yale University Press, 1988), p. 166.

64. The stories are discussed in Mary Cadogan and Patricia Craig, *You're a Brick, Angela!: A New Look at Girls' Fiction from 1839 to 1975* (London: Victor Gollancz, 1976), pp. 132–35. Drotner (*English Children and Their Magazines*, p. 166) gives the dates on which initial *Girls' Friend* sequences began: "Pollie Green," January 4, 1908; "Pollie Green at Cambridge," May 23, 1908; "Pollie Green in Society," December 5, 1908; and "Pollie Green at Twenty-One," July 31, 1909.

65. Quoted in Cadogan and Craig, *You're a Brick, Angela!*, p. 151.

66. Cadogan and Craig, *You're a Brick, Angela!*, p. 129.

67. The label in my copy of Margaret Parker's *For the Sake of a Friend*, for example, which is about a girl sent to Australia's most fashionable boarding school because it also affords the best academic training, indicates that the book was awarded "for regular attendance, progress and good conduct" in 1911 to Adelaide Smith by a local council elementary school in King's Norton.

68. Charlotte Yonge, *What Books to Lend and What to Give* (London: National Society's Depository, [1877]), p. 26.

69. C. R. Coleridge, *The Girls of Flaxby* (London: Walter Smith, 1882), p. 18.

70. Another of the rare pupil-teacher stories is Charlotte Yonge's *Our New Mistress; or, Changes at Brookfield Earl* (London: National Society's Depository, 1888). The book is technically quite interesting: its events

are first told from the pupil teacher's viewpoint and then seen (in a different light) in the notes a well-trained teacher records in her logbook.

71. Jonathan Gathorne-Hardy, *The Old School Tie: The Phenomenon of the English Public School* (New York: Viking, 1978), p. 255.

72. *Girls' Reader*, n.s., 1 (1909): 4.

73. In an E. M. Delafield novel about a girl of the period, eighteen-year-old Monica is allowed to read adult books and is "a little bit ashamed" that she still keeps L. T. Meade on her shelves; see E. M. Delafield, *Thank Heaven Fasting* (1932; reprint, London: Virago, 1988), p. 52.

74. Gill Frith, " 'The Time of Your Life': The Meaning of the School Story," in Carolyn Steedman, Cathy Urwin, and Valerie Walkerdine, eds., *Language, Gender, and Childhood* (London: Routledge & Kegan Paul, 1985), p. 117. Italics in the original.

75. Bobbie Ann Mason, *The Girl Sleuth: A Feminist Guide* (Old Westbury, N.Y.: The Feminist Press, 1975), p. 122.

76. Margaret Cole, *Growing Up Into Revolution* (London: Longmans, 1949), pp. 12–13.

77. Jessie Mansergh, *Pixie O'Shaughnessy* (London: RTS, [1903]), p. 7.

78. Mason, *The Girl Sleuth*, p. 125.

79. Rosemary Auchmuty, "You're a Dyke, Angela! Elsie J. Oxenham and the Rise and Fall of the Schoolgirl Story," in *Not a Passing Phase: Reclaiming Lesbians in History, 1840–1985* by the Lesbian History Group (London: Women's Press, 1989), p. 126.

80. Frith, " 'The Time of Your Life,' " p. 118. Italics in the original.

five   *To Be a Boy*

1. Gwen Raverat, *Period Piece: A Cambridge Childhood* (London: Faber & Faber, 1952), p. 129.

2. See, for example, Edith Nesbit, *Long Ago When I Was Young* (1896; reprint London: Ronald Whiting & Wheaton, 1966); Eleanor Farjeon, *A Nursery in the Nineties*, new ed. (Oxford: Oxford University Press, 1980); and several of the memoirs in Margot Asquith, ed., *Myself When Young* (London: Frederick Muller, 1938).

3. Emily Lutyens, *A Blessed Girl: Memoirs of a Victorian Girlhood Chronicled in an Exchange of Letters, 1887–1896* (London: Rupert Hart-Davis, 1953), p. 10.

4. Tierl Thompson, ed., *Dear Girl: The Diaries and Letters of Two Working Women (1897–1917)* (London: The Women's Press, 1987), p. 133.

5. Flora Lucy Freeman, *Religious and Social Work Amongst Girls* (London: Skeffington & Son, 1901), p. 92.

6. Mrs. Atkins, M.D., in *The Mother's Companion* 1 (1887): 151, quoted in Deborah Gorham, *The Victorian Girl and the Feminine Ideal* (Bloomington: Indiana University Press, 1982), p. 71.

7. A Surgeon and Accoucheur, *Girlhood and Wifehood* (London: "Family Doctor" Publishing Co., 1896), p. 85.

8. Mary Toulmin Carbery, *Happy World: The Story of a Victorian Childhood* (London: Longmans, 1941), pp. 197, 221.

9. Asquith, *Myself When Young*, p. 56. Gabrielle Margaret Vere Campbell Long (1888–1952) wrote historical novels, plays, children's books, and a biography of Mary Wollstonecraft: *This Shining Woman* (1937). Her autobiography, as Margaret Campbell, is *The Debate Continues* (1939).

10. See, for example, Beatrix Potter, *The Journal of Beatrix Potter from 1881 to 1897* (London: Frederick Warne, 1966), p. 117; Gertrude Margaret Bell, *The Earlier Letters of Gertrude Bell* (London: Ernest Benn, 1937), p. 66; Raverat, *Period Piece*, p. 129.

11. *Girl's Realm* 3 (1900–1901): 248.

12. Bruce Haley, *The Healthy Body and Victorian Culture* (Cambridge: Harvard University Press, 1978), p. 124.

13. Haley, *Healthy Body*, p. 125. Haley cites a quotation from Anthony Trollope (*British Sports and Pastimes*, 1868) to the effect that cricket is a sport but tennis a game.

14. Kathleen E. McCrone, *Sport and the Physical Emancipation of Victorian Women, 1870–1914* (London: Routledge, 1988), p. 15.

15. Lutyens, *A Blessed Girl*, p. 10.

16. Betty Askwith, *A Victorian Young Lady* (Salisbury: Michael Wilton, 1978), pp. 28–31.

17. J. Hamilton Fletcher, "Feminine Athletics," *Good Words* 20 (1879): 535.

18. McCrone, *Sport*, pp. 27, 38.

19. Gorham, *The Victorian Girl*, p. 91.

20. Gorham, *The Victorian Girl*, p. 91.

21. Evelyn Sharp, *The Making of a Schoolgirl* (1897; new ed. New York: Oxford University Press, 1989), p. 28.

22. "A Girls' Cricket Club," *Girl's Own Paper* 10 (1888–1889): 33–36.

23. One Who Knows Them, *Girls and Their Ways: A Book for and About Girls* (London: John Hogg, 1881), p. 217. Italics in the original.

24. W. T. Pilkington, "Modern Mannish Maids," *Blackwood's Edinburgh Magazine* 147 (1890): 254.

25. "Grace at the Wickets," *Girl's Own Paper* 27 (1905–1906): 27.

26. Isabel Rogers, "A Tomboy's Justification," *School Girls*, n.s., 2 (1895): 84.

27. Edith C. Kenyon, *A Girl in a Thousand* (London: S. W. Partridge, [1904]), frontispiece.

28. Marianne Farningham, *Girlhood* (London: James Clarke & Co., 1869), p. 21.

29. Marianne Farningham, *Girlhood*, rev. ed. (London: James Clarke & Co, 1895), pp. 174–75.

30. One advertiser in the first number of *Sweethearts* (February 19, 1898) was Ottey's Strong Female Pills: "Quickly and certainly remove all obstructions, arising from any cause whatever, where Steel and Pennyroyal fails. Invaluable to married women."

31. "House of Pain," *Girls' Best Friend*, no. 53 (1899): 14.

32. Gordon Stables, *The Girl's Own Book of Health and Beauty* (London: Jarrold & Sons, 1891), p. 58.

33. *Forget-Me-Not* 1, no. 26 (1892): 14.

34. David Rubenstein, *Before the Suffragettes: Women's Emancipation in the 1890s* (Brighton: Harvester, 1986), p. 216. *Girl's Own Paper* in 1896–1897 had a series of articles on touring by cycle and another on bicycle maintenance and repairs.

35. A sixpenny monthly, *Girl's Realm* was published from November 1898 to October 1915.

36. "Chat with the Girl of the Period," *Girl's Realm* 1 (1898–1899): 216.

37. Amy B. Barnard, *A Girl's Book About Herself* (London: Cassell, 1912), p. 9.

38. Pilkington, "Modern Mannish Maids," 257.

39. Barnard, *A Girl's Book About Herself*, p. 66.

40. Dr. D. S. Pembrey, *Times* (London), May 8, 1914, quoted in "On This Day," *Times*, May 8, 1989, p. 14.

41. Dorothy Marsh, "Girls' Reading," *Girl's Realm* 17 (1914–1915): 386.

42. Edward Salmon, *Juvenile Literature as It Is* (London: Drane, 1888), p. 22. The Kingsley title was also perennially popular in girls' reading-and-discussion groups. It appears, for example, in the Girls' Friendly Society Reading Union Leaflet for 1897. *Westward Ho!* presumably gained admittance, despite the blood, miscegenation, and torture, because the author was a clergyman and the history celebrated the glorious conquests made during England's previous imperial era.

43. Eleanor C. Lodge, *Terms and Vacations* (London: Oxford University Press, 1938), p. 11.

44. Quoted in Gorham, *The Victorian Girl*, p. 164.

45. Bell, *Earlier Letters*, 10.

46. Annabel Jackson, *A Victorian Childhood* (London: Methuen, 1932), p. 158.

47. Katherine Furse, *Hearts and Pomegranates: The Story of Forty-Five Years, 1875 to 1920* (London: Peter Davies, 1940), p. 26.

48. Two well-known young readers were Evelyn Sharp and Angela Brazil, both daughters of prosperous merchants.

49. Henrietta Eliza Vaughan Stannard (1856–1911) wrote for the *Family Herald* in the 1870s and 1880s. She became an extremely popular military novelist, described by the *Feminist Companion to Literature in English* as "strongly male-identified, with sentimental representation of male comradeship" (p. 1175). From 1901 to 1903 she was president of the Society of Women Journalists.

50. John Strange Winter, "A Golden Silence," *Atalanta* 1 (1887–1888): 180–86.

51. Claudia Nelson, *Boys Will Be Girls: The Feminine Ethic and British Children's Fiction, 1857–1917* (New Brunswick: Rutgers University Press, 1991), p. 101.

52. Dorothy Marsh, "Girls' Reading," *Girl's Realm* 17 (1914–1915): 386.

53. Blanche Willis Howard, "A Battle and a Boy," *Atalanta* 5 (1891–1892).

54. Laura Alex. Smith [*sic*], "Women Soldiers," *Girl's Own Paper* 15 (1893–1894): 67–68.

55. Edith Hughes, "A Brave Royalist," *School Girls*, n.s., 2 (1895): 79–80.

56. Nelson, *Boys Will Be Girls*, p. 103.

57. Amy B. Barnard, *The Girl's Encyclopedia* (London: Pilgrim Press, [1909]), p. 87. Beryl Lee Booker, who "loathed" girls' books (with a few exceptions for American imports), consumed a great deal of Henty and also loved *Midshipman Easy*; see Beryl Lee Booker, *Yesterday's Child, 1890–1909* (London: John Long, 1937), p. 31.

58. See Claudia Nelson's discussion of this issue in *Boys Will Be Girls*, p. 107.

59. She described this as her nighttime "Henty existence": see Raverat, *Period Piece*, p. 167.

60. Eleanor Acland, *Goodbye for the Present: The Story of Two Childhoods* (London: Hodder & Stoughton, 1935), p. 82.

61. G. A. Henty, "A Frontier Girl," *Girl's Realm* 3 (1900–1901): 176.

62. Esmè Stuart, *Harum Scarum: A Poor Relation* (London: Jarrold & Sons, 1896), pp. 60, 63. Amelia Clair Leroy (who used the pseudonym Esmè Stuart) was an active supporter of women's suffrage.

63. Cynthia M. Westover, *Bushy; or, The Adventures of a Girl* (London: Chapman & Hall, 1897), p. 307.

64. Bessie Marchant, *Juliette, the Mail Carrier* (London: Collins' Clear-Type Press, 1907), p. 286.

65. Bessie Marchant, *The Youngest Sister: A Tale of Manitoba* (Glasgow: Blackie & Son, 1913). J. S. Bratton discusses Marchant's merging of domestic and imperialistic values in "British Imperialism and the Reproduction of Femininity in Girls' Fiction, 1900–1913," in *Imperialism and Juvenile Literature*, ed. Jeffrey Richards (Manchester: Manchester University Press, 1987), pp. 195–215.

66. Rose Kerr, *The Story of the Girl Guides* (London: The Girl Guides Association, 1932), p. 22. A recent biography by Tim Jeal provides evidence that Robert Baden-Powell was thinking about scouting as youth training before General Allenby told him the scouting games his son and Katharine Loveday practiced. Jeal does, however, quote Baden-Powell's acknowledgment that Charlotte Mason had used his *Aids to Scouting* to help teachers in "character training"; see Tim Jeal, *The Boy-Man: The Life of Lord Baden-Powell* (New York: William Morrow, 1990), pp. 367, 382, 532.

67. Eustace Miles, "The Girl and the Rifle. Are They Incongruous?" *Girl's Realm* 10 (1907–1908): 657.

68. McCrone, *Sport*, pp. 46. *Girl's Own Paper* 29 (1907–1908): 4–6 had an article on a village rifle club popular with ladies.

69. Laurence Saunders, "A Drill Brigade for Girls. Girls Who Seriously Play at Soldiers," *Girl's Realm* 10 (1907–1908): 881–84.

70. Kerr, *Story*, p. 156.

71. Kerr, *Story*, p. 59.

72. Kerr, *Story*, p. 158.

73. Alfred Harmsworth (1865–1922) was by this time Viscount Northcliffe and owner of the *Times*—and still a dedicated jingo.

74. Quoted in Mary Cadogan and Patricia Craig, *You're a Brick, Angela!: A New Look at Girls' Fiction from 1839 to 1975* (London: Victor Gollancz, 1976), p. 141.

75. Kerr, *Story*, p. 30.

76. Agnes Baden-Powell and Robert Baden-Powell, *Girl Guides: A Suggestion for Character Training for Girls* (London: Bishopsgate Press, [1909]), p. 17. Italics in the original.

77. Kerr, *Story*, p. 31.

78. Kerr, *Story*, p. 12.

79. Baden-Powell and Baden-Powell, *Girl Guides*, p. 3.

80. Jeal, *The Boy-Man*, p. 469.

81. Jeal, *The Boy-Man*, pp. 547–48.

82. Baden-Powell and Baden-Powell, *Girl Guides*, p. 9.

83. Agnes Baden-Powell, *Handbook for Girl Guides; or, How Girls Can Help Build the Empire* (London: Thomas Nelson, 1912), pp. v–vi.

84. Elsie Oxenham, *The Tuck-Shop Girl: A School Story of Girl Guides* (London: W & R Chambers, [1916]), p. 136.

85. Robert Baden-Powell, *Girl Guiding: The Official Handbook* (London: C. A. Pearson, 1918), p. 51, and Robert Baden-Powell, *Scouting for Boys: A Handbook for Instruction in Good Citizenship*, 9th ed. (London: C. A. Pearson, 1918), p. 6.

86. Baden-Powell, *Girl Guides*, p. 4.

87. Katharine Tynan, *Heart O'Gold; or, The Little Princess: A Story for Girls* (London: S. W. Partridge), p. 84.

88. Florence B. Low, "The Reading of the Modern Girl," *Nineteenth Century* 59 (1906): 279.

89. Farjeon, *A Nursery in the Nineties*, p. 331.

90. Daughter of the eminent mathematician George Boole, Ethel Boole Voynich (1864–1960) was a governess in St. Petersburg and married a Polish revolutionary.

91. Cadogan and Craig, *You're a Brick, Angela!*, p. 59.

92. May Wynne, *An English Girl in Serbia: The Story of a Great Adventure* (London: Collins, [1916]), p. 43.

93. May Wynne, *Life's Object; or, Some Thoughts for Young Girls* (London: James Nisbet, 1899), p. 16.

94. Dorothea Moore, *Wanted, an English Girl: The Adventures of an English Schoolgirl in Germany* (London: S. W. Partridge, 1916).

95. Kerr, *Story*, p. 74.

96. Edith C. Kenyon, *Pickles: A Red Cross Heroine* (London: Collins' Clear-Type Press, [1916]), p. 9.

97. Pilkington, "Modern Mannish Maids," 254.

98. Graham Moore, *The Human Girl* (London: Elliot Stock, [1909]), p. 8.

99. *Royal Annual* (London: John Shaw, 1913), p. 119.

100. *Girl's Own Paper* 12 (1890–1891): 4, quoted in Gorham, *The Victorian Girl*, p. 56.

101. Jane Ellen Harrison, *Reminiscences of a Student Life* (London: Hogarth Press, 1925), p. 45.

102. Ellen Creathorne Clayton, *Female Warriors: Memorials of Female Valour and Heroism, from the Mythological Ages to the Present Era* (London: Tinsley, 1879), 1:3.

103. Rosaline Orme Masson, *Leslie Farquhar* (London: J. Murray, 1902), p. 63.

104. *Girl's Own Paper* 9 (1887–1888): 380–81.

105. Agnes Baden-Powell, *Handbook for Girl Guides*, p. 340.

106. Robert Baden-Powell, *Scouting for Boys*, p. 204.

107. Masson, *Leslie Farquhar*, p. 8.

108. Lucy White Palmer, "A Word in Behalf of the Little Girls," *The Mother's Companion* 3 (1889): 95, quoted in Gorham, *The Victorian Girl*, p. 80.

109. Elsie Oxenham, *The Tuck-Shop Girl*, p. 72.

110. Carbery, *Happy World*, pp. 51–52.

111. *Forget-Me-Not*, March 24, 1906, 535. The advertisement was for a novelette published in the "Handy Library."

112. "Handsome Harry, the Girl-Man," *Girls' Home* 1 (December 10, 1910): 340.

113. Julie Wheelwright, *Amazons and Military Maids: Women Who Dressed as Men in the Pursuit of Life, Liberty, and Happiness* (London: Pandora, 1990), p. 9.

114. Elizabeth Crosthwait, "'The Girl Behind the Man Behind the Gun': The Women's Army Auxiliary Corps, 1914–1918," in *Our Work, Our Lives, Our Words: Women's History and Women's Work*, ed. Leonore Davidoff and Belinda Westover (Totowa, N.J.: Barnes & Noble, 1986), p. 172.

115. Beryl Lee Booker, *Yesterday's Child, 1890–1909* (London: John Long, 1937), p. 22.

116. Asquith, *Myself When Young*, p. 220.

117. Moore, *The Human Girl*, p. 3.

118. Evelyn Everett-Green, *Sister: A Chronicle of Fair Haven* (London: T. Nelson, 1898), p. 28.

119. First published serially in *Girl's Own Paper* 7 (March 21–September 26, 1885).

120. Acland, *Goodbye for the Present*, p. 201.

121. Bell, *Earlier Letters*, p. 66.

122. "Cranks and Crazes," *North American Review* 161 (1895), quoted in McCrone, *Sport*, p. 178.

123. Emma Marshall, *Eastward Ho! A Story for Girls* (London: J. Nisbet, 1890), p. 29.

124. Furse, *Hearts and Pomegranates*, pp. 2, 26.

125. Margaret Wynne Nevinson, *Life's Fitful Fever: A Volume of Memories* (London: A & C Black, 1926), p. 17.

126. Phyllis Bottome, *Search for a Soul* (London: Faber & Faber, 1947), p. 95.

127. Mary Butts, *The Crystal Cabinet: My Childhood at Salterns*, new ed. (Boston: Beacon Press, 1988), p. 79.

128. "Handsome Harry, the Girl-Man," 339.

six   *Reading Feelings*

1. Caroline Louise Timings, *Letters from the Past: Memories of a Victorian Childhood*, ed. Edward K. Timings (London: Andrew Melrose, 1954), pp. 29, 38.

2. Helen Corke, *In Our Infancy: An Autobiography* (Cambridge: Cambridge University Press, 1975), pp. 97–98.

3. Florence Thorne Ring, "The Factory Girl and Her Reading," *Girls' Club Journal* 1 (1909): 51.

4. One Who Knows Them, *Girls and Their Ways: A Book for and About Girls* (London: John Hogg, 1881), p. 189. Italics in the original.

5. See, for example, Jeanie Douglas Cochrane, *Peerless Women: A Book for Girls* (London: Collins' Clear-Type Press, [1904]); Millicent Garrett Fawcett, *Some Eminent Women of Our Times* (London: Macmillan, 1889); Joseph Johnson, *Clever Girls of Our Time, and How They Became Famous Women* (London: Darton & Hodge, 1863); William M. Thayer, *Women Who Win; or, Making Things Happen* (London: T. Nelson & Sons, 1897).

6. Corke, *In Our Infancy*, p. 139.

7. Lucy Soulsby, *Stray Thoughts for Girls*, new ed. (London: Longmans, Green & Co., 1907), p. 55. Italics in the original.

8. "Comrades in Council," *Friendly Leaves* (January 1898): 18–22.

9. Albert Dawson, "What They Read in the East End: An Interview with the Lady Librarian at the People's Palace," *Young Woman* 1 (1892–1893): 411.

10. "Books I Like to Read," *Girl's Realm* 17 (1914–1915): 817.

11. Emily Elizabeth Constance Jones, *As I Remember: An Autobiographical Ramble* (London: A & C Black, 1922), p. 33.

12. When *The Story of an African Farm*, newly published, was "smuggled" into Cheltenham Ladies' College, Annabel Jackson remembered, "the whole sky seemed aflame and many of [the girls] became violent feminists"; see *A Victorian Childhood* (London: Methuen, 1932), pp. 160–61. Working-class Ruth Slate read Schreiner's book in 1908. "Am I presumptious," she wrote in her diary, "in feeling that *much* of what I have been thinking so strongly is here expressed?" (Tierl Thompson, *Dear Girl: The Diaries and Letters of Two Working Women [1897–1917]* [London: The Women's Press, 1987], p. 117).

13. Christabel Coleridge, *Charlotte Mary Yonge: Her Life and Letters* (London: Macmillan, 1903), p. 121.

14. See, for example, Lilian M. Faithfull, *In the House of My Pilgrimage* (London: Chatto & Windus), pp. 32–33.

15. George Bainton, ed., *The Art of Authorship* (London: James Clarke & Co., 1890), p. 157.

16. Thompson, *Dear Girl*, pp. 53, 62.

17. Maude Stanley, *Clubs for Working Girls* (London: Macmillan, 1890), p. 40.

18. Margaret Haig, Viscountess Rhondda, *This Was My World* (London: Macmillan, 1933), p. 36.

19. J. S. Bratton, *The Impact of Victorian Children's Fiction* (Totowa, N.J.: Barnes & Noble, 1981), p. 177.

20. Frances H. Low, "Journalism as an Occupation for Girls," *Girl's Realm* 4 (1901–1902): 1009–10.

21. Marion Leslie, "Women Who Work," *Young Woman* 3 (1894–1895): 233.

22. Even that novel did not put the emotions to rest; Voynich's *Put Off Thy Shoes* (1945) added further scenes, mostly involving Gemma (the woman of *The Gadfly*).

23. Sylvia Brooke, *Sylvia of Sarawak* (London: Hutchinson, 1936), p. 77.

24. Dorothea Deakin, *The Poet and the Pierrot* (London: Chatto & Windus, 1905), p. 14.

25. Sonia Keppel, *Edwardian Daughter* (London: Hamish Hamilton, 1958), pp. 22–23.

26. Keppel, *Edwardian Daughter*, p. 96.

27. Anne Mozley, "On Fiction as an Educator," *Blackwood's Edinburgh Magazine* 108 (1870): 450.

28. Aside from every woman's own observations, Lyn Mikel Brown and Carol Gilligan cite multiple references from psychological literature in *Meeting at the Crossroads: Women's Psychology and Girls' Development* (Cambridge: Harvard University Press, 1992), p. 2.

29. "The China Cupboard," *Monthly Packet*, n.s., 1 (1891): 668.

30. L. T. Meade, "From the Editor's Standpoint," *Atalanta* 6 (1892–1893): 842. Italics in the original.

31. *Young Woman* 9 (1900–1901): 157.

32. E. M. Delafield, "The Tragic Years," in *Little Innocents: Childhood Reminiscences*, ed. Alan Pryce-Jones (1932; reprint Oxford: Oxford University Press, 1986), p. 103.

33. Brooke, *Sylvia of Sarawak*, p. 57.

34. Kathleen Woodward, *Jipping Street* (1928; reprint London: Virago, 1983), p. 61.

35. Charlotte Yonge, "Class Literature of the Last Thirty Years," *Macmillan's Magazine* 20 (1869): 451. Yonge takes the appeal of the pathetic as primitive or unsophisticated; it doesn't seem to occur to her

that servants (especially young servants) may often be unhappy and powerless, while also being forced to hide their feelings and lacking friends to console them. See my discussion of *A Noble Life* in *Dinah Mulock Craik* (Boston: G. K. Hall, 1983).

36. Amy Cruse, *After the Victorians* (London: G. Allen & Unwin, 1938), p. 161.

37. Caroline Austin, *Cousin Geoffrey and I* (London: Blackie & Son, 1890), p. 19.

38. Austin, *Cousin Geoffrey*, p. 109.

39. Beatrice Marshall, *Emma Marshall: A Biographical Sketch* (London: Seeley, 1900), p. 296.

40. Henry Cooper [Mabel St. John, pseud.], *Mabel St. John's Schooldays* (London: Girls' Friend Library, [1921]), p. 53.

41. Katherine Dalsimer, *Female Adolescence: Psychoanalytic Reflections on Literature* (New Haven: Yale University Press, 1986), pp. 6–7.

42. Hesba Stretton, *Jessica's First Prayer* (London: Religious Tract Society, [1867]), p. 33.

43. Bratton, *Impact*, p. 86.

44. I use *screen* in a sense adapted from psychoanalytic terminology, as allowing the projection of relatively safe memory or fantasy while simultaneously concealing more significant and threatening material.

45. Bratton, *Impact*, p. 20.

46. Amy B. Barnard, *A Girl's Book About Herself* (London: Cassell, 1912), p. 51.

47. *Girls' Home* 1 (April 9, 1910): 42.

48. Corke, *In Our Infancy*, p. 60. Italics in the original.

49. Evangelical writer Charlotte Maria Tucker, who used the pseudonym A.L.O.E. ("A Lady of England") produced tales in which the actors were bees or rats or people named "Truth," "Conscience," or "Hasty Acts." The distance of that remove from direct hectoring of the reader decorates the preaching enough to make it passibly tolerable—but I have yet to find an autobiographer who mentions these stories.

50. Hesba Stretton, *An Acrobat's Girlhood* (London: SPCK, 1889), p. 9.

51. Evelyn Everett-Green, *The Secret of the Old House* (London: Blackie & Son, 1890), p. 193.

52. See my discussion in "Sentiment and Suffering: Women's Recreational Reading in the 1860s," *Victorian Studies* 21 (1977): 29–45.

53. Kimberley Reynolds's study of gender in children's fiction identifies particularly the "authors' recurrent use of temporary paralysis to bring about the reform of the central 'rebel' character." See Kimberley Reynolds, *Girls Only? Gender and Popular Children's Fiction*

in Britain, 1880–1910 (Philadelphia: Temple University Press, 1990), p. 128.

54. Deborah Gorham, *The Victorian Girl and the Feminine Ideal* (Bloomington: Indiana University Press, 1982), p. 86.

55. Judith M. Bardwick, "Psychological Conflict and the Reproductive System," in Judith M. Bardwick and others, *Feminine Personality and Conflict* (Belmont, Calif.: Brooks/Cole, 1970), pp. 36–37.

56. Rosa N. Carey, *No Friend Like a Sister* (London: Macmillan, 1906), p. 355.

57. Gwen Raverat, *Period Piece: A Cambridge Childhood* (London: Faber & Faber, 1952), p. 245.

58. Flora Thompson, *Lark Rise to Candleford*, new ed. (Harmondsworth: Penguin Books, 1973), p. 253.

59. Quoted in Marion Lochhead, *Young Victorians* (London: John Murray, 1959), p. 222.

60. Thompson, *Dear Girl*; see especially chapter 2.

61. Rhondda, *My World*, p. 36.

62. Rolf E. Muuss, *Theories of Adolescence* (New York: Random House, 1962), p. 24.

63. Patricia Meyer Spacks, *Myths of Youth and the Adult Imagination* (New York: Basic Books, 1981), p. 7.

64. Mary Wood-Allen, M.D., *What a Young Woman Ought to Know*, rev. ed. (London: Vir Publishing Company, 1913), pp. 124, 151.

65. Elizabeth Garrett Anderson, "Sex in Mind and Education: A Reply," *Fortnightly Review*, n.s., 15 (1874): 890, quoted in Spacks, *Myths of Youth*, p. 33.

66. Rhondda, *My World*, p. 9.

67. Margot Asquith, *Myself When Young* (London: Frederick Muller, 1938), p. 60.

68. Leonora Eyles, *The Ram Escapes: The Story of a Victorian Childhood* (London: Peter Nevill, 1953), p. 144.

69. "Handsome Harry, the Girl-Man," *Girls' Home* 1 (December 3, 1910): 327.

70. Mary Agnes Hamilton, *Remembering My Good Friends* (London: Jonathan Cape, 1944), p. 46.

71. L. T. Meade, *A Sweet Girl Graduate*, new ed. (New York: A. L. Burt, n.d.), p. 310. Tennyson's piece was, interestingly, actually performed by Girton students during Lent term of 1891 to an audience of women from Newnham and Girton; see M. C. Bradbrook, *"That Infidel Place": A Short History of Girton College, 1869–1969* (London: Chatto & Windus, 1969), p. 95.

72. Corke, *In Our Infancy*, p. 90.

73. Rosaline Orme Masson, *Leslie Farquhar* (London: J. Murray, 1902), pp. 62, 63.

74. Mary Butts, *The Crystal Cabinet: My Childhood at Salterns*, new ed. (Boston: Beacon Press, 1988), p. 79.

75. Jessie Mansergh, *The Love Affairs of Pixie* (London: RTS, [1915]), p. 23. Italics in the original.

76. Mansergh, *The Love Affairs of Pixie*, p. 83.

77. Charlotte Yonge, *The Heir of Redclyffe*, new ed. (London: Macmillan, 1894), p. 71.

78. When Florence Low surveyed high-school girls in 1906 about their favorite novels, *Donovan* and its sequel, *We Two*, were named more often than any other books; see Florence B. Low, "The Reading of the Modern Girl," *Nineteenth Century* (1906): 279.

79. Edna Lyall, *Donovan*, 24th ed. (London: Hurst and Blackett, 1897), p. 2.

seven   *Conclusion: Time and Change*

1. Elizabeth Sloan Chesser, *From Girlhood to Womanhood* (London: Cassell & Company, 1913), p. 77. Chesser, who studied medicine at Glasgow University, had a London practice at 13 Harley Street and wrote the medical column for *Girl's Realm* in 1906–1907.

2. Chesser, *From Girlhood to Womanhood*, p. 80.

3. In Margot Asquith, ed., *Myself When Young* (London: Frederick Muller, 1928), pp. 75, 76, 79.

4. Amy B. Barnard, *A Girl's Book About Herself* (London: Cassell & Company, 1912), pp. 182, 184.

5. Barnard, *A Girl's Book About Herself*, p. 28.

6. Barnard, *A Girl's Book About Herself*, p. 94.

7. Barnard, *A Girl's Book About Herself*, p. 100.

8. Barnard, *A Girl's Book About Herself*, p. 64.

9. Barnard, *A Girl's Book About Herself*, pp. 74–75.

10. Barnard, *A Girl's Book About Herself*, p. 65.

11. Barnard, *A Girl's Book About Herself*, pp. 21–22.

12. *The School and the World* (London: Simpkin Marshall & Co., 1872), pp. 189–90.

13. Barnard, *A Girl's Book About Herself*, p. 173.

14. Barnard, *A Girl's Book About Herself*, p. 218.

15. Brian Harrison, "For Church, Queen, and Family: The Girls' Friendly Society, 1874–1920," *Past and Present* 61 (1973): 109.

16. James Shelley, "From Home Life to Industrial Life with Special Reference to the Adolescent Girl," in *The Young Wage Earner*, ed. J. J. Findlay (London: Sidgwick & Jackson, 1918), pp. 17–20.

17. Emily Matthias, "The Young Factory Girl," in *Young Wage Earner*, ed. Findlay, p. 85.

18. Gillian Freeman, *The Schoolgirl Ethic: The Life and Work of Angela Brazil* (London: Allen Lane, 1976), p. 72.

19. Alec Ellis, *Library Services for Young People in England and Wales, 1830–1970* (London: Pergamon Press, 1971), p. 55.

20. Joseph McAleer, *Popular Reading and Publishing in Britain, 1914–1950* (Oxford: Clarendon Press, 1992), p. 216.

21. Mrs. George Curnock, *A Girl in Her Teens, and What She Ought to Know* (London: Cassell, 1907), p. 77.

22. "A Page for Flappers," *Home Notes* 71 (September 7, 1911): 464.

23. Elizabeth Ewing, *History of Children's Costume* (London: B. T. Batsford, 1977), p. 134.

24. "The War and Women: The Influence of the World-Conflict on Women's Status and Work," *Girl's Realm* 17 (1914–1915): 45–46.

25. Susan Kingsley Kent, *Making Peace: The Reconstruction of Gender in Interwar Britain* (Princeton: Princeton University Press, 1993), p. 15.

26. Leslie Oyer, "The Prince from the Skies," in *Empire Annual for Girls*, ed. A. R. Buckland (London: RTS, 1915), pp. 9–19.

27. *Girl's Realm* 17 (1914–1915): x.

28. Chesser, *From Girlhood to Womanhood*, p. 14.

29. Chesser, *From Girlhood to Womanhood*, pp. 25, 125.

30. Kent, *Making Peace*, p. 99.

31. Ann Phillips, ed., *A Newnham Anthology* (Cambridge: Cambridge University Press, 1979), p. 118.

32. Robert Baden-Powell, *Girl Guiding: The Official Handbook* (London: C. A. Pearson, 1918), p. 176. Italics in the original.

33. R. Baden-Powell, *Girl Guiding*, p. 176.

34. Girl Guides Association, *The Girl Guides: Rules, Policy, and Organisation* (London: Girl Guides Association, 1918), p. 65.

35. R. Baden-Powell, *Girl Guiding*, p. 178.

36. See, for example, Katharine Cochran Dewar, *The Girl* (London: G. Bell & Sons, 1921), p. 64.

37. A letter home by N. McC. Smith on March 5, 1917, reported: "College Meeting in the evening. Our Petition granted, and all the idiotic chap. rules are extinct." Quoted in Phillips, *A Newnham Anthology*, p. 102.

bibliography

GIRLS' MAGAZINES & PERIODICALS

Atalanta. 1887–1898.
British Girl's Annual. 1918.
Empire Annual for Girls. 1915.
Every Girl's Magazine. 1882–1884.
Forget-Me-Not. 1891–1918.
Friendly Leaves. 1876–1917.
Girls' Best Friend. 1898–1899. (continued as *Girls' Friend*)
Girl's Favourite. 1898.
Girls' Friend. 1899–1931.
Girls' Gossip. 1902–1903.
Girls' Home. 1910–1915.
Girl's Own Paper. 1880–1908.
Girl's Own Paper and Women's Magazine. 1908–1927.
Girls' Reader. 1908–1915.
Girl's Realm. 1898–1915.
Girls' Weekly. 1912–1922.
Golden Stories. 1898–1913.
Home Friend. 1880–1919.
Monthly Packet. 1851–1898.
Our Girls. 1915–1918.
Our Magazine. 1875–1923.
Our Sisters. 1896–1898.

Royal Annual. 1913.
School Girls. 1894–1895.
Sisters. 1895–1896. (continued as *Our Sisters*)
Sweethearts. 1898. (continued as *Girl's Favourite*)
Young Gentlewoman. 1892–1915.
Young Ladies' Journal. 1864–1920.
Young Woman. 1892–1915.

FICTION

Adams, Ellinor Davenport. *A Girl of To-Day*. London: Blackie & Son, 1899.
———. *Miss Secretary Ethel: A Story for Girls of Today*. London: Hurst & Blackett, 1898.
———. *A Queen Among Girls*. London: Blackie & Son, 1900.
Albanesi, E. Maria. *Envious Eliza*. London: E. Nash, 1909.
Alcott, Louisa May. *Jo's Boys*. 1886. New ed. Boston: Little, Brown, 1908.
———. *Little Women*. 1868. New ed. Boston: Little, Brown, 1912.
———. *An Old-Fashioned Girl*. 1870. New ed. Boston: Little, Brown, 1911.
Alford, Elizabeth Mary. *Dorothy: The Coombehurst Nightingale*. London: S. W. Partridge "True Grit" Series, 1899.
Argles, Margaret. *A Troublesome Girl*. London: F. V. White, 1889.
Armstrong, Annie E. *Madge's Mistake: A Recollection of Girlhood*. London: Blackie & Son, 1884.
———. *Three Bright Girls: A Story of Chance and Mischance*. London: Blackie & Son, 1892.
———. *A Very Odd Girl; or, Life at the Gabled Farm*. London: Blackie & Son, 1893.
Armstrong, Frances. *A Girl's Loyalty*. London: Blackie & Son, 1897.
Austin, Caroline. *Cousin Geoffrey and I*. London: Blackie & Son, 1890.
Baldwin, May. *A City Schoolgirl and Her Friends*. London: W & R Chambers, 1912.
———. *Dora: A High School Girl*. London: W & R Chambers, 1906.
———. *Golden Square High School*. London: W & R Chambers, 1908.
———. *"Miss Peter."* London: W & R Chambers, 1917.
———. *A Plucky Girl*. London: W & R Chambers, 1902.
———. *The Sunset Rock*. London: W & R Chambers, 1903.
Beale, Anne. *Gladys the Reaper*. 3 vols. London: Bentley, 1860.
Bramston, Mary. *A Girl's Outlook*. London: Wells Gardner, Darton & Co., 1903.
———. *The Heroine of a Basket Van*. London: National Society's Depository, [1886].

———. *Lottie Levison: A Story of South London for Young Women and Older Girls*. London: National Society's Depository, 1892.

———. *Rosamond's Girls: A School Story*. London: SPCK, [1905].

———. *Wanted: A Sphere*. London: SPCK, 1890.

———. *A Woman of Business*. London: SPCK, [1885].

Brazil, Angela. *The Fortunes of Philippa*. 1907. New ed. London: Blackie & Son, n.d.

———. *A Fourth Form Friendship*. London: Blackie & Son, 1914.

———. *The Manor House School*. London: Blackie & Son, 1911.

———. *A Terrible Tomboy*. New ed. London: Henry Frowde, 1915.

Briggs, Alice J. *Bessie's Ministry*. London: Robert Culley, [1898].

Brontë, Charlotte. *Jane Eyre*. 1847. New ed. New York: W. W. Norton, 1971.

Brown, Helen Dawes. *Two College Girls*. Boston: Ticknor & Co., 1886.

Burnett, Frances Hodgson. *Little Lord Fauntleroy*. London: Warne, 1886.

———. *A Little Princess*. London: Warne, 1905.

———. *The Lost Prince*. London: Hodder & Stoughton, 1915.

———. *Sara Crewe*. London: Fisher Unwin, 1887.

———. *The Secret Garden*. London: Heinemann, 1911.

Card, Susan. *Agnes's Dilemma*. London: Drane's, 1913.

Carew, Maud [Florence King]. *Little King Richard*. London: SPCK, [1899].

Carey, Rosa Nouchette. *Aunt Diana*. London: Religious Tract Society, [1888].

———. *Nellie's Memories*. 3 vols. London: Tinsley, 1868.

———. *No Friend Like a Sister*. London: Macmillan, 1906.

———. *Not Like Other Girls*. 3 vols. London: Bentley, 1884.

———. *Queenie's Whim*. 3 vols. London: Bentley, 1881.

Champney, Elizabeth. *Three Vassar Girls Abroad, with Their Haps and Mishaps*. Boston: Estes & Lauriat, 1883.

———. *Three Vassar Girls in England*. Boston: Estes & Lauriat, 1884.

Clarke, Amy. *A Clever Daughter*. London: The Sunday School Union, [1896].

———. *A High School Girl; or, The Secret of the Old Bureau*. London: The Sunday School Union, [1896].

———. *The Mystery of the Manor House*. London: Blackie & Son, 1899.

———. *The Ravensworth Scholarship*. London: Blackie & Son, [1894].

Clayton, Ellen. *A Ministering Angel*. London: Dean and Son, [1895].

Coleridge, C. R. *The Girls of Flaxby*. London: Walter Smith, 1882.

Colville, Harriet E. *Molly: The Story of a Wayward Girl*. London: S. W. Partridge, 1906.

Cook, Emily C. "A Modern High-School Girl." *National Review* 17 (1891): 370–78.

Cooper, Henry [Mabel St. John, pseud.]. *Mabel St. John's Schooldays*. London: Girls' Friend Library, [1921].

Corkran, Alice. *Margery Merton's Girlhood*. London: Blackie & Son, 1888.

Craik, Dinah Mulock. *John Halifax, Gentleman*. 3 vols. London: Hurst & Blackett, 1852.

———. *A Noble Life*. 2 vols. London: Hurst & Blackett, 1866.

Cummins, Maria Susanna. *The Lamplighter*. Boston: J. P. Jewett, 1854.

Davidson, Lillias Campbell. *A Girl's Battle*. London: S. W. Partridge, [1904].

Deakin, Dorothea. *The Poet and the Pierrot*. London: Chatto & Windus, 1905.

Delafield, E. M. *Thank Heaven Fasting*. 1932. Reprint, London: Virago, 1988.

Doudney, Sarah. *Michaelmas Daisy: A Young Girl's Story*. London: Griffith & Farran, 1882.

———. *Monksbury College: A Tale of Schoolgirl Life*. London: Sunday School Union, [1878].

———. *Thy Heart's Desire: A Story of Girls' Lives*. London: Isbister [1888].

———. *Under False Colours: A Story from Two Girls' Lives*. London: Blackie & Son, 1889.

Drower, Ethel Stefana [E. S. Stevens, pseud.]. *"—And What Happened."* London: Mills & Boon, 1916.

Du Maurier, George. *Trilby*. London: Osgood, McIlwaine, 1895.

Dunsmuir, Amy [Amy M. Oliphant Smith]. *Vida; Study of a Girl*. 2 vols. London: Macmillan, 1880.

Edwardes, Annie. *A Girton Girl*. *Temple Bar* 73–75 (1881). 3 vols. London: Bentley, 1885.

Enock, Esther E. *Those Dreadful Girls*. London: RTS, 1913.

Evelyn, Constance. *Miss Nettie's Girls: A Story of London East-End Life*. London: RTS, 1887.

Everett-Green, Evelyn. *Adventurous Anne*. London: Stanley Paul, 1916.

———. *Called of Her Country: The Story of Joan of Arc*. London: S. H. Bousfield, [1903].

———. *Carol Carew; or, Was It Imprudent?*. London: S. W. Partridge, [1907].

———. *The Castle of the White Flag: A Tale of the Franco-German War*. London: Thomas Nelson, 1904.

———. *Dorothy's Vocation*. Edinburgh: Oliphant & Co., 1890.

———. *The Head of the House: The Story of a Victory Over Passion and Pride*. London: RTS, [1886].

———. *Judith: The Money-Lender's Daughter*. Edinburgh: Oliphant & Co., 1895.

———. *The Secret Chamber at Chad*. London: T. Nelson & Sons, 1894.

———. *The Secret of the Old House*. London: Blackie & Son, 1890.

———. *Sister: A Chronicle of Fair Haven*. London: T. Nelson, 1898.

——. *True Stories of Girl Heroines*. London: Hutchinson & Co., 1901.

Ewing, Juliana Horatia. *Six to Sixteen*. London: SPCK, 1876.

Fielding, Sarah. *The Governess; or, Little Female Academy*. 1749. Facsimile reproduction with introduction by Jill E. Grey. London: Oxford University Press, 1968.

Filleul, Marianne. *Ellen Tremaine*. London: RTS, [1884].

Foley, Kathleen P. *A Girl Soldier*. London: F. V. White, 1903.

Forbes, Ethel M. *A Daughter of the Democracy*. London: Cassell, 1911.

Freeman, Flora Lucy. *Polly: A Study of Girl Life*. Oxford: A. R. Mowbray, 1904.

Gellie, Mary E. *The New Girl; or, The Rivals*. London: Griffith & Farran, 1878.

Gerard, Morice [John Jessop Teague]. *Ruth Gwynnett, Schoolmistress*. London: S. W. Partridge, [1905].

Giberne, Agnes. *Miss Con; or, All Those Girls*. London: Nisbet, 1887.

Greville, Violet. *Zoe: A Girl of Genius*. 3 vols. London: Bentley, 1881.

Grey, Rowland [Lilian Kate Rowland Brown]. *The Story of Chris*. London: Methuen, 1892.

Hall, Edith. *That Examination Paper! A Story for Girls*. London: Blackie & Son, 1900.

Hampden, Mary. *The Girl with a Talent*. London: RTS, 1894.

Hart, Mabel. *Sister K*. London: Methuen, [1909].

Haverfield, Eleanor Luisa. *Audrey's Awakening*. Oxford: Humphrey Milford, [1910].

Heddle, Ethel F. *Girl Comrades*. London: Blackie & Son, 1907.

——. *An Original Girl*. London: Blackie & Son, 1902.

——. *The Pride of the Family*. London: James Bowden, 1899.

——. *Three Girls in a Flat*. London: Gardner, Darton & Co., 1896.

Hocking, Salome. *Norah Lang: The Mine Girl*. London: Andrew Crombie, [1886].

Hodgkinson, Florence. "The Adventures of Joan." *Girl's Realm* 10 (1907–1908): 555ff.

Hone, Annie M. *Our Nellie; or, Found in the Factory*. London: Gall & Ingalls, [1886].

Irvine, Amy. *The Probationer*. London: S. W. Partridge, [1910].

Keary, Annie. *Sidney Grey: A Tale of School Life*. London: David Bogue, 1857.

——. *A York and a Lancaster Rose*. London: Macmillan, 1876.

Kenealy, Arabella. *Dr. Janet of Harley Street*. London: Digby, Long, [1893].

Kenyon, Edith C. *A Girl in a Thousand*. London: S. W. Partridge, [1904].

——. *Pickles: A Red Cross Heroine*. London: Collins' Clear-Type Press, [1916].

Kipling, Rudyard. *The Light That Failed*. London: Macmillan, 1891.

LeFeuvre, Amy. *A Bit of Rough Road*. London: RTS, 1908.

——. *A Daughter of the Sea*. London: Hodder & Stoughton, 1902.

——. *Heather's Mistress*. London: Leisure Hour Library, 1911.

Legh, M. H. Cornwall. *An Incorrigible Girl*. London: RTS, [1899].

Leslie, Emma. *Brought Out of Peril*. London: RTS, [1907].

——. *Elsie's Scholarship and Why She Surrendered It*. London: Gall & Ingles, [1898].

——. *The Gipsy Queen*. London: Partridge, 1884.

Lyall, Edna. *Donovan*. 1882; 24th ed., London: Hurst & Blackett, 1897.

——. *We Two*. 1884; 23rd ed., London: Hurst & Blackett, 1898.

Mackenzie, Hannah B. *Crowned Victor: A Story of Strife*. Edinburgh: Oliphant & Anderson, 1894.

Mansergh, Jessie. *About Peggy Saville*. London: RTS, [1900]. (First published in *Girl's Own Paper*, 1898.)

——. *Betty Trevor*. London: RTS, [1907].

——. *The Love Affairs of Pixie*. London: RTS, [1915].

——. *Rhoda, a Public School Story*. *Girl's Realm* 3 (1900–1901).

——. *Sisters Three*. London: Cassell & Co., 1900.

——. *Tom and Some Other Girls: A Public School Story*. London: Cassell & Co., 1901.

Mansergh, Jessie [as Mrs. George de Horne Vaizey]. *A College Girl*. London: RTS, 1913.

—— [as Mrs. George de Horne Vaizey]. *The Daughters of a Genius: A Story of Brave Endeavour*. London: Chambers, 1903.

—— [as Mrs. George de Horne Vaizey]. *Etheldreda the Ready: A School Story*. London: Cassell, 1910.

—— [as Mrs. George de Horne Vaizey]. *A Houseful of Girls*. London: RTS, [1902]. (First published in *Girl's Own Paper*, 1900–1901.)

—— [as Mrs. George de Horne Vaizey]. *Pixie O'Shaughnessy*. London: RTS, [1903]. (First published in *Girl's Own Paper*, 1901–1902.)

Marchant, Bessie. *A Canadian Farm Mystery; or, Pam the Pioneer*. London: Blackie & Son, 1917.

——. *Cecily Frome, the Captain's Daughter*. Edinburgh: W. P. Nimms, Hay, & Mitchell, [1900].

——. *A Courageous Girl: A Story of Uruguay*. London: Blackie & Son, 1909.

——. *The Girl Captives: A Story of the Indian Frontier*. London: Blackie & Son, 1900.

——. *A Girl Munition Worker*. London: Blackie & Son, 1916.

——. *Juliette, the Mail Carrier*. London: Collins' Clear-Type Press, 1907.

———. *Molly Angel's Adventures: A Story of Belgium Under German Occupation.* London: Blackie & Son, 1915.

———. *The Secret of the Everglades: A Story of Adventure in Florida.* London: Blackie & Son, [1902].

———. *Three Girls on a Ranch: A Story of New Mexico.* London: Blackie & Son, 1901.

———. *The Youngest Sister: A Tale of Manitoba.* Glasgow: Blackie & Son, 1913.

Marshall, Emma. *Abigail Templeton; or, Brave Efforts.* London: W & R Chambers, 1896.

———. *Alma; or, The Story of a Little Music Mistress.* London: Sonenschein & Co., 1888.

———. *The Close of St. Christopher's: A Story for Girls.* London: J. Nisbet, 1894.

———. *Eastward Ho! A Story for Girls.* London: J. Nisbet, 1890.

———. *A Good-Hearted Girl; or, A Present-Day Heroine.* London: W & R Chambers, 1899.

———. *Those Three; or, Little Wings: A Story for Girls.* London: Nisbet, 1891.

Marshall, Frances [Alan St. Aubyn, pseud]. *Fortune's Gate.* London: Chatto & Windus, 1898.

—— [Alan St. Aubyn, pseud]. *The Harp of Life.* London: F.B. White, 1908.

—— [Alan St. Aubyn, pseud]. *The Junior Dean.* New ed. London: Chatto & Windus, 1892.

—— [Alan St. Aubyn, pseud]. *The Master of St. Benedict's.* London: Chatto & Windus, 1893.

—— [Alan St. Aubyn, pseud]. *A Proctor's Wooing.* London: F. B. White, 1897.

Martin, Mary Emma. *An Unlessoned Girl.* 2 vols. London: Marcus Ward, 1881.

Masson, Rosaline Orme. *Leslie Farquhar.* London: J. Murray, 1902.

Meade, L. T. *Bess of Delany's.* London: Digby, Long, 1905.

———. *A Brave Poor Thing.* London: Isbister, 1900.

———. *Catalina: Art Student.* London: W & R Chambers, 1896.

———. *The Chesterton Girl Graduates.* London: W & R Chambers, 1913.

———. *The Children's Pilgrimage.* London: Nisbet, 1883.

———. *Corporal Violet.* London: Hodder & Stoughton, [1912].

———. *Daddy's Girl.* London: Newnes, 1901.

———. *Engaged to Be Married: A Tale of To-day.* London: Simpkin, Marshall, 1890.

———. *Four on an Island.* London: W & R Chambers, [1892].

———. *A Girl from America.* London: W & R Chambers, 1907.

———. *A Girl in Ten Thousand. Young Woman* 3 (1894–1895): 12ff.

———. *A Girl of the People.* London: Metheun, 1890.

———. *The Girls of Merton College*. London: W & R Chambers, 1911.

———. *The Girls of St. Wode's*. London: W & R Chambers, 1898.

———. *The Honourable Miss*. 2 vols. London: Metheun, 1891.

———. *Jill, a Flower Girl*. London: Isbister, [1893].

———. *A Little Mother to the Others*. London. F. V. White, 1896.

———. *The Little Princess of Tower Hill*. London: Partridge, 1889.

———. *The Little School-Mothers*. London: Cassell, 1907.

———. *The Maid with the Goggles*. London: Digby, Long & Co., 1906.

———. *Mary Gifford, M.B.* London: Wells Gardner, 1898.

———. *The Medicine Lady*. 3 vols. London: Cassell, 1892.

———. *Merry Girls of England*. London: Cassell, 1896.

———. *Nurse Charlotte*. London: John Long, 1904.

———. *Polly: A New-Fashioned Girl*. London: Cassell, 1889.

———. *A Princess of the Gutter*. London: Wells Gardner, Darton & Co., 1895.

———. *Red Rose and Tiger Lily*. London: Cassell, 1894.

———. *"Ruffles."* London: Stanley Paul & Co., [1911].

———. *The School Favourite*. London: W & R Chambers, 1908.

———. *A Sister of the Red Cross*. London: T. Nelson & Sons, 1900.

———. *Sue: The Story of a Little Heroine and Her Friend*. London: W & R Chambers, 1906.

———. *A Sweet Girl Graduate*. 1891. New ed. New York: A. L. Burt, n.d.

———. *A Very Naughty Girl*. London: W & R Chambers, 1901.

———. *A Wild Irish Girl*. London: W & R Chambers, 1910.

———. *Wild Kitty*. London: W & R Chambers, 1897.

———. *A World of Girls*. London: Cassell, 1886.

Miall, Agnes M. *Meddlesome Mattie*. London: S. W. Partridge, [1913].

Miles, Alfred H. *Fifty-Two Stories of Courage and Endeavour for Girls*. London: Hutchinson, [1901].

Mockler, Geraldine. *Cousin Betty: A Tale for Girls*. London: Thomas Nelson, 1913.

———. *The Four Miss Whittingtons*. Glasgow: Blackie & Son, [1899].

———. *The Girls of Saint Bede's*. London: Jarrold & Sons, 1899.

———. *Proud Miss Sydney*. London: Blackie & Son, 1896.

———. *The Rebellion of Margaret*. London: Jarrold & Sons, [1910].

Molesworth, Mary Louisa. *Imogen; or, Only Eighteen*. London: W & R Chambers, 1892.

Montgomery, Florence. *Misunderstood*. London: Richard Bentley, 1869.

Moore, Dorothea. *Captain Nancy: A Story of the 'Forty-Five*. London: J. Nisbet, 1914.

———. *The Lucas Girls; or, The Man of the Family*. London: S. W. Partridge, [1911].

———. *Mistress Dorothy: The Story of a Brave Heart*. London: National Society's Depository, [1902].

———. *A Plucky School-Girl*. London: James Nisbet, 1908.

———. *Terry the Girl-Guide*. Foreword by Agnes Baden-Powell. London: James Nisbet & Co., 1912.

———. *Wanted, an English Girl: The Adventures of an English Schoolgirl in Germany*. London: S. W. Partridge, 1916.

Moore, Graham. *The Human Girl*. London: Elliot Stock, [1909].

Nesbit, E. "The Girton Girl." *Atalanta* 8 (1895): 755–59.

Oxenham, Elsie. *The Conquest of Christina*. London: Collins, [1909].

———. *Expelled from School*. London: Collins, [1919].

———. *Girls of the Hamlet Club*. London: W & R Chambers, 1914.

———. *The Girl Who Wouldn't Make Friends*. London: Nelson, [1909].

———. *A Go-Ahead Schoolgirl*. London: W & R Chambers, 1919.

———. *A Holiday Queen*. London: Collins, 1910.

———. *A School Camp Fire*. London: W & R Chambers, 1917.

———. *Schoolgirls & Scouts*. London: Collins, [1914].

———. *The Tuck-Shop Girl: A School Story of Girl Guides*. London: W & R Chambers, [1916].

Oyer, Leslie. "The Prince from the Skies." In *Empire Annual for Girls*, ed. A. R. Buckland, pp. 9–19. London: RTS, 1915.

Parker, Margaret. *For the Sake of a Friend: A Story of School Life*. London: Blackie & Son, 1896.

Porter, Gene Stratton. *Freckles*. New York: Doubleday, Page & Co., 1904.

———. *A Girl of the Limberlost*. New York: Doubleday, Page & Co., 1909.

Prentiss, Elizabeth. *Stepping Heavenward*. New York: A. D. F. Randolph, 1869.

Read, Mrs. R. H. *Dora: A Girl Without a Home*. London: Blackie & Son, 1883.

Rossetti, Christine. *Maude: A Story for Girls*. London: James Bowden, 1897.

Ruck, Berta. *Arabella the Awful*. London: Hodder & Stoughton, 1918.

School-Girl Life and Incident. London: Strahan & Co., [1880].

School Girls All the World Over. London: Routledge & Sons, 1884.

Schreiner, Olive. *The Story of an African Farm*. 1883. New ed. London: Penguin, 1982.

Sergeant, Adeline. *No Ambition*. Edinburgh: Oliphant, Anderson & Ferrier, 1895.

Sewell, Anna. *Black Beauty*. London: Jarrold & Sons, 1877.

Seymour, Mary Corbet. *A Girl's Kingdom*. London: Blackie & Son, 1897.

Sharp, Evelyn. *The Making of a Schoolgirl.* 1897. New ed. New York: Oxford University Press, 1989.

———. *The Youngest Girl in the School.* London: Macmillan, 1901.

Slater, Catherine P. *A Friendly Girl.* London: National Society's Depository, 1896.

Smedley, Constance. *On the Fighting Line.* London: G. P. Putnam's Sons, 1915.

———. *The June Princess.* London: Chatto & Windus, 1909.

Stowe, Harriet Beecher. *Uncle Tom's Cabin.* Boston: J. P. Jewett, 1852.

Streatfeild, Lilian Cecil. *Evelyn's Quest.* London: H. J. Glaisher, 1906.

Stretton, Hesba. *An Acrobat's Girlhood.* London: SPCK, 1889.

———. *Alone in London.* 1869. 39th Impression. London: Religious Tract Society, 1914.

———. *Cassy.* [1874]. New ed. London: Religious Tract Society, n.d.

———. *Jessica's First Prayer.* London: Religious Tract Society, [1867].

Stronach, Alice. *A Newnham Friendship.* London: Blackie & Son, 1901.

Stuart, Esmè [Amelia Claire Leroy]. *Harum Scarum: A Poor Relation.* London: Jarrold & Sons, 1896.

Surrey, Margaret. *A Modern Atalanta.* London: RTS, 1908.

———. *The Soul of a Girl.* London: Marshall Brothers, 1907.

Swan, Annie S. *Elizabeth Glen, M.B.* London: Hutchinson, 1895.

———. *Mrs. Keith Hamilton, M.B.* London: Hutchinson, 1897.

Taylor, Lucy. *Fairy Phoebe; or, Facing the Footlights.* New ed. London: John F. Shaw, 1887.

Taylor, Mary. *Miss Miles.* 1890. Introduction by Janet H. Murray. New York: Oxford University Press, 1990.

Thompson, Flora. *Lark Rise to Candleford.* 1939–1943. New ed. Harmondsworth: Penguin Books, 1973.

Three Stories for Working Girls. London: SPCK, [1887].

Travers, Graham [Dr. Margaret Todd]. *Mona Maclean, Medical Student.* 3 vols. London: Blackwood, 1892.

Tynan, Katharine. *Heart O'Gold; or, The Little Princess: A Story for Girls.* London: S. W. Partridge, 1912.

———. *Kitty Aubrey.* London: J. Nisbet, 1909.

———. *Love of Sisters.* London: Smith, Elder, 1902.

Tytler, Sarah [Henrietta Keddie]. *Girl Neighbours; or, The Old Fashion and the New.* London: Blackie & Son, 1888.

——— [Henrietta Keddie]. *The Girls of Inverbarns.* London: John Long, 1906.

——— [Henrietta Keddie]. *In Clarissa's Day.* London: Chatto & Windus, 1903.

Voynich, Ethel. *The Gadfly.* New York: Henry Holt, 1897.

———. *An Interrupted Friendship.* London: Hutchinson, 1910.

Walton, Catherine Augusta. *Christie's Old Organ*. London: Religious Tract Society, [1882].

———. *Nobody Loves Me*. London: Religious Tract Society, 1883.

———. *A Peep Behind the Scenes*. [1877]. Reprint, London: Religious Tract Society, n.d.

———. *Taken or Left*. London: Religious Tract Society, 1885.

Ward, Mary. *Marcella*. 1894. Reprint, London: Virago, 1984.

Warden, Florence [Florence Price James]. *The Bohemian Girls*. London: F. V. White & Co., 1899.

Warner, Susan. *The Wide, Wide World*. 1850. New ed. New York: The Feminist Press, 1986.

Westover, Cynthia M. *Bushy; or, The Adventures of a Girl*. London: Chapman & Hall, 1897.

Whiting, Mary Bradford. *Meriel's Career: A Tale of Literary Life in London*. London: Blackie, 1914.

Williamson, Alice. *The Newspaper Girl*. London: C. A. Pearson, 1899.

Wood, Ellen Price. *East Lynne*. 1861. New ed. New Brunswick: Rutgers University Press, 1984.

Woods, Margaret L. *The Invader*. London: William Heinemann, 1907.

Wotton, Mabel E. *A Girl Diplomatist*. London: Chapman & Hall, 1892.

Wynne, May. *An English Girl in Serbia: The Story of a Great Adventure*. London: Collins, [1916].

———. *The Honour of the School*. London: Nisbet, [1918].

———. *Honour's Fetters*. London: Stanley Paul & Co. [1911].

Yonge, Charlotte M. *The Clever Woman of the Family*. 2 vols. London: Macmillan, 1865.

———. *The Daisy Chain*. 1856. New ed. London: Macmillan, 1890.

———. *Heartsease*. 2 vols. London: John W. Parker & Son, 1854.

———. *The Heir of Redclyffe*. 1853. New ed. London: Macmillan, 1894.

———. *Modern Broods; or, Developments Unlooked For*. London: Macmillan, 1900.

———. *Our New Mistress; or, Changes at Brookfield Earl*. London: National Society's Depository, 1888.

———. *Scenes and Characters*. London: James Burns, 1847.

Young, Amelia and Rachel Trent. *A Home Ruler: A Story for Girls*. London: W. H. Allen, 1881.

OTHER PRIMARY AND SECONDARY SOURCES

(Including Autobiographies, Advice Manuals, History, Criticism)

Acland, Eleanor. *Goodbye for the Present: The Story of Two Childhoods*. London: Hodder & Stoughton, 1935.

Adam, Ruth. *A Woman's Place, 1910–1975*. London: Chatto & Windus, 1975.

Alderson, Brian. "Tracts, Rewards, and Fairies: The Victorian Contribution to Children's Literature." In *Essays in the History of Publishing*, edited by Asa Briggs, pp. 245–82. London: Longman, 1974.

Aldis, M. S. "University Education of Women: Complements and Compliments." *Westminster Review* 136 (1891): 173.

Anderson, Gregory. *Victorian Clerks*. Manchester: Manchester University Press, 1976.

Ashwell, F. E. "The Girl Graduate: A Reply." *National Review* 16 (1891): 609–13.

Askwith, Betty. *A Victorian Young Lady*. Salisbury: Michael Wilton, 1978.

Asquith, Margot, ed. *Myself When Young*. London: Frederick Muller, 1938.

Auchmuty, Rosemary. "You're a Dyke, Angela! Elsie J. Oxenham and the Rise and Fall of the Schoolgirl Story." In *Not a Passing Phase: Reclaiming Lesbians in History, 1840–1985* by the Lesbian History Group, pp. 119–41. London: Women's Press, 1989.

Avery, Gillian, *Childhood's Pattern: A Study of the Heroes and Heroines of Children's Fiction, 1770–1950*. London: Hodder & Stoughton, 1975.

——. *Nineteenth Century Children*. London: Hodder & Stoughton, 1965.

Baden-Powell, Agnes. *Handbook for Girl Guides; or, How Girls Can Help Build the Empire*. London: Thomas Nelson, 1912.

Baden-Powell, Agnes and Robert Baden-Powell. *Girl Guides: A Suggestion for Character Training for Girls*. London: Bishopsgate Press, [1909].

Baden-Powell, Robert. *Girl Guiding: The Official Handbook*. London: C. A. Pearson, 1918.

——. *Scouting for Boys: A Handbook for Instruction in Good Citizenship*. 9th ed. London: C. Arthur Pearson Ltd., 1918.

Bainton, George, ed. *The Art of Authorship*. London: James Clarke & Co., 1890.

Bardwick, Judith M., Elizabeth Douvan, Matina S. Horner, and David Gutmann. *Feminine Personality and Conflict*. Belmont, Calif.: Brooks/Cole, 1970.

Barlow, Amy. *Seventh Child: The Autobiography of a Schoolmistress*. London: Gerald Duckworth, 1969.

Barnard, Amy B. *A Girl's Book About Herself*. London: Cassell, 1912.

——. *The Girl's Encyclopedia*. London: Pilgrim Press, [1909].

Barr, Barbara. *Histories of Girls' Schools and Related Biographical Material*. Leicester: School of Education Library, 1984.

Beale, Dorothea. *Reports Issued by the Schools' Enquiry Commission on the Education of Girls*. London: David Nutt, 1869.

———. "Schools of To-Day." *Atalanta* 3 (1889–1890): 315–17.

Beale, Dorothea, Lucy H. M. Soulsby, and Jane Frances Dove. *Work and Play in Girls' Schools*. London: Longmans, 1898.

Bell, Gertrude Margaret. *The Earlier Letters of Gertrude Bell*. Edited by Elsa Richmond. London: Ernest Benn, 1937.

Bellairs, Lady. *Gossips with Girls and Maidens, Betrothed and Free*. London: Blackwood, 1887.

Bennett, E. A. *Journalism for Women: A Practical Guide*. London: John Lane, 1878.

Black, Clementina. "Typewriting and Journalism for Women." In *Our Boys and Girls and What to Do with Them*, edited by John Watson, pp. 35–45. London: Ward, Lock & Co., 1892.

Black, Helen C. "Mrs. L. T. Meade." In *Pen, Pencil, Baton, and Mask: Biographical Sketches*, pp. 222–29. London: Spottiswoode, 1896.

———. *Notable Women Authors of the Day*. London: Maclaren & Company, 1906.

Blackburn, Helen. *A Handbook for Women Engaged in Social and Political Work*. Bristol: J. W. Arrowsmith, 1881.

Blackburne, G. M. *A Girl's Difficulties*. London: Wells Gardner, Darton & Co., 1895.

Blackie, Agnes C. *Blackie and Son: A Short History of the Firm, 1809–1959*. London & Glasgow: Blackie & Son, 1959.

Blain, Virginia, Patricia Clements, and Isobel Grundy. *The Feminist Companion to Literature in English*. New York: Yale University Press, 1990.

Boas, George. *The Cult of Childhood*. London: The Warburg Institute, 1966.

Bondfield, Margaret. *A Life's Work*. London: Hutchinson, 1949.

Booker, Beryl Lee. *Yesterday's Child, 1890–1909*. London: John Long, 1937.

Bott, Alan, ed. *Our Mothers*. London: Victor Gollancz, 1932.

Bottome, Phyllis. *Search for a Soul*. London: Faber & Faber, 1947.

Boucherett, Jessie. *Hints on Self Help: A Book for Young Women*. London: S. W. Partridge, 1863.

Bradbrook, M. C. *"That Infidel Place": A Short History of Girton College, 1869–1969*. London: Chatto & Windus, 1969.

Bramston, Mary. *A Girl's Outlook*. London: Wells Gardner, 1903.

Bratton, J. S. "British Imperialism and the Reproduction of Femininity in Girls' Fiction, 1900–1930." In *Imperialism and Juvenile Literature*, edited by Jeffrey Richards, pp. 195–215. Manchester: Manchester University Press, 1989.

———. *The Impact of Victorian Children's Fiction*. Totowa, N.J.: Barnes & Noble, 1981.

Brazil, Angela. *"Little Women:* An Appreciation." *Bookman* 63 (December 1922): 139–40.

———. *My Own Schooldays.* London: Blackie, 1925.

"Brilliant Sketch." *Shafts,* September 1893, 136.

Brittain, Vera. *The Women at Oxford: A Fragment of History.* London: George G. Harrap, 1960.

Brooke, Sylvia. *Sylvia of Sarawak.* London: Hutchinson, 1936.

Broome, Mary Anne. *Colonial Memories.* London: Smith, Elder, 1904.

Brown, Lyn Mikel and Carol Gilligan. *Meeting at the Crossroads: Women's Psychology and Girls' Development.* Cambridge: Harvard University Press, 1992.

Brown, Penny. *The Captured World: The Child and Childhood in Nineteenth-Century Women's Writing in England.* New York: Harvester Wheatsheaf, 1993.

Browne, Phillis [Sarah Sharp Hamer]. *What Girls Can Do.* London: Cassell, [1880].

Burstall, Sara Annie. *English High Schools for Girls: Their Aims, Organization, and Management.* London: Longmans, 1907.

———. *Retrospect and Prospect: Sixty Years of Women's Education.* London: Longmans, Green & Co., 1933.

Burstyn, Joan N. *Victorian Education and the Ideal of Womanhood.* New Brunswick: Rutgers University Press, 1984.

Butler, Christina V. *Domestic Service: An Inquiry by the Women's Industrial Council.* London: G. Bell, 1916.

Butts, Mary. *The Crystal Cabinet: My Childhood at Salterns.* 1937. New ed. Boston: Beacon Press, 1988.

Cadbury, Edward and others. *Women's Work and Wages.* 2nd ed. London: Unwin, 1908.

Cadogan, Mary and Patricia Craig. *You're a Brick, Angela!: A New Look at Girls' Fiction from 1839 to 1975.* London: Victor Gollancz, 1976.

"Cambridge and Degrees for Women." *Spectator* 78 (1897): 535–36.

Carbery, Mary Toulmin. *Happy World: The Story of a Victorian Childhood.* London: Longmans, 1941.

Carpenter, Humphrey and Mari Prichard. *The Oxford Companion to Children's Literature.* New York: Oxford University Press, 1984.

Cartwright, Julia, ed. *The Journals of Lady Knightley of Fawsley.* London: John Murray, 1915.

Caulfeild, S. F. A. *Directory of Girls' Societies, Clubs, and Unions.* London: Griffith & Farran, [1886].

Cawelti, John G. *Adventure, Mystery, and Romance: Formula Stories as Art and Popular Culture*. Chicago: University of Chicago Press, 1976.

Central Rules and Constitution of the Girls' Friendly Society. London: Hatchards, 1880.

Chesser, Elizabeth Sloan. *From Girlhood to Womanhood*. London: Cassell & Company, 1913.

Chinn, Carl. *They Worked All Their Lives: Women of the Urban Poor in England, 1880–1939*. Manchester: Manchester University Press, 1988.

Chisholm, Catherine, B.A., M.D. *The Medical Inspection of Girls in Secondary Schools*. London: Longmans, 1914.

Cholmondeley, Mary. *Under One Roof: A Family Record*. London: John Murray, 1918.

Christian-Smith, Linda K. *Becoming a Woman Through Romance*. New York: Routledge, 1990.

Clayton, Ellen Creathorne. *Female Warriors: Memorials of Female Valour and Heroism, from the Mythological Ages to the Present Era*. 2 vols. London: Tinsley, 1879.

Clough, Anne Jemima. "Women's Progress in Scholarship" (1890). In *The Education Papers*, edited by Dale Spender, pp. 295–304. New York: Routledge & Kegan Paul, 1987.

Clough, Blanche Athena. *A Memoir of Anne Jemima Clough*. London: Arnold, 1897.

Cobbe, Frances Power. "The Education of Women, and How it Would Be Affected by University Examinations" (1862). In *The Education Papers*, edited by Dale Spender, pp. 37–49. New York: Routledge & Kegan Paul, 1987.

Cochrane, Jeanie Douglas. *Peerless Women: A Book for Girls*. London: Collins' Clear-Type Press, [1904].

Cole, Margaret. *Growing Up Into Revolution*. London: Longmans, 1949.

Coleridge, Christabel. *Charlotte Mary Yonge: Her Life and Letters*. London: Macmillan, 1903.

"College for Women, at Hitchin, Hertfordshire." Committee Room, 9, Conduit Street, London: November, 1869. (prospectus).

"College for Working Women." *Englishwoman's Review*, n.s., 15 (1884): 38–39.

"Comrades in Council." *Friendly Leaves*, January 1898, 18–22.

Cook, Emily T. *From a Woman's Note-Book: Studies in Modern Girlhood and Other Sketches*. London: George Allen, 1903.

Copping, Alice M. *The Story of College Hall, 1882–1972*. London: Newman Books, 1974.

Corke, Helen. *In Our Infancy: An Autobiography*. Cambridge: Cambridge University Press, 1975.

Courtney, Janet E. *Recollected in Tranquility*. London: Heinemann, 1926.

Craig, Patricia, and Mary Cadogan. *The Lady Investigates: Women Detectives and Spies in Fiction*. Oxford: Oxford University Press, 1986.

Crask, Mary. "Girl Life in a Slum." *Economic Review* 18 (1908): 184–89.

Crisp, Jane. *Rosa Nouchette Carey*. Victorian Fiction Research Guides, no. 16. University of Queensland, Department of English, 1989.

Crosthwait, Elizabeth. "'The Girl Behind the Man Behind the Gun': The Women's Army Auxiliary Corps, 1914–1918." In *Our Work, Our Lives, Our Words: Women's History and Women's Work*, edited by Leonore Davidoff and Belinda Westover, pp. 161–81. Totowa, N.J.: Barnes & Noble, 1986.

Cruse, Amy. *After the Victorians*. London: G. Allen & Unwin, 1938.

Cunnington, Phillis and Anne Buck. *Children's Costume in England, 1300–1900*. London: A & C Black, 1965.

Curnock, Mrs. George. *A Girl in Her Teens, and What She Ought to Know*. London: Cassell, 1907.

Dalsimer, Katherine. *Female Adolescence: Psychoanalytic Reflections on Literature*. New Haven: Yale University Press, 1986.

Davidson, J. E. *What Our Daughters Can Do For Themselves: A Handbook of Women's Employments*. London: Smith, Elder, 1894.

Davies, Celia. *Clean Clothes on Sunday*. Lavenham: Terence Dalton, 1974.

Davies, Emily. "The Influence of University Degrees on the Education of Women." *Victoria Magazine* 1 (1863): 260–71.

———. *Thoughts on Some Questions Relating to Women, 1860–1908*. 1910. Reprint, New York: Kraus Reprint Co., 1971.

Davis, Gwenn and Beverly A. Joyce. *Personal Writings by Women to 1900*. London: Mansell, 1989.

Dawson, Albert. "What They Read in the East End: An Interview with the Lady Librarian at the People's Palace." *Young Woman* 1 (1892–1893): 411–14.

Dewar, Katharine Cochran. *The Girl*. London: G. Bell & Sons, 1921.

Dixon, Ella Hepworth. "Why Women Are Ceasing to Marry." *The Humanitarian* 14 (1899): 391–96.

Drotner, Kirsten. *English Children and Their Magazines, 1751–1945*. New Haven: Yale University Press, 1988.

Dyhouse, Carol. *Girls Growing Up in Late Victorian and Edwardian England*. London: Routledge & Kegan Paul, 1981.

Ellis, Alec. *Library Services for Young People in England and Wales, 1830–1970*. London: Pergamon Press, 1971.

Ellis, Sarah Stickney. *The Women of England*. London: Fisher, 1838.

Ellsworth, Edward W. *Liberators of the Female Mind: The Shirreff Sisters, Educational Reform, and the Women's Movement*. Westport, Conn.: Greenwood Press, 1979.

Englishwoman's Year Book. London, 1899, 1901, 1911, 1916.

Escombe, Edith. *"Bits I Remember."* London: Eden, Remington & Co., 1892.

Eugenius. "The Decline of Marriage." *Westminster Review* 135 (1891): 11–27.

Evans, Joan. *Prelude and Fugue: An Autobiography*. London: Museum Press, 1964.

Ewing, Elizabeth. *History of Children's Costume*. London: B. T. Batsford, 1977.

———. *Women in Uniform*. London: B. T. Batsford, 1975.

Eyles, Leonora. *The Ram Escapes: The Story of a Victorian Childhood*. London: Peter Nevill, 1953.

Faithfull, Lilian M. *In the House of My Pilgrimage*. London: Chatto & Windus, 1924.

Farjeon, Eleanor. *A Nursery in the Nineties*. New ed. Oxford: Oxford University Press, 1980.

Farningham, Marianne [Mary Anne Hearne]. *Girlhood*. London: James Clarke & Co., 1869. Revised ed. London: James Clarke & Co., 1895.

Faunthorpe, J. P. "Girlhood and Its Chances." *Sunday Magazine* 27 (1898): 156–59.

Fawcett, Millicent Garrett. "Degrees for Women at Oxford." *Contemporary Review* 69 (1896): 347–56.

———. *Some Eminent Women of Our Times*. London: Macmillan, 1889.

———. "The Use of Higher Education to Women." *Contemporary Review* 50 (1886): 719–27.

———. *What I Remember*. London: T. Fisher Unwin, 1924.

"Female Poaching on Male Preserves." *Westminster Review* 129 (1888): 290–97.

Findlay, J. J., ed. *The Young Wage Earner*. London: Sidgwick & Jackson, 1918.

Firth, Catherine B. *Constance Louisa Maynard, Mistress of Westfield College*. London: Allen & Unwin, 1949.

Fitch, J. G. "The Education of Women." *Victoria Magazine* 2 (1863–1864): 432–53.

Fletcher, J. Hamilton. "Feminine Athletics." *Good Words* 20 (1879): 533–36.

Fletcher, Sheila. *Feminists and Bureaucrats: A Study in the Development of Girls' Education in the Nineteenth Century*. Cambridge: Cambridge University Press, 1980.

———. *Women First: The Female Tradition in English Physical Education, 1880–1980*. London: Athlone Press, 1984.

Flint, Kate. *The Woman Reader, 1837–1914*. New York: Oxford University Press, 1993.

Forrester, Wendy. *Great-Grandmama's Weekly: A Celebration of the Girl's Own Paper, 1890–1901*. Guildford: Lutterworth Press, 1980.

Fortescue, Winifred. *There's Rosemary . . . There's Rue . . .* Edinburgh: Blackwood, 1939.

Freeman, Flora Lucy. *Our Working-Girls and How to Help Them*. London: A. R. Mowbray, 1908.

———. *Religious and Social Work Amongst Girls*. London: Skeffington & Son, 1901.

Freeman, Gillian. *The Schoolgirl Ethic: The Life and Work of Angela Brazil*. London: Allen Lane, 1976.

Friedrichs, Hulda. "A Peep at the Pioneer Club." *Young Woman* 4 (1895–1896): 302–6.

Frith, Gill. "'The Time of Your Life': The Meaning of the School Story." In *Language, Gender, and Childhood*, edited by Carolyn Steedman, Cathy Urwin, and Valerie Walkerdine, pp. 113–36. History Workshop Series. London: Routledge & Kegan Paul, 1985.

Furse, Katherine. *Hearts and Pomegranates: The Story of Forty-Five Years, 1875 to 1920*. London: Peter Davies, 1940.

Gardner, P. "Women at Oxford and Cambridge." *Quarterly Review* 186 (1897): 529–51.

Gathorne-Hardy, Jonathan. *The Old School Tie: The Phenomenon of the English Public School*. New York: Viking, 1978.

Gell, Edith Lyttleton. "Squandered Girlhood." *Nineteenth Century* 32 (1892): 930–37.

Girl Guides Association. *The Girl Guides: Rules, Policy, and Organisation*. London: Girl Guides Association, 1917, 1918.

Girls at Home. Oxford: A. R. Mowbray, 1903.

Girls' Friendly Society. *Report on the Conference of the Department for Members in Professions and Business*. London: Girls' Friendly Society, 1886.

Girls' School Year Book. London, 1906, 1911, 1916.

Girton College Register, 1869–1946. Cambridge: Girton College, 1948.

Glendinning, Victoria. *A Suppressed Cry: Life and Death of a Quaker Daughter*. London: Routledge & Kegan Paul, 1969.

Gordon, Alice M. "The After-Careers of University-Educated Women." *Nineteenth Century* 37 (June 1895): 955–60.

Gordon, Maria. *A Handbook of Employments*. Aberdeen: Rosemount Press, 1908.

Gorham, Deborah. *The Victorian Girl and the Feminine Ideal*. Bloomington: Indiana University Press, 1982.

——. "The Ideology of Femininity and Reading for Girls, 1850–1914." In *Lessons for Life: The Schooling of Girls and Women, 1850–1950*, edited by Felicity Hunt, pp. 39–59. Oxford: Basil Blackwell, 1987.

Grand, Sarah. "The Modern Girl." *North American Review* 158 (1894): 706–14.

Grant, Clara E. *From "Me" to "We" (Forty Years on Bow Common)*. London: The Author, 1940.

Grant, Julia M., ed. *St. Leonards School, 1877–1927*. London: Oxford University Press, [1927].

Grimes, Janet and Diva Daims. *Novels in English by Women, 1891–1920: A Preliminary Checklist*. New York: Garland, 1981.

Grogan, Mercy. *How Women May Earn a Living*. Rev. ed. London: Cassell, 1883.

Gwynn, Stephen. "Bachelor Women." *Contemporary Review* 73 (1898): 866–76.

Haley, Bruce. *The Healthy Body and Victorian Culture*. Cambridge: Harvard University Press, 1978.

Hall, Trevor H. *Dorothy L. Sayers: Nine Literary Studies*. Hamden, Conn.: Archon, 1980.

Hamilton, Cecily Hamill. *Life Errant*. London: J. M. Dent, 1935.

Hamilton, Mary Agnes. *Remembering My Good Friends*. London: Jonathan Cape, 1944.

Harrison, Brian. "For Church, Queen, and Family: The Girls' Friendly Society, 1874–1920." *Past and Present* 61 (1973): 107–38.

Harrison, Jane Ellen. *Reminiscences of a Student Life*. London: Hogarth Press, 1925.

Harte, Negley. *The University of London, 1836–1986*. London: Athlone Press, 1986.

[Haweis, Olive]. *Four to Fourteen: By a Victorian Child*. London: Robert Hale, 1939.

Heather. "How to Train Our Daughters." *Womanhood* 1 (1888–1889): 57.

Heath-Stubbs, Mary. *Friendship's Highway: Being the History of the Girls' Friendly Society, 1875–1925*. London: G. F. S. Central Office, 1926.

"Higher Education of Women." *Westminster Review* 129 (1888): 152–62.

Hogarth, Janet E. "The Higher Education of Women." In *The Woman's Library*. Vol. 1. London: Chapman & Hall, 1903.

Holcombe, Lee. *Victorian Ladies at Work*. Hamden, Conn.: Archon Books, 1973.

Holden, C. M. *The Warfare of Girlhood*. London: H. R. Allenson, 1896.

How a Schoolmistress May Live Upon Seventy Pounds a Year. London: The Education Union, 1887.

Hughes, M. V. *A London Girl of the 1880s.* 1946. New ed. Oxford: Oxford University Press, 1978.

———. *A London Home in the 1890s.* 1946. New ed. Oxford: Oxford University Press, 1978.

Humphry, Mrs. C. E. [Madge of *Truth*, pseud.]. *Manners for Girls.* London: Unwin, 1901.

Hunt, Felicity, ed. *Lessons for Life: The Schooling of Girls and Women, 1850–1950.* Oxford: Basil Blackwell, 1987.

Hutchins, Bessie L. "Higher Education and Marriage" (1912). In *The Education Papers*, edited by Dale Spender, pp. 328–34. New York: Routledge & Kegan Paul, 1987.

Jackson, Annabel. *A Victorian Childhood.* London: Methuen, 1932.

Jackson, Mary V. *Engines of Instruction, Mischief, and Magic: Children's Literature in England from Its Beginnings to 1839.* Lincoln: University of Nebraska Press, 1989.

Jeal, Tim. *The Boy-Man: The Life of Lord Baden-Powell.* New York: William Morrow, 1990.

Jermy, Louise. *The Memories of a Working Woman.* Norwich: Goose & Son, 1934.

Jex-Blake, Sophia. "Medical Women in Fiction." *Nineteenth Century* 33 (1893): 261–72.

John, Angela, ed. *Unequal Opportunities: Women's Employment in England, 1800–1918.* Oxford: Basil Blackwell, 1986.

Johnson, Joseph. *Clever Girls of Our Time, and How They Became Famous Women.* London: Darton & Hodge, 1863.

Jones, Dora M. "The Ladies' Clubs of London." *Young Woman* 7 (1898–1899): 409–13.

Jones, Emily Elizabeth Constance. *As I Remember: An Autobiographical Ramble.* London: A & C Black, 1922.

Kamm, Josephine. *Hope Deferred: Girls' Education in English History.* London: Methuen, 1965.

———. *Indicative Past: A Hundred Years of the Girls' Public Day School Trust.* London: George Allen & Unwin, 1971.

Kanner, Barbara. *Women in English Social History, 1800–1914: A Guide to Research.* 3 vols. New York: Garland, 1987–1990.

Kenney, Annie. *Memories of a Militant.* London: Edward Arnold & Co., 1924.

Kent, Susan Kingsley. *Making Peace: The Reconstruction of Gender in Interwar Britain*. Princeton: Princeton University Press, 1993.

Keppel, Sonia. *Edwardian Daughter*. London: Hamish Hamilton, 1958.

Kerr, Rose. *The Story of the Girl Guides*. London: The Girl Guides Association, 1932.

Keynes, Florence Ada. *Gathering Up the Threads: A Study in Family Biography*. Cambridge: W. Heffer & Sons, 1950.

Kincaid, James B. *Child-Loving: The Erotic Child and Victorian Culture*. New York: Routledge, 1992.

Kirk, Edward B. *A Talk with Girls About Themselves*. London: Simkin Marshall, 1905.

Knollys, B. S. "Ladies' Clubs in London, No. 1: The Pioneer Club in Bruton Street." *The Englishwoman* 1 (1895): 120–25.

Krout, Mary Hannah. *A Looker-On in London*. London: B. F. Stevens & Brown, 1899.

Kumm, Lucy Guiness. *In Perils in the City*. Published under the direction of the Federation of Working Girls' Clubs. London: Headley Brothers, [1909].

Lamb, Ruth. *Servants and Service*. London: RTS, [1889].

Leighton, Clare. *Tempestuous Petticoat: The Story of an Invincible Edwardian*. 1947. Reprint, Chicago: Academy Chicago, 1984.

Leng's Careers for Girls: How to Train and Where to Train. Dundee: John Leng, 1911.

Leonardi, Susan J. *Dangerous by Degrees: Women at Oxford and the Somerville College Novelists*. New Brunswick: Rutgers University Press, 1989.

Leslie, Marion. "Women Who Work." *Young Woman* 3 (1894–1895): 230–34.

Levstik, Linda S. "'I Am No Lady!': The Tomboy in Children's Fiction." *Children's Literature in Education*, n.s., 14 (Spring 1983): 14–20.

Lewis, Jane. *Women in England, 1870–1950: Sexual Divisions and Social Change*. Bloomington: Indiana University Press, 1984.

Linton, Eliza Lynn. "The Higher Education of Women." *Fortnightly Review* 40 (1886): 498–510.

Lochhead, Marion. *Young Victorians*. London: John Murray, 1959.

Lodge, Eleanor C. *Terms and Vacations*. Edited by Janet Spens. London: Oxford University Press, 1938.

London, M. A. "The Girl Graduate: A Few Statistics." *National Review* 16 (1890–1891): 161–65.

Low, Florence B. "The Reading of the Modern Girl." *Nineteenth Century* 59 (1906): 278–87.

Low, Frances H. "Journalism as an Occupation for Girls." *Girl's Realm* 4 (1901–1902): 1009–10.

Lumsden, Louisa. *Yellow Leaves: Memories of a Long Life.* Edinburgh: Blackwood, 1933.

Lutyens, Emily. *A Blessed Girl: Memoirs of a Victorian Girlhood Chronicled in an Exchange of Letters, 1887–1896.* London: Rupert Hart-Davis, 1953.

Mann, Jessica. *Deadlier Than the Male: An Investigation Into Feminine Crime Writing.* Newton Abbot: David & Charles, 1981.

March-Phillips, Evelyn. "Women's Industrial Life." Published serially in *Monthly Packet*, n.s., 13 (1897).

Marshall, Beatrice. *Emma Marshall: A Biographical Sketch.* London: Seeley, 1900.

Marshall, Mary Paley. *What I Remember.* Cambridge: University Press, 1947.

Martin, Frances. "College for Working Women." *Macmillan* 40 (1879): 483–88.

Martineau, Harriet. "The Young Lady in Town and Country: Her Health." *Once a Week* 2 (February 25, 1860): 191–95.

Mason, Bobbie Ann. *The Girl Sleuth: A Feminist Guide.* Old Westbury, N.Y.: Feminist Press, 1975.

Maxwell, Mrs. M. A. "Medicine for Women." In *Our Boys and Girls and What to Do with Them*, edited by John Watson, pp. 113–23. London: Ward, Lock & Co., 1892.

Maynard, Constance L. "From Early Victorian Schoolroom to University: Some Personal Experiences." *Nineteenth Century* 76 (1914): 1060–73.

McAleer, Joseph. *Popular Reading and Publishing in Britain, 1914–1950.* Oxford: Clarendon Press, 1992.

McCrone, Kathleen E. *Sport and the Physical Emancipation of English Women, 1870–1914.* London: Routledge, 1988.

McKenna, Ethel M., ed. *Education and Professions.* Vol. 1 of *The Woman's Library.* London: Chapman & Hall, 1903.

McWilliams-Tullberg, Rita. "Women and Degrees at Cambridge University, 1867–1897." In *A Widening Sphere*, edited by Martha Vicinus, pp. 117–45. Bloomington: Indiana University Press, 1977.

——. *Women at Cambridge: A Men's University—Though of a Mixed Type.* London: Victor Gollancz, 1975.

Meade, L. T. "Girls' Schools of To-day. I.: Cheltenham College." *Strand* 9 (1895): 283–88.

——. "Girls' Schools of To-day. II.: St. Leonards and Great Harrowden Hall." *Strand* 9 (1895): 457–63.

——. "How I Began." *Girl's Realm* 3 (1900): 57–64.

———. "Story Writing for Girls." *The Academy and Literature* 65 (1903): 499.

"Millicent Garrett Fawcett and Her Daughter." *Review of Reviews* 2 (1890): 20.

[Minturn, Eliza T. ?]. "An Interior View of Girton College, Cambridge" (1876). In *The Education Papers*, edited by Dale Spender, pp. 277–83. New York: Routledge & Kegan Paul, 1987.

Mitchell, Hannah. *The Hard Way Up*. Edited by Geoffrey Mitchell. 1968. Reprint, London: Virago, 1984.

Moor, Lucy M. *Girls of Yesterday and To-Day: The Romance of the Y.W.C.A.* London: S. W. Partridge, [1910].

Mozley, Anne. "On Fiction as an Educator." *Blackwood's Edinburgh Magazine* 108 (1870): 449–59.

Murray, Margaret. *My First Hundred Years*. London: William Kimber, 1963.

Musgrove, Frank. *The Migratory Elite*. London: Heinemann, 1963.

Muuss, Rolf E. *Theories of Adolescence*. New York: Random House, 1962.

Nell, Victor. *Lost in a Book: The Psychology of Reading for Pleasure*. New Haven: Yale University Press, 1988.

Nelson, Claudia. *Boys Will Be Girls: The Feminine Ethic and British Children's Fiction, 1857–1917*. New Brunswick: Rutgers University Press, [1991].

Nesbit, E. *Long Ago When I Was Young*. Introduction by Noel Streatfeild. London: Ronald Whiting & Wheaton, 1966. (Originally published in *Girl's Own Paper* in 1896.)

Neubach, John. *The Fin-de-Siècle Culture of Adolescence*. New Haven: Yale University Press, 1992.

Nevinson, Margaret Wynne. *Life's Fitful Fever: A Volume of Memories*. London: A & C Black, 1926.

Nimon, Maureen. "A Chart of Change: The Work of L. T. Meade." *Children's Literature in Education* 18 (1987): 163–75.

Oldfield, Sybil. *Spinsters of This Parish: The Life and Times of F. M. Mayor and Mary Sheepshanks*. London: Virago, 1984.

Oman, Carola. *An Oxford Childhood*. London: Hodder & Stoughton, 1976.

One Who Knows Them. *Boys and Their Ways*. London: John Hogg, 1880.

———. *Girls and Their Ways: A Book for and About Girls*. London: John Hogg, 1881.

Owen, Dorothy. *Letters to School-Girls*. London: Skeffington, 1908.

Parsloe, Muriel Jardine. *A Parson's Daughter*. London: Faber & Faber, 1935.

Peck, Winifred. *A Little Learning; or, A Victorian Childhood*. London: Faber & Faber, 1952.

Pedersen, Joyce Senders. *The Reform of Girls' Secondary and Higher Education in Victorian England: A Study of Elites and Educational Change*. New York: Garland, 1987.

Peel, Dorothy Constance. *Life's Enchanted Cup: An Autobiography (1872–1933)*. London: Bodley Head, 1933.

Peters, Charles, ed. *The Girl's Own Outdoor Book*. London: RTS, 1889.

Pfeiffer, Emily. *Women and Work: An Essay Treating on the Relations to Health and Physical Development, of the Higher Education of Girls*. London: Trübner & Co., 1888.

"Philippa Garrett Fawcett." *Education* 1 (July 1890): 148–51.

Phillips, Ann, ed. *A Newnham Anthology*. Cambridge: Cambridge University Press, 1979.

Pilkington, W. T. "Modern Mannish Maids." *Blackwood's Edinburgh Magazine* 147 (1890): 252–64.

Pinchbeck, Ivy and Margaret Hewitt. *Children in English Society*. Volume II: *From the Eighteenth Century to The Children Act (1948)*. London: Routledge & Kegan Paul, 1973.

Pollard, Alfred W. "Fees, Work, and Wages in Girls' High Schools." *Murray's Magazine* 10 (1891): 576–82.

Pollock, Alice. *Portrait of My Victorian Youth*. London: Johnson, 1971.

Postgate, J. P. "Shall Women Graduate at Cambridge." *National Review* 10 (1887): 191–201.

Potter, Beatrix. *The Journal of Beatrix Potter from 1881 to 1897*. Transcribed from her code writings by Leslie Linder. London: Frederick Warne, 1966.

Proctor, Mortimer R. *The English University Novel*. Berkeley and Los Angeles: University of California Press, 1957.

Pryce-Jones, Alan, ed. *Little Innocents*. 1932. Reprint, Oxford: Oxford University Press, 1986.

Purvis, June. *Hard Lessons: The Lives and Education of Working-Class Women in Nineteenth-Century England*. Cambridge: Polity, 1989.

Quigley, Isabel. *The Heirs of Tom Brown: The English School Story*. London: Chatto & Windus, 1982.

Raverat, Gwen. *Period Piece: A Cambridge Childhood*. London: Faber & Faber, 1952.

Reaney, Isabel. *English Girls: Their Place and Power*. London: Kegan Paul, 1879.

"Registered Medical Women for 1889." *Englishwoman's Review of Social and Industrial Questions* 20 (1889): 65–69.

Reynolds, Kimberley. *Girls Only? Gender and Popular Children's Fiction in Britain, 1880–1910*. Philadelphia: Temple University Press, 1990.

Rhondda, Margaret Haig, Viscountess. *This Was My World*. London: Macmillan, 1933.

Richards, Jeffrey, ed. *Imperialism and Juvenile Literature*. Manchester: Manchester University Press, 1989.

Ring, Florence Thorne. "The Factory Girl and Her Reading." *Girls' Club Journal* 1 (1909): 50–52.

Roberts, Elizabeth. *A Woman's Place: An Oral History of Working-Class Women, 1890–1940*. Oxford: Basil Blackwell, 1984.

Roberts, Elizabeth. *Women's Work, 1840–1940*. London: Macmillan, 1988.

Root, Mary E. S. "Not to Be Circulated." *Wilson Bulletin* 3 (1929): 446.

Rowbotham, Judith. *Good Girls Make Good Wives: Guidance for Girls in Victorian Fiction*. Oxford: Basil Blackwell, 1989.

Rubenstein, David. *Before the Suffragettes: Women's Emancipation in the 1890s*. Brighton: Harvester, 1986.

———. *A Different World for Women: The Life of Millicent Garrett Fawcett*. Columbus: Ohio State University Press, 1991.

———. *School Attendance in London, 1870–1904: A Social History*. New York: Augustus M. Kelley, 1969.

Ruck, Berta. *A Story-Teller Tells the Truth*. London: Hutchinson, 1935.

Salmon, Edward. *Juvenile Literature as It Is*. London: Drane, 1888.

———. "What Girls Read." *Nineteenth Century* 20 (1886): 515–29.

Sayers, Dorothy L. Introduction to *The Omnibus of Crime*. Reprinted in *The Art of the Mystery Story*, edited by Howard Haycraft, pp. 71–109. New York: Simon and Schuster, 1946.

Scannell, Dorothy. *Mother Knew Best: An East End Childhood*. London: Macmillan, 1974.

Scharlieb, Mary, M.D. "Adolescent Girlhood Under Modern Conditions, with Special Reference to Motherhood." *Eugenics Review* 1 (1909–1910): 174–83.

Schellenberger, John. "Fiction and the First Women Students." *New Universities Quarterly* 36 (Autumn 1982): 352–59.

The School and the World. London: Simpkin Marshall & Co., 1872.

Sewell, Elizabeth M. *Note-Book of an Elderly Lady*. London: Walter Smith, 1881.

Sharp, Evelyn. *Unfinished Adventure*. London: John Lane, 1933.

Sidgwick, Eleanor M. *Health Statistics of Women Students of Cambridge and Oxford and of Their Sisters*. Cambridge: University Press, 1890.

Singer, Jerome L. *The Inner World of Daydreaming*. New York: Harper & Row, 1975.

Slung, Michele B. *Crime on Her Mind*. New York: Pantheon, 1975.

Smith-Rosenberg, Carroll. "The Female World of Love and Ritual." In *Disorderly Conduct: Visions of Gender in Victorian America*, pp. 53–76. New York: Oxford University Press, 1985.

Soulsby, Lucy. *Stray Thoughts for Girls*. New ed. London: Longmans, Green & Co., 1907.

———. *Stray Thoughts on Reading*. London: Longmans, Green & Co., 1897.

Spacks, Patricia Meyer. *Myths of Youth and the Adult Imagination*. New York: Basic Books, 1981.

Spender, Dale, ed. *The Education Papers*. New York: Routledge & Kegan Paul, 1987.

Springhall, John. *Coming of Age: Adolescence in Britain, 1860–1960*. Dublin: Gill & Macmillan, 1986.

Stables, Gordon. *The Girl's Own Book of Health and Beauty*. London: Jarrold & Sons, 1891.

Stanley, Maude. *Clubs for Working Girls*. London: Macmillan, 1890.

Stearns, Peter N. "Working-Class Women in Britain, 1890–1914." In *Suffer and Be Still: Women in the Victorian Age*, edited by Martha Vicinus, pp. 100–20. Bloomington: Indiana University Press, 1972.

Stephen, Barbara. *Girton College, 1869–1932*. Cambridge: University Press, 1933.

Stopes, Marie. *Married Love*. London: A. C. Fitfield, 1918.

Strachey, Ray. *The Cause: A Short History of the Women's Movement in Great Britain*. 1928. Reprint, London: Virago, 1978.

Stubbs, Mary Heath. *Friendship's Highway: Being the History of the Girls' Friendly Society, 1875–1925*. London: GFS, 1925.

Stutfield, Hugh. "Psychology of Feminism." *Blackwood's Edinburgh Magazine* 161 (1897): 104–17.

Summerfield, Penny. "Cultural Reproduction in the Education of Girls: A Study of Girls' Secondary Schooling in Two Lancashire Towns, 1900–50." In *Lessons for Life: The Schooling of Girls and Women, 1850–1950*, edited by Felicity Hunt, pp. 149–70. Oxford: Basil Blackwell, 1987.

A Surgeon and Accoucheur. *Girlhood and Wifehood*. London: "Family Doctor" Publishing Co., 1896.

Sutherland, John. *The Stanford Companion to Victorian Fiction*. Stanford: Stanford University Press, 1989.

Swan, Annie S. *My Life: An Autobiography*. London: Ivor Nicholson & Watson, 1934.

Swanwick, Helena Maria. *I Have Been Young*. London: Victor Gollancz, 1935.

"Swimming for Ladies." *Englishwoman's Review*, n.s., 6 (1875): 423–24.

Tanner, J. R. "Degrees for Women at Cambridge." *Fortnightly Review* 67 (1897): 716–27.

Thayer, William M. *Women Who Win; or, Making Things Happen*. London: T. Nelson & Sons, 1897.

Thompson, Tierl, ed. *Dear Girl: The Diaries and Letters of Two Working Women (1897–1917)*. London: The Women's Press, 1987.

Tillotson, Kathleen. "*The Heir of Redclyffe*." In *Mid-Victorian Studies*, edited by Geoffrey Tillotson and Kathleen Tillotson, pp. 49–55. London: Athlone Press, 1965.

Timings, Caroline Louisa. *Letters from the Past: Memories of a Victorian Childhood*. Edited by Edward K. Timings. London: Andrew Melrose, 1954.

Tooley, Sarah A. "Famous Bachelor Women." *Woman at Home* 7 (1899): 685–96.

Tuke, Margaret J. *A History of Bedford College for Women, 1849–1937*. London: Oxford University Press, 1939.

Turner, Barry. *Equality for Some: The Story of Girls' Education*. London: Ward Lock Educational, 1974.

Tyacke, R. and E. *The Book of Service: Talks to Girl Guides*. London: RTS, 1927.

"University Examinations for Girls." *London Review* 7 (1863): 646–47.

"University Successes of June, 1890." *Englishwoman's Review* 21 (1890): 289–93.

Valentine, Laura Jewry, ed. *The Girls' Home Companion: A Book of Pastimes in Work and Play*. New ed. London: Frederick Warne, 1902.

Vanderbilt, Arthur Talbot. *What to Do with Our Girls*. London: Houlston & Sons, 1884.

Vicinus, Martha. "Distance and Desire: English Boarding-School Friendships." In *Hidden from History: Reclaiming the Gay and Lesbian Past*, edited by Martin Duberman, Martha Vicinus, and George Chauncey, Jr., pp. 212–29. New York: Meridian, 1989. First published in *Signs* 9 (1984): 600–22.

———. *Independent Women: Work and Community for Single Women, 1850–1920*. Chicago: University of Chicago Press, 1985.

———. "What Makes a Heroine? Nineteenth-Century Girls' Biographies." *Genre* 20 (1987): 171–87.

Vincent, David. *Literacy and Popular Culture: England, 1750–1914*. Cambridge: Cambridge University Press, 1989.

Walkerdine, Valerie. *Schoolgirl Fictions*. London: Verso, 1990.

Walvin, James. *A Child's World: A Social History of English Childhood, 1800–1914*. Harmondsworth: Penguin Books, 1982.

Ward, Mary Augusta. *A Writer's Recollections*. London: W. Collins, 1918.

Warde, C. Olivia Orde. "A School for Womanhood." *Englishwoman's Review*, n.s., 41 (1910): 98–107.

Watson, John, ed. *Our Boys and Girls and What to Do with Them*. London: Ward, Lock & Co., 1892.

Wheelwright, Julie. *Amazons and Military Maids: Women Who Dressed as Men in the Pursuit of Life, Liberty, and Happiness*. London: Pandora, 1990.

Williams, Perry. "Pioneer Women Students at Cambridge, 1869–81." In *Lessons for Life: The Schooling of Girls and Women, 1850–1950*, edited by Felicity Hunt, pp. 171–91. Oxford: Basil Blackwell, 1987.

"The Woman Journalist." *The Academy and Literature* 63 (1902): 309–10.

"Women and the Universities." *Spectator* 60 (1887) 855–56.

"Women at the Doors of the Universities." *Saturday Review* 81 (1896): 269–70.

Women of Worth: A Book for Girls. London: James Hogg, 1904.

Wood-Allen, Mary, M.D., *What a Young Woman Ought to Know*. Rev. ed. London: Vir Publishing Company, 1913.

Woodward, Kathleen. *Jipping Street*. 1928. Reprint, London: Virago, 1983.

Wordsworth, Elizabeth. "Colleges for Women." *The Monthly Packet*, n.s., 1 (1891): 246–57.

——. *Glimpses of the Past*. London: A. R. Mowbray, [1912].

Wyatt, Jean. *Reconstructing Desire: The Role of the Unconscious in Women's Reading and Writing*. Chapel Hill: University of North Carolina Press, 1990.

Wynne, May [Mabel Knowles]. *Life's Object; or, Some Thoughts for Young Girls*. London: James Nisbet, 1899.

Yates, Margarita. "Do Our Girls Take an Interest in Literature?" *Monthly Review* 23 (April 1906): 120–32.

Yonge, Charlotte M. "Children's Literature of the Last Century." *Macmillan's Magazine* 20 (1869): 229–37, 302–10.

——. "Class Literature of the Last Thirty Years." *Macmillan's Magazine* 20 (1869): 448–56.

——. *What Books to Lend and What to Give*. London: National Society's Depository, [1887].

Zimmeck, Meta. "Jobs for the Girls: The Expansion of Clerical Work for Women, 1850–1914." In *Unequal Opportunities*, edited by Angela John, pp. 153–77. Oxford: Basil Blackwell, 1986.

index

Designer: Linda Secondari
Text: 11.5/14 Fournier
Compositor: Columbia University Press
Printer: Edwards Brothers
Binder: Edwards Brothers